# WHAT ARE THEY SAYING ABOUT AUGUSTINE?

# What Are They Saying About Augustine?

JOSEPH T. KELLEY

Paulist Press
New York/Mahwah, NJ

Cover image: Painting by Antonello da Messina, c. 1472, Museo Nazionale, Palermo, Italy. Photo courtesy Wikimedia Commons.
Cover design by Jim Brisson
Book design by Lynn Else

Library of Congress Cataloging-in-Publication Data

Kelley, Joseph T., 1948–
    What are they saying about Augustine? / Joseph T. Kelley.
        pages cm
    Includes bibliographical references and index.
    ISBN 978-0-8091-4854-7 (pbk. : alk. paper) — ISBN 978-1-58768-328-2 (ebook)
    1. Augustine, Saint, Bishop of Hippo. I. Augustine, Saint, Bishop of Hippo. Works. Selections. English. 2014. II. Title.
    BR65.A9K395 2014
    270.2092—dc23

                                                                    2014004360

ISBN 978-0-8091-4854-7 (paperback)
ISBN 978-1-58768-328-2 (e-book)

Published by Paulist Press
997 Macarthur Boulevard
Mahwah, New Jersey 07430

www.paulistpress.com

Printed and bound in the
United States of America

# CONTENTS

# TO THE AUGUSTINIAN FAMILY AROUND THE WORLD

*In quorum ego caritatem, fateor, facile me totum proicio,*
*praesertim fatigatum scandalis saeculi; et in ea sine ulla*
*sollicitudine requiesco: Deum quippe illic esse sentio,*
*in quem me securus proicio, et in quo securus requiesco.*
LETTER 73.10

# ACKNOWLEDGMENTS

Many Augustinian Friars have been my teachers, mentors, and friends. Through them I have come to know and value the thought and spirituality of Augustine. In particular, I want to thank Donald Burt, John Gavigan, John Rotelle, Robert Russell, and Luc Verheijen (all of happy memory); also, Robert Dodaro, George Lawless, Brian Lowery, Paul Maloney, Gary McCloskey, and Mike Scanlon.

Allan Fitzgerald was most helpful in the guidance and direction he provided for this project. Jane Merdinger, Joseph Farrell, and Patricia Lo were also generous with their time and talent in helping me improve the text. I also want to thank my Augustinian friend and colleague James Wenzel for the McFadden-Wenzel Augustinian Collection in the McQuade Library and for the use of his personal library.

Chris Bellitto, my editor at Paulist, has been a cherished companion along the way. His encouragement, scholarship, and patience I value as a great gift. Lyena Chavez, C. J. Wong, and Christine Condon of McQuade Library have provided much assistance for my research.

Finally, I want to thank my wife Alina and our children Kasia and Patryk for providing the family community of "one mind and heart," without which I could not pursue my work.

*August 28, 2013*
*Methuen, Massachusetts*

# A NOTE ON ENGLISH TRANSLATIONS AND TEXTS

The English translations of Augustine's works cited in this text come from *The Works of Saint Augustine: A Translation for the 21st Century* by New City Press. This translation is under the direction of *The Augustinian Heritage Institute, Inc.*, John E. Rotelle, OSA, (1939–2002) and Boniface Ramsey, editors, and Patricia Lo, president.

Citations of Augustine's works include book, chapter, and paragraph. For example: *Confessions* I.1.1 refers to book I, chapter 1, paragraph 1 of *Confessions*. Augustine divided most of his longer works into books (*liberi*). Chapters were introduced into many manuscripts from the fifteenth century, and paragraphs were numbered within the chapters in the late seventeenth century.

The volumes of the New City Press translations are listed in appendix A, noting which of Augustine's works are included in each volume of the series.

The Works of Saint Augustine in Latin can be found on-line at http://www.augustinus.it in the section *S. Aurelii Augustini Opera Omnia—Editio Latina*. The Latin text is from the volumes on Augustine in the Migne Edition of *Patrologiae Latinae Elenchus* (*PL* Volumes 32–45).

Two projects continue the work of cataloguing and authenticating Augustine's Latin texts. The first is the *Corpus Scriptorum Ecclesiasticorum Latinorum* (CSEL), a long-term project of the Austrian Academy of Sciences in Vienna begun in the mid-nineteenth century. See www.csel.eu. There is also the *Corpus Christianorum Series Latina* (CCL), a more recent project begun in the mid-twentieth century at the Catholic University of Louvain in partnership with the Brepols Publishing Company in Turnhout, Belgium. See www.corpuschristianorum.org; www.brepols.net. CD-ROMs with recent critical editions of Augustine's Latin texts are available from CETEDOC, a project of CCL and Brepols, and are on hand at many academic libraries.

# CHRONOLOGY OF AUGUSTINE'S LIFE

354      Augustine is born on November 13 at Thagaste, modern Souk-Ahras in Algeria.

366–69      Studies grammar at Madauros, modern Mdaourouch, Algeria

369–70      Returns for a year of idleness in Thagaste

370–73      Studies rhetoric in Carthage, near modern Tunis, Tunisia; birth of Adeodatus; reads Cicero's *Hortensius*; joins Manichean sect

373–74      Returns to teach in Thagaste

374–83      Teaches in Carthage; meets Faustus, a Manichean

383–84      Teaches in Rome; falls ill; wins chair of rhetoric in Milan

384–86      Serves as Imperial *Rhetor* at court in Milan; Monica joins Augustine and his family; Augustine meets Ambrose; reads Books of the Platonists; hears about Christian monasticism

386      Conversion in garden at Milan

386–87      Prebaptismal retreat at Cassiciacum, probably modern Cassago Brianza, Italy

387          April 26/27 baptized at Easter Vigil by Ambrose in
             Milan along with son Adeodatus and friend Alypius;
             Monica dies at Ostia in August

387–88       Second stay in Rome

388–90       Returns to Thagaste to establish monastic retreat;
             Adeodatus dies

391          Visit to Hippo to found monastery; ordained priest
             by Bishop Valerius of Hippo

391–95       Priestly ministry at Hippo, modern Annaba, Algeria

395          Ordained co-adjutor bishop; succeeds Bishop
             Valerius

396          Re-reads St. Paul and begins to develop a theology of
             grace

397–400      Writes *Confessions*

403          Council of Carthage

410          Sack of Rome by Alaric and the Visigoths

411          Conference between Donatists and Catholics at
             Carthage

416          Councils of Carthage and Milevis condemn teach-
             ings of Pelagius and Caelestius

418          Beginning of feud with Julian of Eclanum

427          Appoints the priest Eraclius to succeed him

430          Dies at Hippo on August 28 during third month of
             Vandal siege

(Adapted from "Principal Chronological Highlights" in Serge
Lancel, *St. Augustine* [London: SCM Press, 2002], 531–32.)

# INTRODUCTION

What are they saying about Augustine of Hippo? The interrogative in the title prompts a further question: Who are "they" that have something to say about Aurelius Augustinus (354–430)? Who today is thinking and writing about the famous convert to Christianity who became Bishop of Hippo in North Africa and one of the most influential Christians of all times? The answer is an impressive list of theologians, philosophers, and historians as well as scholars in classical studies, philology, linguistics, political science, and other disciplines.

The list comprises Christian clergy of all ranks, including Joseph Ratzinger, Pope Benedict XVI, and Rowan Williams, former Archbishop of Canterbury, both of whom have written extensively about Augustine.[1] Interest in this fifth-century bishop from Roman North Africa also includes scholars from many religious orders in the Catholic Church.[2]

Important twentieth-century philosophers such as Martin Heidegger and Hannah Arendt drew significantly from Augustine's thought.[3] The continental postmodernist Jacques Derrida was particularly interested in the perduring Augustinian philosophical legacy.[4] Throughout the second half of the twentieth century, the list has grown exponentially to encompass women and men from many countries whose diverse scholarly interests or philosophical and religious predilections have drawn them into the field of Augustine Studies.[5]

*List* is perhaps too cold a word. Augustine himself would

prefer *community* to describe the thousands of contemporary scholars who, sixteen hundred years after his death, continue as his conversation partners. His first biographer, Possidius, notes that Augustine loved to engage friends and guests in conversation when they dined with him in the episcopal monastery at Hippo.[6]

The Augustine scholars of today continue dialogue and debate that the Bishop of Hippo began during his lifetime. From table conversation over simple monastic fare in the fifth-century seaport city of Hippo Regius, through scholarly lectures in the medieval classrooms of great European universities, into the fiery debates of the Protestant Reformation, and down to the proceedings of contemporary scholarly conferences and ecclesial retreats, animated Augustinian conversations continue. Believers and skeptics alike continue to scour questions of faith and philosophy, soul and society, human will and divine grace, love and salvation, war and peace, in terms that Augustine first defined or in categories he first delineated. No theologian from the first six centuries of the church has influenced the development of Christian life and thought more than Augustine. His contemporary and sometime correspondent Saint Jerome seems to anticipate this vast influence when he calls Augustine the "second founder of the faith" (*Letter* 195).[7]

So the answer to "What are they saying about Augustine of Hippo?" is an invitation to come to know the ongoing work of that remarkable ecumenical, multidisciplinary, and international community of scholars. They are quite diverse in their religious and philosophical convictions. Yet they are united in their confidence that conversations initiated by Augustine so many years ago still very much matter in today's world and for today's important issues.[8]

The present volume is designed to introduce you to the academic field of Augustine Studies. It focuses on research and writing either originally done in English, or now available in English translation, though there will also be occasional references to the invaluable books and journals in other European languages. I draw from the Augustine scholarship of the past fifty to sixty years, basically the era of the Second Vatican Council and subsequent decades that have witnessed a veritable explosion of research and writing in the field. Major texts and helpful articles are cited to highlight and summarize contemporary trends in Augustine scholarship, and give direction for further study.

We will take a chronological approach, first looking at Augustine's life and his writings, and then tracing his influence over the centuries up to the present day. However, the expansive scholarship on Augustine developed over the past half century will inform each step of our historical review. Thus, our survey will be a three-way conversation. It includes Augustine himself, his interpreters throughout history, and contemporary Augustine scholars. The *they* in *What Are They Saying About Augustine* is a community of scholars from across the centuries, representing diverse perspectives, working at various levels of interpretation and reinterpretation.

Chapter 1 provides an overview of Augustine's life. We know a great deal about the man from his own *Confessions* as well as from his friend, episcopal colleague, and biographer Possidius of Calma (ca. 370–ca. 440).[9] Studies over the past sixty years have probed the religious, political, and social contexts of the fourth and fifth centuries to provide ever clearer focus on the details that help us enter Augustine's life and times. Chapter 2 begins a review of Augustine's writings, concentrating on the major texts *Confessions*, *City of God*, *The Trinity*, *Teaching Christianity*, *Expositions of the Psalms*, and the four books called the Cassiciacum Dialogues. Chapter 3 moves on to his works on theological controversies, written to help clarify the Catholic position on key doctrinal questions that arose in late fourth- and early fifth-century Christianity. This chapter also looks at recent research on the five hundred sermons and more than 250 letters that have been preserved. It ends with a look at *Revisions*, a review of his corpus, which Augustine did in his last years. Given the extent of Augustine's literary output, any summary of his writings and what contemporary scholarship has to say about them is a daunting task. It brings to mind the words of Possidius: "So many are the works he dictated and published, so many the sermons he preached in church and then wrote down and revised,…that even a student would hardly have the energy to read and become acquainted with all of them" (Possidius, *Life*, XVIII.9).

Chapter 4 traces Augustine's theological legacy across the life and thought of the church and society throughout the Middle Ages and into the Renaissance. Continuing research and discoveries by Augustine scholars provide us new insights into his perduring influence during this first millennium after his death. Chapter 5 continues to explore his impact on the Reformation and the persistence of his genius up to the present day.

Chapter 6 looks at the areas in Augustine Studies that have received the most attention from scholars in recent decades. After a look at important shifts in the methodology of the field, we will present what contemporary scholars are saying about the role of Christ in Augustine's thought; his scriptural hermeneutics; his ideas on love; his theology of grace; and his writings about women, marriage, and virginity.

Chapter 7 reviews the many influential biographies of Augustine that have enriched the field over the past fifty to sixty years. We also take a brief look at the vast territory of secondary resources, including scholarly journals, institutes, anthologies, and other collections that introduce readers to Augustine's thought and help them enter and explore the field of Augustine Studies.

In the preface to his new (2000) edition of his original (1967) biography of Augustine, Peter Brown notes that in the intervening thirty-three years, "Entire new perspectives on the study of Augustine have opened up, that complement or correct what [I] first wrote."[10] I hope this text in the Paulist "What Are They Saying About" series opens up for the reader the new perspectives in Augustine Studies that have emerged in recent decades. Infrequent visitors to the field of Patristics can be misinformed by reading old guidebooks or misled by following out-dated maps. Augustine is often presumed to be "only too predictable."[11]

Contemporary scholars invite us to a reconsideration of the man, his world, and his thought. They challenge us not necessarily to join a new consensus. Rather, their work advises a thoughtful openness to the writings and reflections of a bishop who struggled with the implications of faith in Christ in a rapidly changing church and world.

# 1
# LIFE
## *Meeting Augustine*

The iconography of Augustine usually depicts him anachronistically in medieval monastic garb or in episcopal vestments, wearing a towering mitre and grasping a gilded staff—religious and liturgical accretions of a later age. Such religious art and his often pounding rhetoric can present him as a formidable hierarch of Christian hegemony, hammering heretics and laying new doctrinal highways atop old Roman roads across the European landscape.

The story, situation, and intention of the man himself are quite different. His genius shines much more clearly when set in the modest realities of his time and place. He was born and raised not in Europe, but in central North Africa, in a province of the Roman Empire called Numidia. His home town of Thagaste is the present day Souk Ahras, Algeria. The port city of Hippo Regius, where he served as bishop, is today the modern city of Annaba, also in Algeria. Contemporary Algerians are quite fond of their famous son in antiquity who died in 430, one hundred forty years before Mohammed was born in 570, and two hundred years before the spread of Islam across North Africa in the second half of the seventh century.

1

## Early Years

As a youth, Augustine received an education typical for the sons of landed Roman gentry of his day. His early education was in grammar, mathematics, and literature.[1] He attended the local school in Thagaste, hating the common corporal punishments he received (*Confessions* I.9.14—10.16). When he was eleven or twelve, his parents saved enough money to send him about twenty-six miles south to Madauros for more studies in Roman and Greek literature.[2] He returned home when he was fifteen or sixteen to a year of leisure and license since his parents did not have the money to send him on for further studies. He famously writes about his adolescent pranks and sexual awakening at that time (*Confessions* II).

In 371, his father, Patricius, had secured for Augustine the patronage of a wealthy resident of Thagaste, Romanianus by name. This enabled the seventeen-year-old Augustine to study in Carthage, the "second city in the Western Empire," about one hundred fifty miles east of Thagaste.[3] There, like many university students of other centuries, he threw himself into the "cauldron of raging love affairs—*sartago flagitiosorum amorum*" that the big city offered (*Confessions* III.1.1).

Despite the suggestive and alluring passages in *Confessions* about his sexual exploits, Augustine's behavior was more or less typical of a young man in his time and place. He quickly met one girl with whom he fell in love. She bore him a son whom they named Adeodatus, which means "given by God." Augustine remained faithful to her for thirteen or fourteen years until they separated in Milan, under some pressure from his mother, Monica. She knew that he had to secure a proper wife from the social elites of Milan to advance his career (*Confessions* VI.16.25).[4]

A closer reading of *Confessions* shows that it was less his sexual behavior and more the arrogance, pride, and political and social opportunism of his younger years that he regretted and later confessed to God.[5] Augustine presents his sexual desires as one example of concupiscence. Ambition and the use of others to attain his ends and self-advancement were just as, if not more, sinful results of his inordinate desires. "Quite certainly you command me to refrain from concupiscence of the flesh and concupiscence of the eyes and worldly pride" (*Confessions* X.30.41; see also *Confessions* X.35—36).

Augustine's curriculum at Carthage was mostly the study of literature and rhetoric. The wheels of empire turned on the axes of persuasion and power. Young men who studied in places like Carthage learned how to grease and turn these wheels to their advantage and for their advancement as lawyers and politicians. So they memorized vast amounts of prose and poetry and practiced techniques for constructing arguments and composing speeches. Augustine excelled in all this. However, during his studies in Carthage when he was eighteen, Augustine read a work of Cicero, the *Hortensius*. It awakened in him a love for philosophy and an ardent desire to pursue truth and seek wisdom. "I was aroused and kindled and set on fire to love and seek and capture and hold fast and strongly cling not to this or that school, but to wisdom itself, whatever it might be" (*Confessions* III.4.8). He also—on his own— began a study of Aristotle's categories out of his desire to pursue truth as well as rhetoric (*Confessions* IV.16.28). The translation he read was possibly that by Marcus Victorinus.[6] This was a remarkable achievement for a young student who complemented the usual curriculum of rhetoric with his own earnest pursuit of truth. It presaged his brilliance as a teacher and scholar.

## Manicheism

During his studies at Carthage (370–73), the young Augustine joined the Manichean religion, a sect officially outlawed in the Empire, though the ban was not often enforced. The Manicheans preached a somewhat undigested mix of mythology, philosophy, and religion that intrigued Augustine. They presented themselves as rational guides to truth, which certainly would have caught the attention of a bright and earnest student like Augustine. They also understood human behavior to be largely the result of much stronger cosmic forces for good and ill, which mitigated individual moral responsibility. That may have suited Augustine's liberal lifestyle at that time.[7] In addition, the Manicheans were a close-knit community of friends, a social group that would exert a powerful pull on the very social Augustine.[8]

The founder of the sect was a third-century Persian prophet by the name of Mani who had been a member of a Jewish-Christian Church. His teachings spread quickly around the Empire and there were active communities of Manicheans proselytizing in Carthage and in Rome. Manichean teaching was strongly dualistic, delineating two cosmic forces: one of ethereal light and goodness, the other of heavy material darkness and evil. These two forces were in constant conflict, especially in the human being whose soul properly sought release from the body.[9]

The principle of darkness and evil, which they called *Hyle*, existed from all eternity. This principle or power was in endless conflict with the co-eternal God of light and goodness. They identified the evil principle with the God described in the Old Testament. The good God was the one described in the New Testament and preached by Jesus. The evil darkness is mixed in with every human soul, they taught, and is responsible for our tendency to sin. Such moral teaching fit comfortably with the young adult Augustine's sexual practice and political ambition. It shifted moral responsibility for his behavior from himself and onto the evil power that was at war within him against the good God of light (*Confessions* V.10.18).

Augustine reread the scriptures that he would have known as a youth from his mother's church, hoping to find in them some guidance for his search for truth and understanding (*Confessions* III.5.9). However, as a student of rhetoric, he found the Latin Bible of his time to be of inferior literary quality compared to the Latin classics such as Virgil and Cicero.[10] He learned that the

Manicheans rejected the entire Old Testament and parts of the New Testament that contradicted their dualistic doctrines. This dismissal of many parts of the Bible suited Augustine's literary sensitivities and rationalized his professional disdain for the Scriptures at that time of his life (*Confessions* III.5.9). In addition, Manicheans considered themselves to be Christians. Augustine saw himself to be practicing a kind of superior Christianity that was purified of the Catholic superstition of his mother. Indeed, the Manicheans called Catholics "semi-Christians" (*Answer to Faustus* 1.2).

In 373, Augustine finished his studies in Carthage and returned to Thagaste to teach. He had become an avid advocate for Manichean belief and set about trying to convert his friends back home to his newfound religion. This upset Monica to no end—at first she refused to let Augustine move back into her house upon his return from Carthage (*Confessions* III.11.19). Augustine relates how he tried to convince a dear friend, with whom he had grown up in Thagaste, to become a Manichean. The friend took seriously ill and received Catholic baptism. Augustine visited his sick bed and ridiculed him for being baptized. Then, after Augustine had left, his friend suddenly died (*Confessions* IV.4.7–9). This death so devastated Augustine, now age twenty-two, that he left Thagaste and returned to Carthage to teach.

Augustine tells us that he was a member of the Manichean sect for nine years, "from my nineteenth to my twenty-eighth year" (*Confessions* IV.1.1). He was a Manichean "hearer," that is, a member of the general membership as opposed to the elite, ascetical group of the "elect." Yet, even in his early years in the community, Augustine had lots of questions about their teachings and writings. While teaching in Carthage (374–83), he finally got the opportunity to meet a Manichean bishop named Faustus. For years his Manichean associates had promised Augustine that Faustus was an expert who would be able to "sort out and resolve" Augustine's questions (*Confessions* V.6.10). Augustine found Faustus to be an effective public speaker and quite affable, but "ill-educated in the liberal arts, apart from grammar, and even in that schooled only to an average level" (*Confessions* V.6.11). He was unable to satisfy Augustine's intellectual probing of Manichean doctrine. Augustine's disappointment with Faustus had left him disillusioned with the sect. He later realized that this disappointment began to "set him free from the trap" of their doctrine (*Confessions* V.7.13).

By 383, Augustine had grown weary of the students in Carthage who were rowdy and disruptive (*Confessions* V.8.14). So he, an ambitious colonial from the North African outback, set his sights on Rome, where there were better students and more opportunities. Monica was devastated and tried to prevent his going. Augustine lied to his mother to convince her that he was not leaving. That very same night, he slipped aboard a ship bound for Rome. This lie haunted Augustine: "I lied to my mother—and what a mother!" (*Confessions* V.8.15).[11]

## Rome, Milan, Conversion

Upon arriving in Rome, Augustine stayed with the Manichean community there. However, though he maintained his social connections with them, his interest in Manichean teachings continued to wane (*Confessions* V.10.18). While in Rome, he began to find the credulity of the Manicheans off-putting and their teachings more and more fantastic. He moved toward the philosophical skepticism and universal doubt of the Greek Academics, who taught "that no part of the truth could be understood by the human mind" (*Confessions* V.10.19).[12]

It was not the Manicheans, but the pagan Prefect of Rome, Symmachus, who secured for Augustine his big break. Symmachus recommended Augustine for the position of Imperial *Rhetor* in Milan, where the boy Emperor Valentian II and his regent Empress mother Justina held court in those years. Augustine left Rome for Milan in 384 to take his new position at court. This role comprised what we might today call a president's or prime minister's speech writer and spokesperson all in one. So after only a year teaching in Rome, Augustine moved to Milan and to the summit of his secular profession.

However, in God's design, as he later realized, the journey from Rome to Milan was another step on his spiritual pilgrimage. It enabled him finally to get away from the Manicheans on whom he had grown so dependent (*Confessions* V.13.23).[13] It also brought him before Bishop Ambrose, whose teaching was to have a profound effect on the young African.

Though it was difficult to meet one-on-one with the busy bishop, Ambrose's teaching deeply affected Augustine first by its eloquence, then by its content (*Confessions* V.13.23; VI.3.3—5.8).[14] The way Ambrose interpreted scripture in his homilies opened Augustine's eyes to the deeper spiritual, symbolic, and allegorical meanings of the text. Fourth-century North Africans—Catholics, Donatists, and Manicheans—read the Bible in a much more literal fashion. Generally, the Africans of Numidia followed the Syrian-Antiochene approach to reading scripture, which favored a more literal interpretation. The Milanese favored the more analogical and allegorical hermeneutics of the Alexandrian School. Augustine would bring the latter approach back to Africa and employ it in his anti-Manichean and anti-Donatist writing and preaching.

In addition, it was in Milan that Augustine came to read "some books by the Platonists, translated from Greek into Latin" (*Confessions* VII.9.13).[15] Neo-Platonism opened Augustine's mind to the possibility of understanding God as pure spirit, something that he, as a Manichean, had not previously imagined (*Confessions* V.13.23–24; VIII.1.1—2.3; 9.13—10.16; 17.23).[16] These breakthroughs to more sophisticated and subtle biblical hermeneutics and to philosophical metaphysics were the necessary intellectual antecedents for Augustine's religious conversion.

On a personal and ethical level, it wasn't long before the stress of court politics, the pressure of his teaching, the ambiguity of his convictions, and what he would come to identify as the immanent grace of God led him to abandon his career, seek baptism, and dedicate himself to a celibate Christian life of prayer and study in community back home in Africa. He had come to know about the monk Antony of Egypt and about other Roman courtiers and notables who had given up worldly pursuits to follow Christ in humility and simplicity of life (*Confessions* VIII.2.3—7.18). He wanted to follow that course.

Thus, in the spring of 386, his long personal search for meaning and truth climaxed in conversion to Catholic Christianity, the religion of his mother, Monica, and of his childhood (*Confessions* VIII). In the fall of 386, he resigned his position at court and withdrew from teaching. Along with his mother, his son, his lifelong friend and fellow citizen of Thagaste Alypius, and a few others, he retired to a villa in Cassiciasum, north of Milan to prepare for baptism. At the Easter Vigil on April 26/27 of 387, Augustine was baptized in Milan by Bishop Ambrose. Augustine's teenage son, Adeodatus, and Alypius also entered the waters of Baptism on that auspicious night.

Having abandoned his career and separated from the woman who was his companion and mother of their son, the newly baptized Augustine and his retinue returned to Africa in 388 to live an ascetic life of study and prayer in a kind of Christian commune that he set up at the family home in Thagaste. Monica died in the Roman port city of Ostia, as this group of expatriate Africans made their way back to Thagaste (*Confessions* IX). A year or two after their return, Augustine's seventeen-year-old son, Adeodatus, died.[17] Thus between 386 and 390, Augustine's life changed dramatically. Though he gained his faith, he lost his woman, his mother, his son, and his career. He intended a quiet African retreat and retirement. God, he would later realize, had other plans.[18]

In 391, Augustine visited Hippo Regius, a port city about fifty miles north of Thagaste. He had traveled there to recruit a new member and to start a new community in Hippo. While there he was recognized by the local Catholic congregation assembled for worship. They immediately demanded that this somewhat famous

convert be ordained as their priest—a turn of events in which historical evidence suggests Valerius, the elderly bishop of Hippo, was
implicated.[19] He was doing his succession planning, and quite well.
So the thirty-seven-year-old Augustine, standing before the congregation in Hippo in 391, protesting their request for his ordination,
began a new life.[20] His little monastic community of ascetic friends,
the people of his congregation, and the wider church would be the
ones to whom he now dedicated himself.

Augustine spent the next thirty-nine years serving the church
in Hippo. His ordination as priest in 391, and then as bishop in 395
made him a public figure once again. He visited the towns in his
diocese and made frequent journeys to Carthage, at that time the
mother church of central and western North Africa. He worked
closely with Aurelius, the bishop of Carthage, to reform and
strengthen the church in North Africa. As a minister of the Gospel
of Jesus Christ, his days were dedicated to preaching, teaching, and
the celebration of the sacraments. He also brought his immense
intellect and rhetorical skills to help the fifth-century church sort
through religious questions, controversies, and concerns of the day.
There were three major theological controversies that he had to
address as a leader of the church. From his ordination in 391 until
around the year 411, he worked for the unity of the church amidst
the conflict between the Donatist sect and the Catholic Church;
from 410 until he died, he engaged in a theological debate with
Pelagius and his devotees about the nature of divine grace; and, as
refugees from the sack of Rome in 410 began to arrive in Hippo
with their Arian sympathies, he had to address the Catholic teaching on the divine nature of Jesus Christ.

## Donatism

When Augustine was first ordained, Catholics were a minority
sect in the city of Hippo.[21] Soon after becoming a priest, Augustine
had to face the fact that the church in North Africa was split down

the middle in schism. As a young man in Thagaste and Carthage, such a rift in church life would hardly have concerned him. Even upon his return from Italy in 388, when he retired to a life of Christian prayer and study at home in Thagaste, he did not have to deal directly with church politics. However, as soon as he became a priest in service to Bishop Valerius of Hippo, he had to face the painful reality that there were two major Christian churches in North Africa: the Catholics and the Donatists.

Though identical in creed and liturgy, Catholics and Donatists differed on how to understand and live out the mystery of the church, on the role of the one who administered baptism, and on the exclusive primacy of Donatist baptism. Throughout the third century, the Roman Empire initiated persecutions against Christians. Particularly brutal were those imposed during the reigns of the emperors Decius (249–51), Valerian I (253–60), and Diocletian (284–305). Many Christians, both laity and clergy, suffered torture, exile, or execution for their faith. In contrast, others compromised by handing over to Roman authorities the books and properties of the church, or turning in the names of their Christian brothers and sisters.[22] When persecutions subsided, some from among these lapsed believers or traitors sought forgiveness and reintegration into the church community.

In North Africa, the ecclesial response to such requests for forgiveness and reconciliation was mixed. The more rigorous position was that lapsed Christians—clergy or lay—could not be accepted back into the church unless they were in mortal danger. This more rigorous faction also decided that, not only were lapsed clergy forbidden to return to office, but anyone baptized or ordained by a lapsed bishop had to be rebaptized or reordained, since the sacramental ministry of these one-time traitors was considered invalid. Likewise the consecration of a bishop that included a lapsed bishop among the three canonically required to consecrate was fatally compromised and considered invalid. As we shall see, Augustine argued that the power of the sacrament came not through the minister, but through the grace of Christ.

Throughout the third century, many, including Saint Cyprian, bishop of Carthage from around 248 to 258, argued for the church discipline that prohibited lapsed clergy from returning to their ministries, though he allowed for their forgiveness. Cyprian also practiced rebaptism, though he did not make it a point of separation from the wider church or from Rome. Upon his own martyrdom, the controversy grew even worse as clergy who had betrayed the church did, in fact, return to their posts.

After the Diocletian persecution (303–5), which further intensified the protests by rigorists in North Africa, a new bishop of Carthage was consecrated in 311, Caecilian by name. The rigorists rejected his leadership, claiming that one of the three co-consecrators had been a traitor. So they consecrated a rival bishop who died shortly thereafter, but whose immediate episcopal successor was one Donatus Magnus, a charismatic Berber from the southern outback of Numidia. Thus began in Carthage a situation soon to be repeated across North Africa. Eventually, most cities and towns had two bishops, two clergies, two congregations: one Catholic and one rigorist. The latter became known as Donatists.[23]

When Augustine became a priest in 391, the Catholics in Hippo were actually in the minority. As priest and then bishop, Augustine had to argue against the common Donatist practice of rebaptizing Catholics who might join their faction, and to contend with the anti-Catholic prejudice his congregants had to endure. Even more, he also had to protect Catholics from the growing threat of violence against them by a fringe group of Donatists known as *circumcellions*. The latter were bands of nomadic, anti-Roman Berbers who joined forces and identified with the Donatists, attacking, maiming, and killing Catholic clergy and laity.[24] Augustine tells how groups of circumcellions blinded Catholics by throwing a mixture of lime and vinegar into their eyes. He also reports how they burned Catholic homes, set fire to their crops, and smashed valuable large amphorae containing oil and wine (*Letter* 88.8).[25]

In the first decade of the fifth century, the Roman government attempted to curtail the North African sect and control the violence. In 405, the Emperor Honorius signed the "Edict of Union," effectively outlawing Donatism. But skillful Donatist politicking had neutralized enforcement of the edict. Disagreement, disunity, and violence continued.[26]

The Donatist controversy climaxed in an ecclesiastical conference in Carthage in 411. Under the watchful eye of Marcellinus, a representative of Honorius, most of the bishops of North Africa, Catholic and Donatists, assembled to argue their case against each other's positions.[27] Augustine spoke for the Catholics and, according to the decision of Marcellinus, won the argument. After 411, the Roman government began a program to punish Donatist clergy or laity who refused to accept the decision made at Carthage. As we shall see when we review Augustine's anti-Donatist writings, he had very mixed feelings about government-imposed religion.[28]

## Pelagianism

The greatest controversy of Augustine's ministry concerned theological positions associated with Pelagius. This debate, in which Augustine engaged from around 411 until the end of his life, was not so much about church discipline and sectarian strife as in the Donatist controversy. Rather it was a dispute over what Augustine considered the very heart of Christian faith: the nature of divine grace and redemption.

Pelagius was a monk from the British Isles. He was born around 354 and died sometime between 420 and 440—which makes him contemporaneous with Augustine. Arriving in Rome around 380, he became known among Christians there for his asceticism, moral virtue, and teaching.

It was at Rome in 404 or 405 that the first spark of the controversy between Pelagius and Augustine ignited. Pelagius was listening to a reading of Book X of Augustine's *Confessions*, which had begun circulating around 400. Three times in that book

Augustine says "Give what you command and command what you will."[29] According to an eyewitness, Pelagius grew visibly agitated at the phrase and the idea behind it: whatever good we do in our attempt to follow God's will is made possible by God's grace, not by our effort.[30] To Pelagius, such an approach undermined free will. Pelagius would have been primed to detect and react to interpretations of divine grace, for around this same time, he was writing his own *Commentary on the Epistles of St. Paul* and his book *On Nature.*[31] He was more than likely responding in these works to Augustine's writing on *Romans* and on Paul's theology in *Miscellany of Questions in Response to Simplicianus.*[32]

About five years later, in 410, Pelagius left Rome, one of thousands of refugees fleeing the assault by Alaric and the Visigoths. He disembarked at Hippo where he stayed briefly. He then traveled to Carthage with his friend and theological sympathizer Caelestius. As far as we know, Pelagius and Augustine never met face to face. Augustine was not in Hippo when Pelagius passed through, a theological and historical regret if ever there was one. And when both men were in Carthage at the same time in 411, Augustine was busy with preparations for the confrontation with the Donatists at the upcoming conference.

Though he soon left Carthage for Jerusalem, Pelagius's ideas gain a foothold in the North African Church, especially through his friend Caelestius, who stayed on in Carthage. For his proselytizing of Pelagius's ideas on original sin and grace, Caelestius was condemned at an ecclesiastical trial in Carthage late in the fall of 411 and again at councils in Carthage and Melivis in 416. In the section on Augustine's writings on Pelagianism in chapter 3, we will trace the development of his theology of grace. Augustine had already been thinking quite a bit about God's grace, especially in his early years as bishop in the late 390s. To respond to Pelagius's teaching, Augustine returns again and again in subsequent decades to try to plumb the depths of grace and salvation. As we shall see, even in Augustine's old age, he had to contend with continued attacks from supporters of Pelagius.

## Arianism

Arian Christianity was not widespread or popular in North Africa before the sack of Rome by Alaric. Consequently, Augustine's interest in Arianism is less evident than his interest in Donatism and Pelagianism. However, after 410, refugees from Rome and Italy poured into North African ports like Hippo and Carthage. With them came many Christians who subscribed to a different understanding of who Jesus was and what he meant to believers. In response to these new members of African congregations, Augustine took on the teachings of Arius.

Arius (ca. 256–336) was a presbyter of the church in Alexandria, Egypt. His teaching about Jesus Christ emphasized the Son's subordination to God the Father. As a Christian, Arius confessed Jesus to be the Word made flesh. However, he believed the Word or Logos was not coeternal with the Father. There was a time when the Word or Son of God did not exist. The Word or Son was generated from the Father prior to creation, and so was not coeternal or consubstantial with the father. Therefore, Jesus as the incarnate Word was not eternally equal to the Father.

Arius's preaching stirred great controversy that spread around the empire. As the first Christian emperor, Constantine took an unprecedented step to confront this growing division among Christians. In 325, he convened and presided over a church council in Nicea. He wanted to settle the issue and calm the imperial waters whipped up by such a theological storm. This First Council of Nicea condemned Arius's interpretation of Scripture and his teaching on the subordination of the Word of God to God. The Incarnate Word of God was "consubstantial" or one in essence (*homoousion*) with the Father, as Christians still recite in the Nicene Creed. Jesus is equal to the Father.

However, Arius's ideas had taken hold and continued to spread around the Empire. Constantine's immediate successor, Constantius II, who ruled from 337 to 361, was of Arian persuasion, as was the later Emperor Valens who ruled from 364 to 378.

Arius's ideas were eradicated by Emperor Theodosius I (379–95) in the Eastern part of the Empire, but they survived in the West in various iterations, and predominated among the Northern tribes, such as the Goths and the Vandals, who invaded and occupied Italy, Gaul, Spain, and North Africa. Alaric and his Visigoths were Arian Christians, as were the Vandal troops who held Hippo under siege when Augustine lay dying in his city in 430.

Augustine would have first encountered Arian Christians in Milan. In the spring of 386, Bishop Ambrose took a bold political stand against the powerful Empress Justina, regent and mother of Valentian II. Justina was an Arian. She was demanding a church in Milan so that her co-worshippers could celebrate Easter. Monica joined Ambrose and other Catholics in a "sit-in" so that the Arians could not take possession of the particular church building Justina wanted (*Confessions* IX.7.15). Eventually, in the face of the powerful Ambrose, Justina and the imperial soldiers, many of whom were Catholic, stood down. So Augustine certainly knew all about this doctrinal dispute among Christians. But in the spring of 386, he himself was not yet a Christian and his own sense of Jesus' identity was still very much in flux (*Confessions* VII.18.24—21.27). As we shall see, Augustine's sermons and books from the second and third decades of the fifth century reflect the development of his Christology, as he labors to give his congregation a deeper, fuller understanding of the mystery of the Incarnation.

## Beyond Controversies

In the theological controversies that swirled around Donatism, Pelagianism, and Arianism, Augustine took a leading role in outlining arguments, defining terms, and identifying core issues. He wielded his impressive rhetorical skills in defense and advancement of his local church community in Hippo and more widely in North Africa and beyond. However, other churchmen did not always concur or automatically defer to him. He was sometimes challenged, sometimes championed, and sometimes ignored by his clerical colleagues across North Africa.[33] From our twenty-first century perspective, it is important to remember that during his lifetime, Augustine had to argue forcibly for his theological positions, which did not immediately enjoy prominence or authority. The power of his thought and writing can lure us into forgetting that the reforms that he and Aurelius of Carthage envisioned for Numidia required much sustained effort to realize.

The research and discoveries over the past fifty to sixty years have revealed new insights into the life and work of the Bishop of Hippo. We have a better understanding of the wider ecclesial, social, and political contexts of the controversies he faced. We are more attentive to Augustine the pastor who, amidst his composition of famous doctrinal texts, ministered day after day to his people. His role as Christian apologist was an extension of his more basic vocation as preacher of the Word and minister of the sacraments to his congregation. Theological controversy was not for its own sake. Augustine argued and struggled to understand for himself and to teach others what the grace of the Incarnation of God in Christ and the Divine Trinity actually meant for their souls, the church, society, and human history.

Augustine died on August 28, 430. His beloved city of Hippo Regius was under siege by the Vandals who had crossed over from the Iberian Peninsula, led by their chieftain Genseric. Catholic bishops and congregations, along with African Donatists and Manicheans, would suffer at the hands of these Arian tribesmen, who over the next century would use North Africa as a staging area to sail north and bring an end to Rome's domination of the West. They themselves would disappear under the wave of Islam that swept out of Arabia and across North Africa two hundred years later in the second half of the seventh century.

Possidius tells us that Augustine was conscious and alert to the end, and that he died quietly and peacefully, with the words of the penitential psalms written out on sheets attached to the wall of his bedroom and with the attention of his monastic brothers to console him (*Life*, XXXI.5). In a most touching tribute to his life-long friend and fellow bishop, Possidius ends his biography with these words:

> From the writings of this priest, so pleasing and dear to God, it is clear, as far as the light of truth allows humans to see, that he led a life of uprightness and integrity in the faith, hope, and love of the Catholic Church. This is certainly acknowledged by those who read his writings on the things of God. I believe, however, that they profited even more who were able to hear him speaking in church and see him there present, especially if they were familiar with his manner of life among his fellow human beings. (*Life*, XXXI.9)

As we turn now in chapters 2 and 3 to his writings, we can exercise our imaginations to hear him preaching to the people in his Basilica of Peace in Hippo. We can overhear him discussing his latest ideas and compositions with his brother monks and fellow clerics gathered at table for a simple monastic meal. We can, from a distance, watch him in his library laboring long into the African night, dictating and revising his thoughts. From our vantage point, we now know that in that quiet room, filled only with his voice and the stirring of scribes, the way people think about God, faith, and religion was being forever changed.[34]

# 2
# WRITINGS I
*Major Books*

Augustine wrote an enormous amount. Including his sermons and letters, he penned the equivalent of a three-hundred-page book each year from the time of his conversion on. In total his compositions comprise five million words that have survived in a vast array of manuscripts.[1]

He was not a systematic writer, summarizing and correlating his ideas in neatly organized theological tracts like the *Summa* of St. Thomas Aquinas. However, he did think systematically in the sense that he repeatedly explored and refined basic theological ideas that continually emerged in his work in response to constant pastoral problems and challenges.[2] His favorite themes are our free but wounded will, original sin and its effects, our responsibility for sin, the nature of evil, our essential need for God's unlimited grace, and the centrality of God's humility and love revealed in the incarnation and lived-in communion with Christ and the church. Throughout his works, he adjusts and polishes these theological lenses to focus on particular pastoral and doctrinal concerns, and to discern the mysterious presence of God in the depths of human experience.

The power of Augustine's works emerges from his motivations for writing. He felt a deep need to confess, that is, to witness to his faith in the power and goodness of God: "Truth it is that I want to do, in my heart by confession in your presence, and with my pen before many witnesses" (*Confessions* X.1.1). He felt a strong sense of pastoral responsibility for the spiritual welfare of his people and his church: "I don't want to be saved without you" (*Sermon* 17.2). Moreover, frequent personal requests from his many friends and colleagues, and daily pastoral challenges moved him to employ his literary and rhetorical skills in the service of the Gospel: "Pray for me, that as long as there is a soul in this body, and any kind of strength supplied to it, I may serve you in preaching the Word of God" (*Sermon* 335.2.7). That combination of motives produced some of the greatest classics in Christian literature.

In this chapter, we will review five classic works that emerged from Augustine's literary and religious passion. We will provide short commentary to outline and contextualize each book, and suggest contemporary scholarship that has deepened and broadened our understandings of these books. These prominent works include: *Confessions, City of God, The Trinity, Teaching Christianity, Expositions of the Psalms*. We will then look at the four books called the Cassiciacum Dialogues.

## *Confessions*

We know much about Augustine's life up to his conversion (386) and the death of Monica (387) from the first nine books of his *Confessions*. When Augustine succeeded Valerius as bishop in 395, there were many clergy and laity in North Africa who remained suspicious of this former Manichean proselytizer. How to lay their suspicions to rest? From another quarter, Paulinus of Nola, a nobleman and lawyer in Italy who had left his wealth and status for the ascetic life of a monk, had asked Alypius to write an account of his life and how he had converted to Christianity. Alypius, Augustine's longtime friend and brother monk, deferred. So Augustine writes to Paulinus, promising him that he would write the story of his own conversion as well as that of Alypius (*Letter* 27.5).

Between 397/398 and 400, Augustine set about composing the story of how he came to Christian faith and baptism. The result was an astonishing literary work that is still to be found in bookstores and libraries around the globe in all the world's major languages. *Confessions,* though autobiographical, is not autobiography in the modern sense.[3] Augustine does not provide a thorough year-by-year account of his life up to the age of 45 or so. He is selective in what he tells, skillfully using narratives from his life to advance his most deeply held theological and philosophical beliefs.

One could argue that Augustine invented a new literary genre by confessing his sinfulness to God in the "hearing" of his readers with whom he wanted to share his faith and clarify his convictions. In Latin, *confessio/confiteri* not only means "to confess"; it also carries the meaning "to praise and thank." Throughout *Confessions,* Augustine interweaves stories from his life with profound theological reflections and ebullient praise and thanks to God for divine forgiveness and love. So *Confessions* is a kind of prayerful memoir written to tell the truth of his story, and to inspire others to reflect on the presence and power of God in his life and in theirs as well.

The amount of scholarship on *Confessions* is "boundless," but "little consensus" has been reached on questions about the text that have persisted for centuries.[4] For example, what is the unity of the thirteen books? Thirteen books comprise *Confessions*—each book being the length of what today we would call a chapter.[5] Books I to VIII are unified by their climax: Augustine's conversion to Christ. Book IX is dedicated largely to Monica. Book X explains why he wrote *Confessions.* It is a reflection on the nature of memory and of conscience, and leads to an affirmation of Christ as Mediator and nourishment. It contains some of the most poignant expressions of Augustine's experience of God's love and grace. Books XI to XIII are an interpretive commentary on the beginning of the Book of Genesis (1:1—2:3), in the context of time and eternity (Book XI). Augustine extols the goodness of the power of God revealed through creation. He relates the Genesis narrative to Christian re-creation through Baptism, leading to eternal life and rest (Book XIII).

Another major question concerns the rhetorical style of the work. What is the historical authenticity of the personal events he so vividly recounts, such as the famous conversion scene in Book VIII? Is his description of the scene in the garden mostly a dramatic, literary representation? Or did it happen pretty much as he describes? There are even larger questions about the work. Is Augustine's life really the unifying theme? Or is *Confessions* more a dialogue between Augustine and God? Or, should the whole work be read and interpreted in the light of Christian faith in the Trinity?

As a literary classic, we can expect that, "Each generation will see it on the basis of its own premises and therefore read it differently."[6] A recent example of contemporary Augustine scholars wrestling with many of these enduring questions about Augustine's most popular work is *A Reader's Companion to Augustine's Confessions* edited by Kim Paffenroth and Robert Kennedy.[7] The editors assigned each of the thirteen books in *Confessions* to a different scholar (including themselves). Then that scholar was asked to argue that his or her assigned book is the one upon which the unity of *Confessions* as a whole rests. This editorial device produces a fascinating series of essays that help the reader understand the importance of each of the thirteen books and its relationship with the others and with the work as a whole. Most of the persistent questions that readers and scholars have posed about the work are reprised and reconsidered in fresh ways by the contributors. This *Companion* also provides even the frequent reader of *Confessions* with new appreciation of the literary, philosophical, theological, historical, psychological, structural, and rhetorical dimensions of each of the thirteen books.

A different valuable compendium of contemporary scholarship on *Confessions* is found in *Collectanea Augustiniana* edited by Joseph Schnaubelt, OSA, and Frederick Van Fleteren.[8] In part one of this collection of fine essays, scholars from around the world address the many aspects of Augustine's conversion as presented in *Confessions*. In part two, still other scholars analyze the literary structure of the work using different paradigms such as psychobiography, paradox, narrative patterns, and unifying grids in the composition of the work. Together *Collectanea Augustiniana* and *A Reader's Companion to Augustine's Confessions* present new studies on multiple questions about Augustine's classic by twenty-three different contemporary scholars.[9]

Another "companion" to *Confessions* is Margaret Miles's *Desire and Delight: A New Reading of Augustine's Confessions*.[10] Miles spent a summer slowly rereading *Confessions* in Augustine's Latin—on a beach in Greece. She introduces this personal detail to emphasize her reading of the text as a beautifully sensuous experience. Both Augustine's artful language and his use of sometimes selective, tantalizing personal details "function to invite the reader into the text as conversation partner, opponent, supporter, and co-author."[11] She assumes that Augustine, as a skillful writer, is fully aware of the contradictions his text poses. For example, there is his experience and appellation of God as "Beauty" over against an ascetic rejection of the enjoyment of such beauties in creation as human sexuality. Yet, she argues, Augustine chooses to let these contradictions remain so that his readers will experience the ambiguities for themselves. At the same time, Miles provides a feminist critique of the lack of integration of spirit and matter she sees persisting in Augustine's Neo-Platonism. She provides an appreciative but critical reading of *Confessions* using her interpretive lens of beauty and pleasure.

Two other contemporary works deserve mention. The first because it is written by a teacher-scholar whose concern is to bring new generations of students to an appreciation of Augustine. In *Language and Love: Introducing Augustine's Religious Thought Through the Confessions Story*, William Mallard uses *Confessions* as a way of introducing students to the major themes in Augustine's theology.[12] As many others have attempted, Mallard retells Augustine's *Confessions* in contemporary English, while trying to retain some of the rhythm and elegance of the original Latin.[13] His purpose is twofold: He wants young people to find Augustine's story relevant to their own struggles; and he wants to avail them of Augustine's language, especially his theological language about love of God and neighbor, as useful for their own spiritual journeys in today's complex world.

A very different book is by Jaroslav Pelikan (1923–2006): *The Mystery of Continuity: Time and History, Memory and Eternity, in the Thought of St. Augustine.*[14] Pelikan was one of the greatest historians of Christian theology in the twentieth century. His book invites the reader to appreciate the philosophical-theological depth of *Confessions*. He argues that Augustine understood both his own conversion to Christianity as well as the role of Christianity in the history of the ancient Roman world more in terms of continuity than discontinuity. Pelikan sees the power of *Confessions* as a classic to be rooted in Augustine's piercing questions about fundamental categories of human experience. His book provides thoughtful analyses, especially of the themes of memory and time in books X and XI. His analysis of these later, nonnarrative books of *Confessions* prepares the schooled reader to review all of *Confessions* with a sharper theological lens. He also sets these philosophical-theological categories in the context of Augustine's profound influence on the history of thought in the Western world. From *Confessions*, Pelikan moves on to analyze these same themes in *City of God*, *The Trinity*, and in many of Augustine's major works, thus elucidating the development of major Augustinian ideas across the decades of Augustine's writings.

Roland J. Teske, SJ, provides another close, philosophical look at the theme of time in Augustine in his *Paradoxes of Time in Saint Augustine.*[15] Teske has done many translations of Augustine's works for the New City Press series and is one of the leading Augustine scholars in the United States. In this book, he brings his considerable philosophical and theological expertise to this analysis. He also provides a valuable and extensive bibliography of contemporary scholarship on the treatment of time in Book XI of *Confessions*.

In 1992, Oxford University Press published James J. O'Donnell's

*Augustine: Confessions* in three volumes.[16] O'Donnell, a classicist by profession, does not provide a translation, presuming his readers can read Augustine's Latin. Volume 1 is an introduction both to the text of *Confessions* and to O'Donnell's interpretative approach, followed by the complete Latin text of the thirteen books. He also provides an overview of scholarship from the last century on *Confessions*. Volumes 2 and 3 are O'Donnell's word-by-word, phrase-by-phrase masterful commentary on the text. His work has received superlative reviews and is an invaluable resource both for the scholar and for any interested reader who wishes to plumb the depths of Augustine's Latin language and thought. In his explication and interpretation of the text, O'Donnell strives to take Augustine at his word. In this intellectual autobiography, he is confessing to God.[17] So *Confessions* are about Augustine and about God: "more Augustine at the beginning, more God at the end."[18] O'Donnell's quick and witty style will delight the reader who is prepared to do a thorough study of Augustine's classical text.

A comment from O'Donnell's introduction to Augustine's most famous work is good advice to anyone who seeks to study and understand the work: "It is impossible, then, to take the *Confessions* in a vacuum, and it is impossible to give any single interpretation that will satisfy. Even these few paragraphs of summary give a misleading impression of simplicity and directness, for a work that draws its rare power from complexity, subtlety, and nuance."[19]

There are several fine English translations of *Confessions*. The Benedictine nun and hermitess Maria Boulding translated *Confessions* for the New City Press series. It has steadily been gaining recognition as one of the finest new English renditions of Augustine's enduring classic and was republished in 2012 with a very helpful annotated bibliography by William Harmless, SJ.[20] Henry Chadwick did a superb translation of *Confessions*, which was first published in 1991 for the Oxford World's Classic series.[21] As one of the world's leading Augustine scholars, Chadwick offers an accessible English text sensitive to the subtleties of Augustine's brilliant Latin. There is also the benefit of Chadwick's scholarly introduction and valuable notes on Augustine's text to help the reader enter Augustine's theological and philosophical world. Another translation by R. S. Pine-Coffin, a Roman Catholic who studied at Cambridge, continues to wear well since it first appeared in 1961 as part of Penguin Classics.[22] Perhaps the most widely known English translation since its appearance in 1942 is that by Frank J. Sheed, the Australian-British writer and publisher.[23] This was reprinted in 1993 with an introduction by Peter Brown, and again in 2006 with an introduction by Henry Chadwick.

## *City of God*

Augustine called this book his *"magnum opus et arduum"*—a long and difficult work (*City of God*, preface). It is long in two ways. It consists in twenty-two books (again, each book being what we today would call a long chapter), running about a thousand, small-print pages in most English translations. It also took him thirteen or fourteen years to write.

As with so many of his works, the writing was in response to real-life situations. On August 24, 410, Alaric invaded the city of Rome at the head of an army of Visigoths. This unthinkable event shook the entire Roman Empire to its core. Political refugees fled Rome and flooded cities such as Carthage and Hippo Regius that were situated at a safe distance, separated by the Mediterranean Sea, from the rampaging central and northern European tribes. Augustine's congregation in Hippo received many of these refugees.

In addition to the social and economic problems created by the sack of Rome, Augustine felt compelled to deal with the accusations of those who blamed the disaster on the spread of Christianity.[24] Rome fell, they claimed, because Christianity had undermined the traditional religious rites and tributes to the gods and goddesses of their ancestors. In 411 or 412, we find the beginnings of Augustine's reflection on the meaning and causes of the fall of Rome in a letter he wrote to his friend Marcellinus, a Christian who was imperial commissioner in Africa (*Letter* 138).[25]

In 413, Augustine began to write his long work, though his writing would be interrupted by many pastoral duties and concerns. Throughout the work, Augustine develops theological themes in epic fashion. He critiques Roman history, politics, and religion, showing that Rome's fortunes or misfortunes coincide not with human courting of or cavorting with gods and goddesses, but with the quality and exercise of justice in society. He discerns the seeds of divine intervention in history through the virtue of those who love God above all else, and finds the weeds of evil growing among those who love themselves above all else.

The text is not an easy read. Conscious of the length and complexity of the work, and perhaps in response to some daunted readers, Augustine himself provided an outline of the twenty-two books. He does this in the review of his writings *Revisions* 2.43, which he completed in 427, not long after finishing *City of God*. The first five books discuss the Roman cult of divinities and the demise of this cult as the cause of the fall of Rome—as claimed by Roman historians, politicians, and other protagonists of the old civic religion in the Republic and Empire. In Books VI to X, Augustine turns to Greece, its philosophers, and to a consideration of natural religion; that is, religion without the revelation provided by God through Sacred Scripture, climaxing in the Incarnation of Christ. He disputes the efficaciousness of pagan cult and philosophy for the afterlife and happiness with God.[26] "With these ten books, then, those two vain opinions that are inimical to the Christian religion are refuted" (*Revisions* 2.43 [70].1).

Books XI to XIV show the origin of the "two cities." It is in Book XIV that we read the famous words where Augustine defines the two cities: "Two loves, then, have made two cities. Love of self, even to the point of contempt for God, made the earthly city, and love of God, even to the point of contempt for self, made the heavenly city. Thus the former glories in itself, and the latter glories in the Lord" (XIV.28). These two loves are the principles that Augustine uses to interpret human history, society, and power—all of which rise or fall not on the whims of gods and goddesses, nor on military power or political might. Rather, societies rise and fall on the quality of the decisions of the humans who inhabit them. Human volition, aided by necessary divine grace given in and through Christ, thereby makes virtuous decisions that prosper peace and justice. Human volition, resisting grace and ignoring God and the good of the neighbor, reaps conflict and injustice.[27]

Books XV through XVIII follow the growth and development of the two cities. Augustine makes the point again and again that these two cities are not separate, discrete social or political realities that can be identified with any one human society or institution, including the church.

> All the while the Heavenly city lives in exile on this earth, it recruits citizens from every nation, gathering a society of aliens who speak all languages. It takes no account of the differences in their customs, laws and institutions, by which earthly peace is established or maintained. It suppresses none of them, destroys none. Rather, it maintains and observes everything that, though different in different nations, tends to one and the same end, earthly peace, at least provided nothing impedes the religion that teaches us to worship the one true and sovereign God. (*City of God* XIX.17)

These two populations or "cities" are found mixed around the world in all societies, even in the church, like the wheat mixed with the chaff in the Gospel parable (*City of God* I.35). Each city is moving through history toward its destiny, though it is often difficult to discern God's will and divine intervention in the vicissitudes of history and human affairs. Citizens of the City of God travel amid the movements of history as pilgrims on the way to their true home in the Heavenly City and the Eternal Sabbath (*City of God* XXII.29—30). It is only at the end of history that the two cities will be separated, as they reach their separate aims—the theme of Books XIX to XXII.

About ten years after the end of World War II, at a gathering of patristic scholars in Paris, the French historian and Christian humanist Henri-Irenee Marrou (1904–77) called for a contemporary, formal synthesis that would capture the essence of Augustine's *City of God*. Perhaps it is no surprise that after two devastating World Wars, the scourge of National Socialism, the Vichy Government, the tragedy of the Holocaust, the inception of the Cold War, and the use of atomic weapons, a Frenchman would call for renewed study of a classic work by a father of the church that wrestles with questions of politics, empire, history, war, peace, and human destiny.[28]

The synthesis of *City of God* that Marrou called for has not yet been achieved. Nor is it likely to happen. Classics tend to elude formal or final syntheses that organize and summarize their themes in linear fashion. This is as true for *City of God* as it is for *Confessions*. However, Marrou's call for renewed study of *City of God* did mobilize a new generation of scholars who have returned to this classic work of Augustine to discover its continuing relevance. The ongoing collaboration among these scholars has opened new understandings into Augustine's reflection on history, politics, and humanity.

There are two valuable bibliographic summaries of this contemporary scholarship on Augustine's "long and difficult work." Dorothy Donnelly and Mark Sherman edited the volume *Augustine's De* Civitate Dei: *An Annotated Bibliography of Modern Criticism, 1960–1990.*[29] This book provides the researcher with a ready list of the diverse scholarship that followed Marrou throughout most of the second half of the twentieth century. This bibliographic overview continues in *History, Apocalypse, and the Secular Imagina-*

*tion: New Essays on Augustine's* City of God.[30] In her section of the Introduction to this book, Karla Pollmann provides an overview of "The *City of God* in Current Research (1991–1999)." She covers current research in English, Italian, German, and French.[31]

Among this extensive scholarship, the novice reader of *City of God* will find certain works helpful. Peter Brown published his influential biography *Augustine of Hippo* in 1967.[32] A few years later he published *Religion and Society in the Age of Saint Augustine.*[33] With his typical clarity and graceful style, Brown brings the reader into the social and religious contexts out of which Augustine's thinking in *City of God* arises.[34]

Among the most influential scholars on *City of God* is the British historian of Late Antiquity, Robert Markus (1939–2011). His work has generated extensive interest in Augustine's tome as an important centerpiece of late Roman antiquity. In *Saeculum: History and Society in the Theology of St. Augustine,* he shows how Augustine's text relates to prior critical analyses of history and society, and how those other thinkers influenced Augustine in his writing *City of God.*[35] Importantly, he argues that Augustine rejects the sacralization of any social order or political structure, a point often missed by those who cite Augustine's thought as canonizing Constantinian Christianity and government sanctioned religion. Augustine was too suspicious of any human institution, and too conscious of the weakness of human will and the power of ignorance to suggest that any government, political order, or social construct could ensure lasting peace and justice. Markus also invites the reader into a consideration of Augustine's theology of history. Markus's other works provide important commentary on the background, contexts, and themes in *City of God,* especially *The End of Ancient Christianity* and *Sacred and Secular: Studies on Augustine and Latin Christianity.*[36]

Reading both Markus and Brown leads to the important insight that Augustine's purpose in *City of God* is not limited to a critical analysis of the Roman empire, nor to the question of Christianity's role in its collapse, nor to political critique of the role of government—though he comments on all of these and more. Rather, at its deepest levels, Augustine's text is an extended theological reflection on human experience in history, a reflection inspired by his Christian faith. The Latin word *saeculum* (often translated "the present age"), as Augustine uses it, refers not only to political or social structure, and not even to the wider concept of the "secular" world. The word, and Augustine's basic interest throughout his theological masterpiece, concerns the existence and the experience of humanity across its entire history. *City of God* cannot be read without an appreciation of Augustine's ongoing theological project, which is to understand human experience in light of God, creation, and the ultimate destiny of all creation. In *Confessions*, he scrutinizes his personal experience in light of those questions. In *City of God*, he widens his scrutiny to include history, society, and the wielding of power.[37]

In *Christ and the Just Society in the Thought of Augustine*, Robert Dodaro, OSA, continues the work of Markus and Brown.[38] In this book, which continues the analysis begun in his doctoral dissertation at Oxford, Dodaro moves research and writing on *City of God* to a new level. He notes that previous scholarly works on Augustine's political thought "invariably pay little attention to his thinking about Christ and scriptural interpretation, and make almost no effort to ask what role these and other areas in his thought contribute to his political ethics."[39] His method throughout his analysis is to integrate various areas of Augustine's thought, which are usually studied in isolation from each other.

For example, Augustine's concept of justice, so central to the themes he elaborates in *City of God*, cannot be properly understood apart from his theology of Christ whose salvific grace empowers citizens of the Heavenly City to live justly. Human ignorance of mind and weakness of will fuel the selfish, destructive dynamics of the City of Man. Yet such ignorance and weakness are overcome only by the healing and strengthening of divine grace through Christ. Thus the virtues necessary to justice and love, which build up the City of God, are rooted in the mystery of

Christ and the Trinity. Dodaro's work exemplifies the methodological shift to communion, which we will discuss in chapter 6.[40]
Dodaro critiques methodologies that isolate concepts and contexts in Augustine Studies, and he strives to integrate various
aspects of Augustine's theology in ways that better reflect the reality of Augustine's own life and thought.

We referred to several "companion texts" that could be helpful to the reader of *Confessions*. There are also contemporary "companions" to help the reader of *City of God*. Given its length and
complexity, such a "companion" is almost essential to guide a mod-
ern-day reader through Augustine's tome. One such text is Gerard
O'Daly's *Augustine's City of God: A Reader's Guide*.[41] O'Daly, a
Latinist and historian of Late Roman Antiquity, was professor at
University College in London. He has written a "detailed yet accessible" guide to Augustine's "vast and complex masterpiece."[42] His
presumed audience includes scholars from many different academic disciplines, who may not be theologians, as well as serious
students of Augustine and his place in history. The first five chapters provide very helpful overviews of the political, social, literary,
and religious background to Augustine's text. These chapters equip
the reader to delve into Augustine's writing, better prepared to
wrestle with his arguments and positions, and to understand the
historical figures mentioned in the text. In chapters 6 through 10,
O'Daly takes the reader carefully through each of Augustine's
twenty-two books. He provides two final chapters on Augustine's
sources and on the place of *City of God* in Augustine's corpus. This
is a very valuable companion text for anyone—novice or experi-
enced scholar—who wishes to enter Augustine's fifth-century
analyses of society, religion, history, and politics.

There are also recent collections of essays that provide information about topics in *City of God* that intrigue contemporary
scholars and about how Augustine's thought continues to engage
twentieth- and twenty-first-century theologians, philosophers,
historians, political scientists, linguists, and others. The latest of
these collections is edited by James Wetzel of Villanova University.

*Augustine's City of God: A Critical Guide* contains twelve essays by some of the finest scholars in the field.[43] There is also *The City of God: A Collection of Critical Essays* edited by Dorothy F. Donnelly, a professor at the University of Rhode Island.[44] The essays cover political thought, literary and linguistic dimensions of Augustine's writings, and philosophical and theological questions raised by the work. Another collection of essays is the already mentioned *History, Apocalypse, and the Secular Imagination: New Essays on Augustine's City of God.* As the title suggests, these essays cluster around three subjects and disciplines: history, specifically Roman history, the theology of Christian eschatology, and the continuing literary and philosophical influence of Augustine's work in Western civilization. These latter two collections will interest the Augustine scholar or the academic expert who wishes to understand how Augustine's thought impacts his or her field.

Finally, a word about translations. William S. Babcock, a church historian and professor emeritus from Southern Methodist University recently completed the two-volume New City Press translation.[45] Babcock's skillful translation is accessible, without sacrificing the subtlety of Augustine's Latin. His fifty-three-page introduction to the translation and Boniface Ramsey's notes are a treasure trove of the most recent scholarship on this work. In her review of Babcock's translation, Arabella Milbank of Emmanuel College, Cambridge, characterizes it as "lyrical without any sacrifice of sense," and writes that "it compares consistently well with both Dyson and Bettenson and is certainly the most beautiful and up-to-date of the existing versions."[46]

There is also the long-standing translation by Marcus Dods, which first appeared around 1870 and was republished in a new edition in 2009, with some updating of the language.[47] Henry Bettenson did a translation for Penguin Classics that was published in 1972 and reissued with a new introduction in 2003.[48] R. W. Dyson, a political scientist and historian at the University of Durham, produced *Augustine: The City of God against the Pagans* for the Cambridge Texts in the History of Political Thought series.[49] All three are fine translations and each finds its own devotees in the world of Augustine Studies.

## The Trinity

About the time he was finishing *Confessions* in 399 or 400, Augustine began work on another theological treatise that would take him until 419 to complete. It was a long meditation on the nature of God as One, yet Three—Father, Son, and Holy Spirit—as affirmed in Christian faith (Book I). He traces the gradual emergence of Christian belief in the Holy Trinity in the Hebrew Bible or Old Testament (Books II to IV), showing how the wisdom and beliefs of the Old Covenant were a preparation for the New Covenant revealed by Christ.

Books V to VII then go on to analyze the language that his Greek and Latin theological predecessors had used to speak about God. Augustine initially advises his readers about the ultimate inadequacy of such attempts or of any written or spoken language to describe God in human terms (*The Trinity* V.1.2). Augustine continues at some length counseling how careful we must be when using human language to describe God. The language of "position, possession, times, and places," can be applied to God only "by way of metaphor and simile" (V.2.9). However, metaphysical language, referring to God's "goodness, eternity, and omnipotence and…all the predications that can be stated of God" is not by way of metaphor and simile "but properly—if anything, that is, can be said properly about him by a human tongue" (V.2.11).

In his attempt to reflect upon the mystery of the Trinity, Augustine then turns from technical theological terms to human experience. He invites us to think about how it is that we experience ourselves, each other, and the world. In insightful analyses, he finds traces both of divine unity and of divine trinity in human experiences, especially in our experience of love and knowledge, where three separate realities interpenetrate each other in a unified experience (Book VIII). For example, the experience of love comprises the lover, the beloved, and their shared love. "Now love means someone loving and something loved with love. There you are with three, the lover, what is being loved, and love" (*The Trinity* VIII.5.14). In a different take, Augustine argues that in any act of knowing, we can rationally distinguish our capacities of mind, knowledge, and love. The mind both knows and loves that it knows. So in every act of the human mind there is a trinity of mind, knowledge, and love, interpenetrating each other. Yet, our mental appropriation of reality is a unified experience (Books IX and X). For the remainder of the work (Books IX to XV), he elaborates these analogies of trinitarian structure in our experience, which he says can lead us to reflect on the triune nature of the one God.

The best of these analogies, he thinks, is the triad of memory, understanding, and will (*The Trinity* XIV). Each of these ingredients of our capacity to know and to love is a distinct operation. Yet all three are necessary, each penetrating the other two, in our experience of ourselves and of each other. It is when we remember, meditate upon, and choose to love God that this analogy of the divine experience most reveals traces of the Holy Trinity in us who are God's image. However, in the end, Augustine advises that such analogies are only that: faint reflections of the incomprehensible and inexpressible mystery that is God (*The Trinity* XV.3—6).[50]

His long text ends with a prayer to the Trinity, asking God's continued guidance in this work of faith, and forgiveness for any of its shortcoming (*The Trinity* XV.51). It is a difficult book. Augustine himself worried that most readers would find it too difficult to be of any benefit.[51] Yet it shows a theological master and religious genius struggling with the heart of all faith—the mystery of the transcendent. It also reveals a bishop sharing his insights and teaching his people how to think about God in light of scripture and church doctrine.

Mary T. Clark gives a clear and accessible overview of *The Trinity* in her essay "*De Trinitate*" in *The Cambridge Companion* to *Augustine.*[52] Clark's direct and unpretentious style provides the reader with an outline of the main sections of the work and a summary of the main points—no easy achievement, given the complexity and subtlety of Augustine's painstaking review of scriptural texts in light of his Catholic faith in the Trinity, his critical analyses of theological language about the nature of God, and the analogies of Trinity that he elaborates.[53] Her many years of scholarship and teaching are evident in both the style and substance of Clark's essay. She concludes that "the originality of Augustine is mainly found in his doctrine of the Holy Spirit and in the centrality he gave to love in Trinitarian life, and to love as renewing human likeness to the Trinity."[54]

Another valuable article that offers an orientation to the text of *The Trinity* is John Cavadini's article "The Structure and Intention of Augustine's *De Trinitate.*"[55] Like Clark, Cavadini provides an overview of the work and its main themes. However, he also emphasizes the practical or pastoral dimensions of Augustine's motivation in writing the text. His long effort in writing *The Trinity* over many years was not just an exercise in "speculative theology," removed from his cares and concerns as a bishop. Cavadini argues that Augustine's pastoral concern, directed at a limited though important audience of thinkers, is appreciated and achieved when we look at the structure of the work as a whole. As a complete work, the text shows how faith (I—VIII) and reason (IX—XV) are both necessary and complementary guides in the journey of faith toward God. Cavadini's emphases on the unity and integrity of the work is compelling and distinctive.

A more recent article by Cavadini provides further assistance in helping the reader enter the experience of Augustine's reflections on the mystery of God. He elucidates the often-overlooked apologetic function of *De Trinitate* that prompted Augustine's writing. Comparing many parts of the text of *De Trinitate* to Books X and XI of *City of God*, Cavadini provides both refreshing and revealing new insights into Augustine's theology of the Trinity, as well as a helpful overview of the text as a whole. He shows Augustine's apologetic aims in *City of God* and *The Trinity* by highlighting how both texts explore Platonic and Neo-Platonic philosophies of God. Augustine explains how these "pagan" thinkers approach the three-ness in the nature of the Godhead with the use of reason. But they only get so far. Augustine identifies the inadequacy of the philosophers in their failure to move from thought or reasoning about God to an experience of the divine humility expressed in the Incarnation. Cavadini stresses how for Augustine, trinitarian theology reaches its fullness only in the lived, committed experience of the worship of the true God.[56] Faith completes reason, even as reason enriches faith.

Cavadini's analysis not only provides insights into the theology of *The Trinity*. He also illustrates how the text of *City of God* X and XI and the text of *The Trinity* are interrelated. This is a further example of what we will describe in chapter 6 as the methodology of communion, that is, attention to the congruence between and among different texts and themes in Augustine's writings.[57]

## Teaching Christianity

Augustine was a rhetorician—the chief rhetorician or *rhetor* in the empire. When he resigned his imperial post and left his teaching responsibilities in Milan, his intention was to return home to Africa and lead a quiet, secluded life of prayer and study in a community of like-minded friends. He had inherited the family land and holdings and had his pension to pay the bills. He seems to have had no intention of ever employing his professional skills again.

When called to the ministry, he had to rethink his intention. The ministry of the Word required him to preach, first as a priest, and then as bishop.[58] This new public role gave rise to some pressing questions. Should he use his vast rhetorical knowledge and skill in his preaching and teaching? How many, if any, of Cicero's rules of rhetoric, which he had taught to so many young men, could be helpful in his ministry of the Word? Do rhetoric and the liberal arts he had studied and taught have any place in reading and explaining the Bible? To put it in the words of his third-century African predecessor Tertullian: "What has Athens to do with Jerusalem?"[59]

Augustine worked out his answers to such questions, as he did with so many pressing matters, through writing. The result was one of his most influential books *Teaching Christianity*. Like *City of God* and *The Trinity*, this work took many years to complete. He started it as a young bishop in 396 or 397, when preaching and teaching became a daily responsibility. The work was not finished until thirty years later when the elderly bishop was reviewing his literary output and came across Books I to III. He decided to finish Book III and add a fourth. So the text provides the advantage of Augustine's lifelong reflections on how to do the work he was called to do as a pastor—teach Christianity.

In Book I, he stresses the basic principle that Christian preaching must communicate the teachings of the church, which he then lays out in the form of the creed. Book II shows how our understanding of the sacred text and its context can and should be enriched by the study of language, history, philosophy, geography, biology, and literature. No simplistic, literal reading of the Bible! The preacher and teacher must have as thorough an understanding of the text and its meaning or meanings as possible. In Book III, Augustine argues that remaining ambiguities in the scriptural texts about which one is preaching can be clarified by the teachings of the church. To assist in this process of clarification of the text, he recommends (with the appropriate and requisite words of Catholic caution) the seven rules of scriptural interpretation developed by the Donatist theologian Tyconius.[60]

Finally, in Book IV, Augustine comments on the role that he had played so many thousands of times over his long ministerial life: preaching about the Word of God amidst Christians assembled for worship or instruction. He allows the use of rhetorical skill for Christian oratory. Cicero's rules of rhetoric can and should be used to instruct, inspire, and even please or delight those assembled to listen to a homily or to receive instruction in the faith.[61]

Teaching Christianity became one of Augustine's most influential works in the Middle Ages. It was used to construct a school curriculum for Christian students in the centuries after Augustine's death. As the empire came apart, and the church served to keep some order in society, Teaching Christianity became the most common basic text in the monastic and cathedral schools of the Early Middle Ages. It was the first of Augustine's works to be printed, reflecting its continuing importance in theological schools beyond the Middle Ages.[62]

Two translations of Teaching Christianity provide introductions and notes that reflect much recent research and scholarship on the text and its reception over the centuries. R. P. H. Green's translation—he renders Augustine's title for the work as On Christian Teaching—is a smooth and engaging text.[63] The introduction is short but valuable, providing insights into Augustine's words and their late Roman Antique context.

Edmund Hill did the translation of De doctrina christiana for the Works of Saint Augustine: A Translation for the 21st Century series, published by New City Press, entitling Augustine's work Teaching Christianity.[64] Hill, who also translated all of Augustine's sermons and The Trinity for the same series, has a deep knowledge of Augustine's mind. To his scholarship, Hill brings a ministerial colleague's informed affection for Augustine's priestly ministry. His introduction to and notes on the text are among the most thorough and compelling in recent decades, and his translation has won admiration.[65]

Two recent collections of scholarly papers on Teaching Christianity are valuable resources. Duane W. H. Arnold and Pamela Bright edited De doctrina christiana: A Classic of Western Culture, for the Christianity and Judaism in Antiquity series of the University of Notre Dame.[66] Edward D. English edited Reading and Wisdom: The De Doctrina Christiana in the Middle Ages for the same series.[67] These papers trace the importance and influence of the work over the centuries.

## Expositions of the Psalms

The 150 psalms in the Hebrew Psalter were an important part of Augustine's own spiritual life. In *Confessions*, he recounts how emotionally powerful and spiritually important praying the psalms was for him immediately after his conversion experience: "How loudly I cried out to you, my God, as I read the psalms of David, songs full of faith, outbursts of devotion with no room in them for the breath of pride!…How loudly I began to cry out to you in those psalms, how I was inflamed by them with love for you and fired to recite them to the whole world, were I able…" (*Confessions* IX.4.8).[68]

During his ministry, Augustine delivered many homilies and catechetical instructions to his people on the psalms. He also dictated to his scribes his thoughts on the meaning of the psalms. So we have a collection in many volumes of his homilies, commentaries, explanations, and teachings on the psalms, representing a twenty-five-year span of the bishop's reflections.[69] Some of these scriptural commentaries are short and simple. Others are long and complex. All are profound examples of how important the psalms were for Augustine's own spiritual life.

The reader can find in them an ongoing journal of Augustine's life of prayer and worship, and trace in them the development of his journey of faith.[70] A quick look at most any page of *Confessions* shows how often he quotes and paraphrases verses of psalms in this other intimate narrative of his inner life.[71] In similar fashion, reading his *Expositions of the Psalms* is an invitation into the passion of Augustine's soul and the depths of his faith. The psalms form and mold Augustine's own prayers. *Expositions* also show how Augustine read the Old Testament. In the poetry, prophecies, symbols, and figures of the psalms he finds constant prefigures of

Christ. He also understands that the church as the Body of Christ prays the psalms as one with Him.

There has been a surge of interest in the *Expositions on the Psalms* in recent decades. A major and seminal work is Michael Fiedrowicz's *Psalmus Vox Totius Christi: Studien zu Augustins "Ennarrationes in Psalmos."*[72] Fortunately for the English reader, a short summary of the scholarship and insight of Fiedrowicz's research is available in his sixty-page introduction to the New City Press translation of *Expositions.*[73]

Two things are clear regarding Augustine and his understanding and use of the psalms. First, they are embedded in all his main theological works. One can hardly find a page in *Confessions* that does not have a verse of one psalm or another. They also run throughout *The Trinity* and *City of God.*[74] They are so pervasive in his homilies that his congregation would often shout out the second part of a psalm verse that Augustine had started.[75] The psalms literally inform Augustine's writing, preaching, and praying. They shape his thinking. They are like scaffolding that support the weight of his theology. So any insights into Augustine's treatment of the psalms provide insights into his theology in general.

The second important point that emerges from a close reading of *Expositions on the Psalms* is the centrality of Christ. We will return to the important and expanding study of Augustine's Christology in chapter 6.

## Cassiciacum Dialogues

After his conversion in 386, Augustine decided to resign his position as *rhetor*, leave his post in the Imperial Court, and seek baptism: "I would then resign in the regular way, but return no more to offer myself for sale, now that you had redeemed me....At last the day arrived which was to set me free in fact from the profession of rhetor..." (*Confessions* IX.2.2 and 4.7). Together with Monica, his son Adeodatus, his brother Navigius, his friend Alypius, two cousins, and two pupils, Augustine left Milan and traveled about twenty-five miles north to the country estate of Verecundus, a Milanese grammarian. The region was known as Cassiciacum, probably in the region of the present day town Cassago Brianza.[76] Augustine and his group stayed there from September 386 to January or February 387.

The little party settled into a quiet rustic life. Augustine, in the fashion of a retired academic and courtier, decided to use his newly won free time to write his reflections on the meaning of his adoption of Christianity. From September 386 until his baptism in April 387, he produced four books: *The Happy Life, Answer to the Academics, On Order*, and *Soliloquies*.

Each of these works is a remarkable piece in itself. In *The Happy Life*, Augustine seeks to find his place as a Christian philosopher addressing the venerable question that Greek and Roman writers had asked: What does it mean to be happy? His answer reflects his recent conversion. To be happy is to find Christ. Such a simple answer, however, can distract from the rich and complex literary and revolutionary way that Augustine constructs and unfolds his answer.[77] In *On Order*, he raises more philosophical questions about the order of the universe and of our lives, and how evil might have crept in—a question left over from his Manichean days, and one to which he will soon return in his anti-Manichean writings.

*Answer to the Academics* is the longest and most philosophically challenging of the Cassiciacum writings. Augustine displays his erudition regarding Greek and Roman philosophy and history, and reveals how he worked his way through and beyond the school of the academic skeptics. This long and complex work ends by affirming that we can acquire knowledge and that we do so both through reason and faith. He confesses Christ as his authority (III.43).[78]

These three works are all dialogues. Augustine, in the manner of Plato and Cicero, explores ideas and arguments together with his pupils. As dialogues, the works embrace an element of theater with distinct and different voices having their say. The plurality of voices must be given their place in imaginative readings of the texts.[79] When the element of theater, the role of Monica as a "wise woman" with her own important speaking role, and Augustine's constant turning over of ideas in these conversations are all considered together, the dialogues can be appreciated for the dynamic intellectual explorations they comprise.[80]

Equally dynamic, but quite different, is the fourth work, for which Augustine invented a neologism: *soliloquia*, or "talking with/to myself." *Soliloquies* is an internal dialogue, a conversation between Augustine and reason, as he seeks for meaning and truth. Book II of *Soliloquies* opens with his famous prayer: "God, who is always the same, may I know myself, may I know you. This is my prayer" (II.1.1).

A persistent question in Augustine Studies has been the seeming disconnect between the highly philosophical speech of these earlier dialogues and the deeper theology and biblical language of his later writings. Augustine himself noted the difference: "The evidence of what I did there [in Cassiciacum] in the way of literary work is to be found in the books that record disputations held between those there present, and deliberations alone with myself in your sight; it was work unquestionably devoted by now to your service, but still with a whiff of scholastic pride about it...." (*Confessions* IX.4.7). Pride or no, even a quick perusal of the dialogues shows that they lack the "interspersion" of scriptural text and Augustine's own words so typical of *Confessions*.[81] The French Jesuit scholar Pierre Courcelle used the more philosophical language of the dialogues to boost his argument that Augustine's conversion, at least initially, was to philosophical Neo-Platonism rather than to biblical Christianity.[82] More recent research, which we will consider later, argues more for continuity and growth rather than discontinuity and disjunction between the Augustine of the dialogues and the Augustine of the *Confessions*.[83]

There is one more dialogue that Augustine wrote. However, he did not write it in Cassiciacum. After his baptism and return to

Africa in 388, and before his call to ministry in 391, his son Adeodatus died at the age of seventeen or eighteen. We do not know if
Augustine finished the *The Teacher* before his son's death. But the
book is a dialogue between a doting father and a brilliant son: "There
is a book of ours entitled *The Teacher*, in which he converses with
me" (*Confessions* IX.6.14). The dialogue does not give hints into
Augustine's teaching techniques or style. Rather, the book goes to the
heart of what he thinks constitutes learning. For Augustine, learning
takes place deep in the soul of the learner, where "Christ the
Teacher" instructs the student who is empowered by the divine
inner light to recognize Truth and affirm it for him or herself.

Augustine moves from a Platonic understanding of learning
as remembering at the instigation of the teacher, to learning as
inner enlightenment and construction of knowledge. We learn
not because a teacher gives us words to name things. Students
learn by judging what they hear and observe from a teacher and
then comparing it to what they come to know deep within themselves by contemplating inner Truth (*The Teacher* 45).[84] His little
community of ascetics and scholars, now in Thagaste, must have
felt quite empty for Augustine after the death of Adeodatus. However, Augustine continues to pursue a life dedicated to prayer and
scholarship, and is comforted that his beloved son enjoyed full
union with Christ: "Very soon you took him away from this life on
earth, but I remember him without anxiety, for I have no fear
about anything in his boyhood or adolescence; indeed I fear nothing whatever for that man" (*Confessions* IX.6.14).

He begins to respond to questions sent to his monastic
homestead from Christians in the wider world who wanted his
understanding of various matters. Thus, in Thagaste during those
brief years between his return to Africa and his ordination, the
scattered manuscripts that he would later gather into a book
known as *Eighty-Three Diverse Questions* begin to accumulate.
And he continues a project he had begun while waiting in Rome
for a ship back home. He had to address his Manichean past.

# 3
# WRITINGS II
*Theological Controversies,*
*Sermons and Letters, and* Revisions

Over the course of his life and ministry, Augustine was drawn into four seminal controversies about the nature of religion, faith, and God. These lively and long discussions also inspired some of his most powerful writings as he helped the church think through the implications of Christian faith and forge understandings of topics such as the nature of good and evil; the mission of church, ministry, and sacraments; the power of sin and divine grace; and, the mystery of God and of Christ. The debates he entered over these topics stirred Augustine to reengage the rhetorical skills from which he had intended to retire upon leaving the imperial court.

Augustine was drawn into many public confrontations with Manicheans, Donatist leaders, Pelagian thinkers, and Arian Christians. However, his motivation for engaging others in argument is best understood as a positive, pastoral response rather than a negative reaction. Augustine, along with Bishop Aurelius of Carthage and the rest of the North African episcopacy, sought to carry out a renewal of the church in Numidia. Frequent church synods in the region guided the project. Augustine's polemical works must be read and interpreted within the context of this program of church renewal. His argumentation in the so-called polemical works had the pastoral purpose of helping his congregation and other Christians understand the problems with what he and his fellow bishops considered erroneous thinking.

So as a pastor and teacher, Augustine returns time and again to rebut, rebuke, and reframe what he saw as the core theological issues and questions raised by Manicheism, Donatism, Pelagianism, and Arianism.[1] We will review Augustine's major works that trace the development of his thought on these topics.

We will then consider Augustine's many sermons and letters, and their place in his life and work. Recent research has provided new insights and perspectives on the daily concerns and ministry of the Bishop of Hippo. Finally, we will look at *Revisions*, a book he wrote in his final years, cataloguing and commenting on his literary corpus.

## Theological Controversies

### Manicheism

After his conversion in 386 and upon his baptism in 387, Augustine, the former Manichean, had some explaining to do. He set out from Milan to return home to Africa in the summer of 387. A naval blockade of Ostia, the port of Rome, delayed him and his party for a year. As he tells us, Monica died during this time: "And while we were at Ostia on the Tiber my mother died" (*Confessions* IX.8.17).

Since Augustine had to spend the year waiting for passage to Africa, the Manichean community in Rome would have learned of and reacted to their former member's conversion. How came their famous co-religionist to reject the teachings of Mani and adopt the "semi-Christianity" of Catholics, whose "father is the serpent" (*Answer to Faustus, A Manichean* I.3)? When he finally arrived back in his home town of Thagaste in 388, how did he explain his new faith to former Manichean associates in Africa? What did he say to all the Catholics who had previously been subjected to his aggressive Manichean proselytizing?

To address this confusion among others and to explain the change in his own thinking, Augustine begins a writing project *contra Manichaeos* or "against the Manicheans" that would last from 388 until 411. Actually, his Manichean past dogged him even into his last years when it came up during the Pelagian debates. Julian of Eclanum charged that Augustine's idea of original sin sounded very much like the Manichean idea of primordial evil (*To Florus* by Julian of Eclanum as cited in Augustine's *Unfinished Work in Answer to Julian*, especially Book V).[2]

He begins his anti-Manichean writing while stranded in Rome. In 387/388 he writes *The Catholic Way of Life and the Manichean Way of Life*. This work consists in two books of considerable length. In book one, he argues for the superiority of Catholic Christianity, based on reason and scripture. He explains the continuity and harmony of the Old and New Testaments, and argues that the followers of Mani, because of their rejection of so much of scripture, are not really Christians at all (*The Catholic Way of Life and the Manichean Way of Life* I.30.62).[3]

In book two, he rejects the Manichean principle of evil as a primordial being co-eternal with God, explaining that evil is not anything existent in itself. What we call evil is rather a "falling away from being" or a lack of goodness (II.2.6). What's more, from his observations, Manichean communities were filled with members who were deceitful, insidious, and malicious, despite their arcane liturgical and strict dietary observances (II.19.67). Certainly there are Catholics who sin. But, Augustine's observation was that hypocrisy, jealousy, and sexual predation were endemic among Manicheans, even and especially among the elect—and he provides some vivid detail of their escapades (II.19.70—20.75).

The following year in 388/389, when back in Thagaste, he wrote his first book on Genesis, *On Genesis: Refutation against the Manichees*. This initial foray by Augustine into scriptural commentary was written to help ordinary Catholics understand and accept the first book of the Bible that the Manicheans rejected and derided. To do so, he takes a figurative approach to the text of Genesis 1:1 to 3:24, showing that scripture can be read in different ways.[4] In this work, Augustine demonstrates an ability to engage and explain sacred texts, a gift that would become a signature of his theological genius. The Manicheans held to a strict literal interpretation of the Genesis text, and admitted no figurative or symbolic interpretations. This restrictive approach to scripture left many inconsistencies and contradictions, and so bolstered the Manichean argument that Genesis must be rejected. Augustine does an end run around their exclusively literal reading of the Old Testament, and invites Christians into ever richer ways of engaging and exploring the various levels of meaning in the text.

Augustine's writing style in these first two anti-Manichean texts is very different from the high rhetorical manner and philosophical content of the Cassiciacum Dialogues, written just a year or two previously. These early anti-Manichean texts are not addressed to an audience of socially elite intellectuals, the kind of audience he would have presumed for the dialogues. Rather, the newly baptized Augustine is concerned about the people whom he had previously led into the Manichean sect, and about those Catholics of lesser learning who were quite susceptible to Manichean preaching.[5] Augustine's first two anti-Manichean texts are basically catechetical works written to help Christian laity understand the real differences between Catholics and Manicheans.

Augustine's central criticism of Mani's teaching emerges with clarity and power in these early writings composed soon after his baptism. It has to do with the nature of God. If God is constantly threatened by this dogged foe, Hyle, the co-eternal principle of evil, then God is not all-powerful. Rather, the good God as the Manicheans understood him is corruptible, that is, capable of changing and being changed by the advances and attacks of the evil one. Augustine rejects this understanding of

God as contradictory (*The Catholic Way of Life and the Manichean Way of Life* I.20.21). He argues that it is of the very nature of divinity to be both infinite and incorruptible. The Manichean notion of God as corporeal, corruptible, and threatened is illogical and unreasonable. Evil, moreover, far from being an eternal principle in opposition to the goodness of God, is a deficit. Evil is the lack of goodness (*The Catholic Way of Life and the Manichean Way of Life* I.1.1—10.19).

*True Religion* is another work that Augustine composed after returning to Thagaste. It is addressed directly to his old patron from Thagaste, Romanianus, whose benefice enabled Augustine to study at Carthage almost twenty years previous. Augustine had dedicated his philosophical dialogue *Argument with the Skeptics* to Romanianus. In this second work honoring his old neighbor, compatriot, and Manichean co-religionist, he tries to show Romanianus the inferiority of Manicheism and the superiority of a contemplative, Neo-Platonic Christianity, such as Augustine had encountered in Milan. It is the last book in which Augustine draws so explicitly from Neo-Platonic thought in his theological arguments.

Augustine continues his attacks on Manichean thought after his ordination to the priesthood in 391. Between 391 and 395, he writes *The Two Souls*. In this book, he extends his argument against the Manichean teaching of two co-eternal principles of good and evil to an argument against their dualistic understanding of human nature. He interprets the struggle between good and evil not as a cosmic conflict localized in each person, but as the voluntary act of each person's human will. Moral evil is the result of sin, that is, of our free choice to act unjustly (*The Two Souls* 11.15).[6] In this work, Augustine again expresses particular concern for his friend and benefactor Romanianus, and also for Honoratus whom he had converted to Manicheism, and who he now hopes will follow him into the Catholic faith.

*A Debate with Fortunatus, A Manichean* is the stenographic record of a debate held in August of 392. Fortunatus was a successful Manichean proselytizer in Hippo whom the young priest Augustine engaged in public contest. The usual topics of the origin of evil and the nature of God were central in this debate. According to the record, Augustine routed Fortunatus, who then left Hippo never to return. At about the same time, Augustine wrote *Answer to Adimantus, A Disciple of Mani.* In this work, Augustine critiques the Manichean text known as the *Discussions of Adimantus.* Adimantus was one of the original twelve disciples of Mani, sent to preach in Egypt. His writings were known in Africa, and highlighted the Manichean rejection of the Old Testament. In his response, Augustine further explores the figurative, analogical interpretation of scripture that he had begun a few years earlier in *On Genesis: Refutation against the Manicheans.*

Just after he became a bishop in 395/396, Augustine continued his anti-Manichean arguments with a formal response to *The Foundation.* This was Mani's basic text, which survives because Augustine quotes it, probably in its entirety, in order to refute it point by point. Augustine's *Answer to the Letter of Mani Known as "The Foundation"* reprises previous arguments against the Manichean understandings of evil and God, and critiques their claim to present a "reasonable" faith and cosmology. He pleads with his friends and former co-religionists to listen to his arguments, expressing empathy for how difficult the search for the light of Truth can be (2.2—3.3).

As we have seen, in the late 390s, Bishop Augustine begins writing his *Confessions,* finishing them around 400. The first-time reader of *Confessions* might find the amount of space that Augustine gives to the errors of Manichean teaching somewhat distracting from the more narrative portions of the narrative. Yet, his arguments against Manichean teaching not only serve to illustrate his own detour into the sect as a young man searching for truth. They also support the more catechetical purposes of *Confessions.* He uses his life story as a pastoral tool to instruct his readers about the truth in Christ, which he has found and to which he is passionately committed. So *Confessions,* especially Books III, IV, and

V, can be listed among the anti-Manichean works that Augustine pens to distance himself from the teachings and practices of his former associates. He hopes to spare his readers the same deviation in their lives by exposing the inconsistencies of Manichean thought. In *Confessions*, Augustine employs the same arguments against Manichean teachings found in the other anti-Manichean writings of his first decade and a half as a Christian. He roundly criticizes their belief in two co-eternal principles of good and evil, their rejection of the Old Testament, and their dualistic understanding of the person and diminution of free will.

In the year 404, Augustine produces three more anti-Manichean works: *The Nature of the Good*; *Answer to Felix, a Manichean*; and *Answer to Secundinus, a Manichean*. *The Nature of the Good* is a summary of Augustine's anti-Manichean arguments, not occasioned by any specific challenge or debate. It provides long quotes from Manichean texts, such as Mani's *Treasury* and *The Chapters* by Faustus (see below). Augustine elaborates his explanation of evil as the corruption of limit, form, and order (*The Nature of the Good* 4), and offers a robust critique of the Manichean notion of a God limited by evil as madness and blasphemy (*The Nature of the Good* 41 and 42).

*Answer to Felix, a Manichean* is the record of Augustine's debate with Felix in December 404 in Hippo, part of which was held in Augustine's church the Basilica of Peace. The text shows Augustine's developing Christology, his understanding of salvation, and the distinctions he makes among the concepts of creation, generation, and making as applied to the Word of God and creation.

Augustine held *Answer to Secundinus, a Manichean* to be his favorite among all his writings against the sect (*Revisions* II.10.37). Secundinus, a thoughtful and intelligent Manichean hearer, had sent Augustine a respectful letter, begging him to reconsider and return to the teachings of Mani. Augustine responds with a long letter, which he later catalogs as a book that expresses all his previously developed anti-Manichean arguments.

*Answer to Faustus, a Manichean* is a long work of thirty-three books, written by Augustine probably between 408 and 410. While still a young teacher, Augustine had met his fellow North African Faustus in Carthage around 383. Augustine had anticipated this meeting in his earnest search for answers about Manichean doctrine (*Confessions* V.6.10—7.1). Several years after his visit with Augustine, the Manichean bishop was exiled for a year to an island in the Mediterranean. There he wrote a book called *The Chapters* in which he formulates his replies to a former Manichean who had converted to Catholicism—possibly Augustine himself. Augustine responds to the thirty-three "chapters" by reproducing them in his own text in order to refute them one by one. Augustine's argument shows his command of scripture as he expounds his figurative interpretation of the Old Testament and its prefiguring of Christ.[7]

Nothing more is heard from or about Faustus after the publication of *The Chapters*. But Manichaenism itself would persist in the Roman Empire for centuries to come. The cult survived in the West, especially among military troops, into the seventh century. It also spread eastward to China, Siberia, and Manchuria. There is archeological evidence of its presence in China until the thirteenth century.[8] Manichean-like teachings of dualism and gnosticism emerged again in Medieval Europe in the religious purist movements of the Cathari in France and the Rhineland, and of the Bogomils in Bulgaria and Byzantium. Even today the term *Manichean* is applied to religious movements or philosophical systems that emphasize metaphysical dualism and esoteric teachings.

### Donatism

Though he considered it his personal and pastoral responsibility to refute Manichean teaching, Augustine, the new priest and bishop, had to deal with other religious issues as well. Among the most pressing of these was the Donatist controversy, which he had to address soon after his move from Thagaste to Hippo.

One of his early letters, written while still a priest, was to Maximinus, the Donatist bishop of Siniti, near Hippo. Augustine asks him not to rebaptize a Catholic deacon who had joined the Donatist congregation in Siniti (*Letter* 23). This letter shows how quickly after his ordination Augustine was drawn into the controversy. Also while still a priest, in 393, Augustine penned a catechetical poem that helped Catholic laity counter Donatist teaching. *Psalm against the Donatist Party* is a modest literary-lyrical achievement in alphabetic form. It gave the Catholics of Hippo something to sing and chant against the Donatist congregation who derided Catholic liturgical singing as rather too sober (*Letter* 55.34).

As a bishop, Augustine develops his argument against Donatism in various books that he writes in the first decade of the fifth century.[9] He begins with *Response to the Letter of Parmenianus* (ca. 400) in which he first outlines the main points of his criticism of the sect. His arguments were that Donatist policies are inconsistent regarding rebaptism, since they rebaptized Catholics, but not members of other groups that had splintered off from Donatist churches;[10] that because of their policy of rebaptism, they were not in communion with the Catholic Church outside of Africa; and, that they were complicit in the violence of the circumcellions.

In *Baptism* (401–2), Augustine expands his critique of the Donatist practice of rebaptism by examining the history of the subject in North Africa starting with Saint Cyprian of Carthage. Cyprian, who was revered by both Catholics and Donatists, had in fact practiced rebaptism. However, though this practice was different from the practice in Italy and the rest of the church at that time, Cyprian did not allow this difference to become cause of schism, as the Donatists would later do (*Baptism* VI—VII). He tolerated fellow North African bishops who did not agree with him about rebaptism. He did not excommunicate them, but only tried to persuade them to his point of view. Even though Augustine disagreed with Cyprian about rebaptism, he extols his *caritas*, and so "claims" him for the Catholic side. In this work, Augustine also develops his theology about the role of the minister of the sacrament. Christ is the source of the grace of the sacrament, not the minister who is but an instrument.[11] Also in 401, he writes a handbook for his fellow bishops on the issues raised by the Donatists entitled *The Unity of the Church*, emphasizing the universality of the Catholic Church as opposed to the sectarian nature of Donatism.

In 402–3, he finished a book entitled *Answer to the Writings of Petilian*. Petilian was the Donatist bishop of Constantine, a city about a hundred miles southwest of Hippo. He had written a textbook of talking points for Donatist bishops to use in their debates with Catholic bishops. It was also directed at Catholic laity to convince them of the superiority of the Donatist church. Augustine's response is a point-by-point defense of Catholicism. He shows how scripture does not always have to be read literally, and how figurative and allegorical readings open up deeper meanings of the text. In reading this book, one gets a taste of the public rhetorical repartee typical in Roman society and state. Both Petilian, in his offense, and Augustine, in his defense, strike low *ad hominem* blows. Surely Augustine was drawing on his previous profession as teacher of rhetoric and imperial *rhetor* to make his points against Petilian and the Donatists stick.

In 405, Augustine writes *Answer to Cresconius*. Cresconius was a well-educated Donatist layman who was also a grammarian and rhetorician. Augustine thought it important to respond to such a potentially powerful spokesman for the sect. *One Baptism* (410–11) treats the question of salvation outside the church. St. Paul (Acts 17:23) and Justin Martyr (*First Apology* 46 and *Second Apology* 10) had recognized that God's saving activity was not limited to the confines of the church, though one should encourage conversion. So how could the Donatists argue, asks Augustine, for an even more limiting interpretation of the action of divine grace by restricting it to their sect alone? In *Letter* 105, an open address to the Donatists written late in 406, Augustine cites the parables of Jesus to remind the Donatists that the church is not a society of perfect Christians, but is God's field with weeds among the wheat

(Matt 13:24–30); it is the chaff among the good grain on the threshing floor (Matt 3:11–13); it is God's fishing net containing all sorts of things before the sorting (Matt 13:47–48).[12]

As we have seen, the controversy among Catholics and Donatists in North Africa climaxed in the ecclesial conference at Carthage in June of 411.[13] About six months after the conference, Augustine published his own summary of the proceedings in a work entitled *Summary of the Conference with the Donatists*. In this review of what transpired at the meeting, much shorter than the official minutes of the event, Augustine skillfully highlights the main points of the argument, with his own editorial comments. He thus provided history with the more influential summary of the event. He follows up a few months later in 412 with a summary treatise on the conference and on all the major issues in the controversy, the *To the Donatists after the Conference*.

In 417, Augustine wrote a letter to Count Boniface (*Letter* 185), which he later entitled as a book *Corrections of the Donatists*. In this work, Augustine elaborates the argument for the use of civil power to enforce legitimate church doctrine and discipline. Boniface was enforcing the directives of the Conference of Carthage, and Augustine provides a theological justification for that enforcement. He writes that one could "persecute out of love" in order to bring the person or group in error back to the truth (*Letter* 185.11). The argument in this letter became an Augustinian text identified with later historical excesses based on the theological position that state authority and power can be used to enforce church doctrine and discipline.

However, a closer look at Augustine's struggle with how to handle church discipline and how to counter the violence that so often erupted among church communities shows a much more nuanced position. In 408, Augustine wrote to the proconsul Donatus that "to force without teaching was the result of a zeal more harmful than advantageous" (*Letter* 101.2). Reason was always to be preferred to force. Augustine wrote a number of letters in which he pleaded with civil authorities not to use capital punishment, even against circumcellions who had killed Catholics.[14] An "eye for an eye" was not the guiding principle in disciplining Donatists. Rather, they should be given every opportunity to change and desist from violence, not be killed or maimed, even if convicted of such crimes themselves (*Letter* 133.1; see also *Letter* 100). Augustine had two goals: to bring peace and unity to the church in North Africa and to protect Catholic congregations from the terror of Donatist violence.[15]

But, as Serge Lancel points out in his analysis of the Donatist controversy, reason usually took a back seat to the social, political, and economic forces seething under the surface of North African religious sectarianism.[16] Augustine's appeal to state authority to help quell the violence and enforce the decisions of the Conference of Carthage must be critiqued and understood in its fifth-century North African context, and not uncritically applied to later European Christian institutions such as the Inquisition. Lancel ends his analysis of the Donatist controversy and Augustine's role in it by asserting that Augustine's anti-Donatist writings "must be read while keeping in mind the strict demands that dictated them," and remembering that these texts, "never caused, either directly or indirectly, any physical attack, still less any death."[17]

The Donatist church persisted in North Africa. There is evidence for its existence well beyond Augustine's death into the late sixth century. The Donatist–Catholic divide more than likely made the conquest of the province easier for the Vandals who were Arian Christians. The social and political context for Donatism in the colonial resistance of Africa is important for understanding the ecclesial situation.[18] Some scholars trace today's Islamic divide between North Africa and Europe back to the early Christian African "national churches" such as the Donatists, Manicheans, Monophysites, Nestorians, and Montanists.[19] In the history of religions, the zeal and quest for purity becomes problematic when it leads to exclusion, strife, and violence, even as we see today in many world religions. Augustine's response to rigorist, exclusionary religion, documented in his

anti-Donatist writings, arises out of his compassionate understanding of human nature and its weaknesses. His understanding
of the pervasive effects of original sin, his invocation of Jesus'
parable of the wheat and the chaff growing together, and his belief
that the church must be *semper reformanda*—always reforming
itself—reveal his realistic expectations of church life and his more
inclusive ecclesiology.[20]

## Pelagianism

After the Conference of Carthage in 411, Augustine continues to repeat in letters and sermons the arguments against
Donatism that he had developed in these major works. However,
the Pelagian controversy begins to take up more of his time and
energy. Becoming more aware of the implications of Pelagian
ideas, and at the request of others like his friend Marcellinus, the
same Roman tribune who had presided at the Catholic–Donatist
showdown in Carthage, Augustine begins to respond.

Between 411 and 418, he writes a number of important
books in which he engages the thought of Pelagius and its implications for Christian soteriology. These include *The Punishment and
Forgiveness of Sins and the Baptism of Infants* (411), *The Spirit and
the Letter* (412), *Nature and Grace* (415), *The Perfection of Human
Righteousness* (415), *The Deeds of Pelagius* (416–17), and *The
Grace of Christ and Original Sin* (418).[21]

In these works, the sheer number of which shows his theological and pastoral concern, Augustine presents and elaborates three
main points in his response to the ideas of Pelagius and Caelestius;
these are the effects of original sin, the extent of free will, and the
need for infant baptism. Pelagius's position was that original sin
does not corrupt human nature nor compromise our free will and
natural ability to do what is right. So guided by God's grace, we
come to know the right thing to do and then freely choose to do it.
Finally, infant baptism is not imperative since Adam's sin had not
corrupted human nature.

By contrast, Augustine understood the effects of original sin to corrupt our nature and radically weaken our will. We need divine grace, not only to enlighten our minds about what is the right thing to do, but also to empower our weak and sin-prone wills to do it. And, infant baptism is imperative in order to share Christ's saving grace with children as soon as possible.

Early in this dispute, Augustine seems to try for mutual understanding and agreement. In a letter written around 411 or 412 to Marcellinus, Augustine acknowledges the exemplary life and virtue of the British monk (*Letter* 140). In these earlier anti-Pelagian works, Augustine critiques Pelagian ideas without explicitly identifying them with Pelagius himself, since he had not yet read Pelagius's work *De Natura*, which he received only in 414.

As Augustine sees it, grace is necessary not only to enlighten our mind to know the good and the true; it is also necessary to empower our will to choose the good and the true. His analysis in *The Grace of Christ and Original Sin* (418) is that Pelagius, whom he now identifies by name with this erroneous teaching, has it half right when he acknowledges the necessity of grace for enlightenment. Pelagius has only to extend the effects of grace to the will and he and Augustine will not be far from agreement: "Let him, as I said, agree that God also helps the will and the action and helps them in such a way that we will or do nothing good without that help, and let him agree that this is the grace of God through our Lord Jesus Christ, by which he makes us righteous with his own righteousness, not with ours,....Then no point of controversy will, as far as I can see, be left between us regarding the help of God's grace" (*The Grace of Christ and Original Sin* I.47.52).

It is important to note that Augustine's ideas on grace elaborated in these early works against Pelagian thought are not new in his thinking.[22] Augustine had already written two works on Paul's Letter to the Romans. These were *Commentary on Some Statements in the Letter to the Romans* (394–95) and *Unfinished Commentary on the Letter to the Romans* (394–95). He had also commented on Romans in *Eighty-three Diverse Questions* (questions number 66–68) written early in his monastic life and priestly ministry. But Augustine was dissatisfied with his own treatment of Paul in these works. So he took a request from his mentor and friend Simplicianus as the opportunity to dive into a thorough study of Romans and of Paul's thoughts on divine grace.

Simplicianus was the elderly priest who had helped him as a catechumen in Milan, and who had succeeded Ambrose as bishop in 397. Simplicianus requested of Augustine clarification on several scriptural texts, including Paul's letter to the Romans, chapters 7 and 9. In his *Miscellany of Questions in Response to Simplician*, written sometime between 396 and 398, Augustine sends his revered mentor, now a fellow bishop, an extensive treatise on divine grace.

This analysis marks a significant shift in his thinking about free will and grace, which some have even called a third "conversion" in his life—counting the first two as his early conversion to Manicheism and then his conversion to Christianity. Wrestling with Paul's text in Romans, he concludes that it is only by God's grace that we are able to turn from sin and do good. Free will has been irrevocably weakened by original sin, which has left humanity like a "lump of mire" and a "mass of sin" (*Response to Simplician* I.2.21). Only God's grace can empower our will to choose the good.

Augustine's theology of grace as it developed soon after his episcopal ordination in the mid-390s is clear. It is not by our own will, but only by God's grace, which heals and strengthens our will that we are able to believe and live good lives according to God's will. His books in response to Pelagius and Caelestius, written between 411 and 418, provided him with further opportunities to elaborate that conviction. He believed Pelagian theology left no role for Christ in our salvation. As Augustine saw it, Pelagius reduced Christianity to spiritual enlightenment followed by a self-willed morality that presumably merited God's love and heavenly reward.

After the Council of Milevis in 416, the North Africans, Augustine among them, asked Pope Innocent I to affirm their own regional condemnation of the teachings of Caelestius and

Pelagius, which the Pope did. Augustine then considered the matter closed, since Rome had agreed with the North African bishops. He refers to the matter in *Sermon* 131 that he preached in Carthage on September 23, 417: "For already on this matter two councils have sent to the Apostolic See, whence also rescripts have come. The cause is finished" (*Sermon* 131:10).[23]

But it was not finished. When Innocent I died in March of 417, Caelestius appealed to his successor Pope Zosimus. Initially Zosimus was inclined to review the matter, especially since his predecessor had left the door open for reconciliation if the two returned to orthodox teaching. Furthermore, Pelagius still had many sympathizers in Italy. However, upon pressure from the African Church, and probably from the Emperor Honorius, the pope sided with the Africans. In 418, the teachings of Caelestius and Pelagius were pronounced heretical, and the two were excommunicated. As in the case of Donatism, the church avoided a split between Africa and Italy with the pope's eventual agreement with the Africans led by Augustine.

The matter once again seemed settled, as Augustine had hoped. But Pelagius and Caelestius still had their allies in Italy who were angered at what they considered to be Rome's capitulation to the North Africans. One of them was to prove a formidable opponent to Augustine and his anti-Pelagian stance. This was Julian of Eclanum in the Campania region of southern Italy. In 418, Julian was a young, married, rich, and very well-educated bishop and son of a bishop. Offended by the condemnation of Pelagius and Caelestius at the instigation of Africans, whom he considered socially inferior, Julian begins a campaign in defense of Pelagius by attacking Augustine. For Julian, nothing was off limits: Augustine's Manichean past, the revelations in *Confessions* of his preconversion life, even Monica's adolescent imbibing from her father's wine supply (*Unfinished Work in Answer to Julian* I.68; *Confessions* IX.8.17). An able rhetorician and writer himself, Julian mounts a surly offensive against Augustine who responds in kind.

This begins a second round of anti-Pelagian volleys that thunder on throughout the last decade of Augustine's life. These include Augustine's books *Marriage and Desire* (419–21), *Answer to Two Letters of the Pelagians* (421), *Answer to Julian* (421–22), and the massive tome *Unfinished Work in Answer to Julian* (429–30). In the latter two works against Julian, Augustine takes on the themes of original sin, grace, human freedom, and predestination with the full power of his theological and rhetorical maturity: all themes he had already addressed in previous books, letters, and sermons. Both Augustine and Julian exaggerate each other's positions for effect, and some of Augustine's less persuasive ideas emerge in the process: his more extreme teachings on predestination, for example, about which the Catholic Church has always been cautious.[24]

Some contemporary theologians encourage a more balanced summary of Pelagian ideas that reaches back beyond the unpleasant theological and personal exchanges between Augustine and Julian in an attempt to understand Pelagius on his own terms.[25] Most of his ideas come to us filtered through Augustine and the documents of subsequent church councils and synods. We have little of what Pelagius wrote, save his commentary on Paul's letter to the Romans, which has appeared in a new critical edition of the Oxford Early Christian Studies series.[26] While these reconsiderations of Pelagius and his thoughts are valuable, Augustine's theological and pastoral concern was with the more extreme interpretations of ideas that rightly or wrongly were associated with the British monk.

The Pelagian controversy continued after Augustine's death in 430. Prosper of Aquitaine in Gaul was a disciple and literary correspondent of Augustine. Prosper championed Augustine's anti-Pelagian positions against a kind of compromise between Augustine and Pelagius that grew up in Southern Gaul. Church historians from the sixteenth century named this compromise semi-Pelgianism. It held that a person can exercise free will to make the initial turn to God in faith and baptism, but beyond this initial conversion, God's grace was necessary for any growth in faith and spiritual or moral development.[27]

A century later, Caesarius (470–542), bishop of Arles in southern Gaul, won approval of Augustine's theology of grace and free will at the Second Council of Orange in 529. The Council reaffirmed previous church rejection of Pelagian thought. It also rejected the semi-Pelagian compromise as not orthodox Christian doctrine. Casearius helped ensure that Augustine's theological legacy would continue to grow in influence in succeeding centuries.[28]

## Arianism

In addition to his theological and pastoral writings against the Manicheans, Donatists, and Pelagians, Augustine also addressed Arian teaching. His writings on this topic are not as extensive as his other polemical works, but are nonetheless an important part of his literary corpus.

Sometime in the first decade of the fifth century, Augustine wrote a letter to Pascentius, a member of the imperial court who was an Arian believer (*Letter* 238). Pascentius had challenged Augustine to a debate. They met in Carthage and discussed their doctrinal differences over dinner. Pascentius, however, did not want their conversation recorded. So Augustine replied with this long letter to provide a written account of their meeting. He lays out the differences between orthodox teaching about Christ and the Arian teaching. Pascentius had offered the common Arian objection to the Nicean formulation that the Son was *homoousion* (consubstantial) with the Father. *Homoousion* was not found in Sacred Scripture, he protested, and so should not be used by Christians. Augustine's response was that the equality of Father and Son is made clear throughout the New Testament, and that even Arians use words not found in scripture, such as "unbegotten" (*Letter* 238.5).

So sometime between 400 and 410, even before the flood of immigrants from Europe fleeing Alaric's invasion, Augustine engages briefly in the Arian debate. However, it is after 416 that we find Augustine preaching more regularly against Arian Christology in a variety of sermons.[29] Presumably these sermons were in part a pastoral response to the growing numbers of Arian Christians among the congregation at his church in Hippo.

Throughout his great work *The Trinity*, Augustine is very conscious of Arian Christology and addresses it directly. This is true in Books V, VI, and VII, which he was writing probably during the second decade of the fifth century. Other Christological writings from these middle, mature years of his episcopal ministry also address the Arian controversy, such as his *Homilies on the Gospel of John* and his *Expositions of the Psalms*.[30]

In 419, a summary presentation of Arian Christology, especially the version popular in the Western Empire, referred to as Homoian Christology, was circulating in North Africa. Augustine responds directly to this "Arian Sermon," as it was called, with his *Answer to an Arian Sermon*. Augustine addresses each of the Arian propositions in the order they were presented in the Sermon.

About ten years later, in 427 or 428, Augustine comes out of retirement to debate an Arian bishop by the name of Maximinus. The latter had come to Africa from Italy, with Count Sigiswulf, a Goth, who led a Roman military force to handle an uprising in Africa. Maximinus was much younger than Augustine and a good rhetorician, well educated in scripture and theology. Augustine's *Debate with Maximinus* (427–28) records their public discussion in Hippo. Maximinus returned to Carthage bragging that he had won the debate against the old Bishop of Hippo. So Augustine felt it necessary to further clarify the issue with another book, *Answer to Maximinus the Arian*. Augustine begins the book by accusing Maximinus of verbosity and evasion during their debate, and by setting out a clear exposé of the errors of Arian Christology.

The fullness of Augustine's understanding of Christ cannot be appreciated without understanding the central role that Jesus played in Augustine's own life of faith and in his ministry. The centrality of Christ in Augustine's life and thought goes far beyond the doctrinal positions he makes clear in his anti-Arian writings.[31] An important development in contemporary Augustine Studies has been a creative, new exploration of Augustine's Christology, which we will explore in chapter 6.

Augustine is known to many historians and scholars largely through the theological positions that he developed and elaborated throughout the many decades of these controversies. Indeed, until the revival of Augustine Studies since the Second Vatican Council, the Bishop of Hippo had been largely identified with his repudiation of Manichean dualism, his victory over the Donatist schism, and his theological pounding of Pelagius. Augustine's emphasis on the pervasive effects of original sin, our radical need for divine grace, and the wounded nature of our human will were developed and clarified in the midst of these debates. However, part of the richness of more recent research is the discovery of a more pastoral Augustine, which recontextualizes his doctrinal positions and theological ideas, and recasts their importance in light of his Christology and his pastoral concerns.

## Sermons and Letters

Recent decades have seen a whole new interest in Augustine's sermons and letters. Careful study of Augustine's sermons and correspondence is a way into the daily context or, to use Brown's lovely phrase, the "unremitting circumstantiality" of Augustine's life and work.[32] New scholarship on Augustine's preaching and correspondence is producing information and insight into the events and relationships in his life that help us understand the circumstances and incentives for his other writings.

We have the texts of about five hundred sermons that Augustine preached, and that the school of scribes who worked for the church in Hippo dutifully copied as he spoke. Augustine himself would have edited many of these transcriptions later.[33] The sermons fill eleven thick volumes in the New City Press series.[34] This is the first time all of the known sermons have been translated into English, a monumental task accomplished by the English Dominican Friar Edmund Hill. Hill chose to translate Augustine's words in a "colloquial, informal style" because he thinks this "approximates most closely to Augustine's own Latin style as a preacher."[35] Though a skilled and practiced public orator, Augustine the bishop addressed his congregation in its own manner of speaking, rather than in the inflated, dramatic technique of late Roman public oratory. Hill attempts to capture this style in his translation.[36] Even the reader with an intermediate reading knowledge of Latin can appreciate the significant stylistic differences between the flowing, poetic prose of *Confessions*, and the shorter, punctuated, direct conversational homilies to the people.[37]

In addition to the volumes of sermons, there are also the 124 *Homilies on the Gospel of John* as well as the ten *Homilies on the First Epistle of John*.[38] Augustine's Johannine writings have also been largely ignored until recently.[39] We will return to themes found in these homilies and the powerful insights they reveal when we look at Augustine's theology of love in chapter 6.

The new interest in Augustine's sermons greatly increased when in 1990 François Dolbeau discovered a manuscript in the Municipal Library of Mainz containing twenty-six previously lost sermons. Most were completely unknown, and a few known only in extracts quoted by theologians and philosophers over the centuries. Augustine preached some of these sermons in Carthage around 397 when he was a new bishop. The others come from his preaching in Carthage and more rural areas of Numidia in 403 and 404. Dolbeau's research on the authenticity of these sermons was published in his *Vingt-six sermons au people* in 1996.[40] In 2008, six more sermons by Augustine were discovered in Erfurt during the ongoing project of the Austrian Academy of Sciences to catalog medieval manuscripts that contain his works. The sermons, which deal with the theme of active charity and almsgiving, are analyzed and authenticated in scholarly German publications.[41]

We have the text of 252 letters written by Augustine to others, and another forty-nine that others sent to him. Twenty-nine were discovered as recently as 1975 and published in 1981 by Johannes Divjak. All these known letters fill four volumes of the New City Press translation series. Fr. Roland Teske, SJ, did the translation, notes, and a valuable introduction to this genre of Augustine's writings.

Like the sermons, Augustine's letters are a window into his daily life, ministry, and relationships. All sorts of fourth- and fifth-century personages walk into the spotlight of history as Augustine responds to their questions and worries, their troublesome behaviors and family problems, their desire to know Christ and how to pray. Reading the letters, we can sometimes hear the distant thunder of theological rhetoric and the clash of concepts in the background. Sometimes the clap of thunder breaks into the very text of a letter, as when Augustine writes to Crispinus, a Donatist bishop (*Letter* 51), or in his long letter to Vincent, bishop of a sect that had split from the Donatists (*Letter* 93).

An invaluable book on the letters is Jennifer Ebbeler's *Disciplining Christians: Correction and Community in Augustine's Letters*.[42] Ebbeler's expertise in the classical epistolary genre, and her long interest in Augustine's letters in particular, equip her to show how Augustine shaped the genre to his own theological and pastoral purposes. His letters become public forums in which important issues can be set forth and argued. She argues persuasively that Augustine understood his letters to be works of charity in which he hoped to lead his correspondents and the wider audience to truth and wisdom. Ebbeler pays special attention to his correspondence with Jerome, with the Donatists, and with Pelagian sympathizers.

Several recent papers also provide valuable guidance on how to read and interpret Augustine's letters to women. In *Voices in Dialogue: Reading Women in the Middle Ages* Catherine Conybeare, a classicist at Bryn Mawr, brings her distinctive sensitivity and insight to textual hermeneutics in her "Spaces Between Letters:

Augustine's Correspondence with Women."[43] The "spaces between letters" refers to the fact that the letters from women *to* Augustine have not survived. Conybeare carefully studies Augustine's text in his letters to women to draw inferences about who these women were and what their social role and intellectual accomplishment might have been. In the same book, Mark Vessey responds to Conybeare.[44] Together Conybeare and Vessey highlight Augustine's respect for his female correspondents' comprehension of Latin and of religious and theological issues. Both argue, each in a different way, that these women were accomplished at many levels of literacy and theological interpretation. His letters show that Augustine willingly engaged them as partners in his conceptual and pastoral projects. Their two essays help move the scholarship on Augustine beyond the usual images of him surrounded solely by male clerics oblivious to the perspectives, insights, and experience of women.

*Feminist Interpretations of Augustine* contains two essays that shed light on the letters. In "Augustine's Letters to Women," Joanne McWilliam provides helpful commentaries on the fourteen letters in which Augustine corresponds with women.[45] McWilliam's overview of these letters reveals the range of the projects about which Augustine wrote to women, including the nature of prayer, problems of dissension and discipline within the church in North Africa, controversy with the Donatists, and his deep theological disagreement with those who promoted the understanding of Christ and of salvation associated with Pelagius. In the same volume, E. Ann Matter's "*De cura feminarum*: Augustine the Bishop, North African Women, and the Development of a Theology of Female Nature" expands the contexts of the theological and pastoral issues that appear in Augustine's letters to women.[46] Matter recommends that for a broader understanding of Augustine's relationships with women, one must go beyond "sex and his mother" and entertain the insights afforded by a careful study of his letters to women in the context of his pastoral work and theological study.

Peter Brown, in the second edition of his biography (2000), adds two chapters to his original work (1967). These two chapters are entitled "New Evidence" and "New Directions." The new evidence is the discovery of the Dolbeau sermons and the Divjak letters. In light of these discoveries, and of renewed attention to Augustine's letters and sermons, Brown admits that his biography overlooked "the more humdrum, the less successful and the more gentle, painstaking aspect of Augustine's life as a bishop in North Africa."[47] With the benefit of recent research by a great number of scholars, Brown says that he comes to "hear" the sermons less as "*ex cathedra* statements of the representative of a securely established Catholic hierarchy…," and more as "dialogues with the crowd."[48] One of the Dolbeau sermons (*Sermon* 359B.3) reveals how restless the congregation could get in Carthage where Augustine was a visiting preacher.

In the Divjak letters, which were written from about 412 to about 430, Brown finds a wholly unexpected picture of Augustine in his final decade of life. They reveal "a very different, more attractive, because so poignantly painstaking, side of the old man."[49] We find him interviewing a little girl who had been kidnapped by slave traders and later rescued and bought back by the members of Augustine's own congregation (*Letter* 10*.3). We notice how attentive he is to the school homework of a teenage son of one of his correspondents, Firmus (*Letter* 2*.12–13).

The detail in these sermons and letters also provide a wider understanding of the context in which bishop Augustine wrote and preached. Neither he nor other North African bishops were anything like their episcopal successors who ruled medieval Europe as bishop-princes. Often oppressed, like their congregations, by the political and economic machinery of the Roman Empire, these fifth-century "Catholic bishops of North Africa had remained little men with little power."[50] They did not live, minister, or preach in a totally Christianized society where church and state were inextricably mixed. Brown shows that Augustine's fiery rhetoric *had* to be strong and assertive just to be heard amidst the competing religious entities and political powers of late Roman antiquity. These new discoveries of sermons and letters remind us that in reading Augustine's more polemical texts one must remember Augustine's context. Roman orators were expected to argue long and forcibly for the communities of thought and faith that they represented. Both constituents and opponents expected no less.[51]

The Divjak letters and Dolbeau sermons, as they are now known, seemed to have been largely ignored in the Middle Ages for the very same reasons that contemporary scholars find them so fascinating. They reveal Augustine, both as a young bishop and then after many years of ministry, dealing with the day-to-day struggles, questions, concerns, and problems of the people he served and the surprisingly diverse and religiously pluralistic society in which he and they lived. Such details were only of marginal interest to medieval theologians, so they rarely quoted these texts. Hence, their fall into obscurity. Renewed study of the sermons and letters has opened new pathways into understanding the complexity and diversity of the society that Augustine had to negotiate as a leader of a minority religion in a smaller port city of the empire.

## Revisions

In 426 or 427, the elderly bishop began a review and commentary on his vast literary output—another innovation in the history of scholarship. He called it *Retractationes*, which does not translate so much as "retractions" but rather "reconsiderations" or "revisions."[52] So we have Augustine's own catalog of his works, as well as his commentary on certain ideas and language that he had rethought. He did not canonize his own compositions as the final word on any topic. Augustine understands his writing as a way of working through ideas, rather than as expressing truth in final form: "I admit I strive to be among those who write as they progress and progress as they write" (*Letter* 143.2). His *Revisions* reflect that conviction about his writings.[53]

Boniface Ramsey did the translation of *Revisions* in the New City Press series (vol. I/2) and he provided a very helpful introduction. In addition, each of the translations of Augustine's works throughout the volumes of the series is preceded by the elderly bishop's own commentary on that particular work, taken from *Revisions*. This editorial decision gives the reader the advantage of Augustine's own look back at his writing, and how he approved, amended, or contextualized the writing of his previous years.

History also had the benefit of another list of Augustine's writings provided by his friend and first biographer Possidius, Bishop of Calama. This *Indiculus* or Index, as Possidius called it, is a list of the works found in Augustine's own library in Hippo. He appends it to his *Life of Saint Augustine*. Though not a complete list of all of Augustine's works, it complements Possidius's biography as well as Augustine's *Revisions*. It is another helpful source to scholars who survey and study his vast literary output.

It is remarkable that the majority of Augustine's books survived, especially in the political and social upheaval that characterized the disintegration of the Roman Empire after his death. His library survived the siege of Hippo—Augustine died on August 28, 430, during that siege.[54] His books were quite possibly transported, along with his remains, across the sea to Sardinia sometime not too long after his death.[55] His many works are used and widely cited in the centuries after his death by such theologians as Gregory the Great, Isidore of Seville, and Bede the Venerable among others.[56]

# 4
## LEGACY I
*Middle Ages and Renaissance*

Augustine's influence on Christian theology and on the history of Western civilization has been vast and significant.[1] Indeed, other than Sacred Scripture itself, Augustine was the primary authority for Western Christian theologians for almost a thousand years after his death in 430. Even after the European rediscovery of Aristotle and the "new" theology of Albert the Great and Thomas Aquinas during the High Middle Ages, Augustine's writings remained important for Christian thought. In the sixteen hundred years since his death, major philosophers, theologians, and other thinkers have invoked his authority, rejected his positions, or modified his language and concepts to express the deeper dimensions of human experience.

Any brief survey of Augustinian influence can highlight only the main points. This chapter will do just that: provide a summary overview of how scholars in successive centuries have taken account of the Bishop of Hippo's writings. The main Augustinian themes that have continued to occasion, inspire, or aggravate academic and ecclesial conversations are his insistence on the primacy of divine grace for salvation, the corrosive effects of sin on free will, the divine indwelling at the core of human subjectivity, the central importance of Sacred Scripture, the authority of the church, and the primacy of the eternal will of God expressed in the doctrine of predestination.

We will follow these themes as they emerge again and again over the years to engage successive generations. Our review is enriched by the work of hundreds of scholars who have traced Augustinian paths and roads across the map of Western civilization. Again, this survey is from a higher altitude. Each line on the map deserves a closer look than is possible here. The cited sources provide ways of focusing in closer on particular thinkers, movements, or schools that have affirmed, modified, extended, or rejected Augustine's positions.

We will use discrete periods of history to organize our survey—though such divisions do not always reveal the currents of thought that run across and under chronological lines, deep beneath the surface of historical designations. These periods are from Augustine's death in the fifth century to the eleventh century, the so-called Early Middle Ages. Then we will look at the changing role of Augustine's thought with the rise of the universities and scholastic theology in the twelfth to fourteenth centuries of the High Middle Ages. During this period, what has come to be known as the "Augustinian School" emerged in the major universities of Europe. It will occupy us for a few pages. We will then briefly consider how the Renaissance rediscovered a different Augustine.

In chapter 5, we move to the Reformation and the Council of Trent in the sixteenth century. Augustinian theology was an important factor in both. We will then consider Augustine's influence on Descartes's turn to the subject and the rise of the modern period up to the Second Vatican Council. Our survey will end with the return of Augustinian interests that emerge amidst postmodernism and other twentieth- and twenty-first-century academic movements.

Augustine is an example of what Hegel called "a world historical figure" whose ideas have become a fundamental part of Western Christianity and Western civilization.[2] In her groundbreaking new work, the *Oxford Guide to the Historical Reception of Augustine*, Karla Pollmann refers to Augustine's "protean authority."[3] Edited by Pollmann of the University of St. Andrews (Editor-in-Chief), in collaboration with Willemien Otten of the University of Chicago (Editor) and twenty co-editors, this collection presents the scholarship of more than four hundred international experts who document Augustine's influence and legacy on a great variety of fields, including political theory, ethics, music, education, semiotics, literature, philosophy, psychotherapy, religion, and popular culture. The short review in this and the following chapter provides the highlights of his continuing influence.

## The Early Middle Ages (500–1100)

### The Spread of Augustine's Writings

Augustine's influence would have waned if his writings had not survived. During his lifetime, Augustine's works were copied many times over as various people and churches requested them. Augustine mentions that his patron Romanianus, who had financed his education at Carthage, assumed financial responsibility for copying and circulating his works (*Letter* 27.4; See also Possidius, *Life*, XVIII.9).

Producing a written text in Augustine's time was not inexpensive. Stenographers (*notarii*) took notes in the shorthand of the day as Augustine dictated in his study or preached in the church. Subsequently they wrote it out in longhand, correcting and editing the text, using ink on expensive parchment made from calf or sheep skins. Augustine himself would often have a hand in this editing process. Given the expense and the effort he put into writing, it makes sense that Augustine carefully catalogued and chronicled his works over the years, keeping them in the episcopal library at Hippo.[4] During his lifetime, Augustine's works were copied many times over in response to requests for his writings.[5] Thus many different copies of his books, sermons, and some of his longer letters circulated around the Mediterranean, eliciting comments and requests for further clarifications from the busy bishop.

After his death, Augustine's many works continued to be read and studied. His corpus of writings is to be found in Rome by the second half of the fifth century. This collection quite possibly contained original manuscripts rescued from his library in Hippo, and saved from destruction during the invasion by the Vandals.[6]

In subsequent centuries, Augustine's admirers in various dioceses and monasteries around Europe continued to copy his writings. Certain books became more influential because they were more frequently copied and circulated. These include *Confessions, City of God, Teaching Christianity, Free Will, True Religion*, and *The Literal Meaning of Genesis*.[7] Influential scholars also began to produce anthologies of his writings and to choose important passages from his books, sermons, and letters. These were known as *florilegia* (poetically called "collections of flowers," or "bouquets") and *sententiae* (important statements or sayings). Many such collections appeared across Europe.

The best known and most influential of early collections of Augustine's words are the *Book of Sentences* or *Liber Sententiarum* of Prosper of Aquitaine (390–455) and the *Excerpta* of Eugippius (ca. 455–ca. 535). Prosper, an educated layman in Southern Gaul, had corresponded with Augustine and championed the bishop's theology of grace against what he considered to be Pelagian sympathies among Gallican monks. Thus, through his *Liber Sententiarum* and his later *Epigrammatica*, Prosper ensures that Augustine's theology of grace is extended and appreciated into the second half of the fifth century.[8] Prosper has been called the first representative of Medieval Augustinianism.

Eugippius was also an early advocate, instrumental in assuring the spread of Augustine's theology. Eugippius was the head of a monastic community at Naples, Italy. He and his monks collected and copied Augustine's writings into a collection entitled

*Excerpts from the Works of Saint Augustine.* This catalogue of Augustine's thought, especially his scriptural hermeneutics, became an important link between medieval Christian Europe and Augustine's late Roman time and place.

From our contemporary perspective, the excerpts from Augustine's writings found in the *sententiae* and *florilegia* are limited or compromised because they have been extracted from their original literary setting and historical context. These collections often even fail to mention the name of the particular book, letter, or sermon that was the original locus of the text. The compiler who produced the anthology might choose texts in support of a particular doctrine of the church with the apologetic intent of refuting heretical teaching of some sort. Our contemporary concern for text in its historical context was not a primary consideration for these scribes of the Early Middle Ages. However, their diligence and products are an important part of the preservation and transmission of Augustine's thought. They extended Augustine's influence into the monastic and cathedral schools of the fifth to the eleventh centuries, where scribes produced still more copies.

There were subsequent periods of special interest in and reproduction of Augustine's writings, such as during the Carolingian flowering of the ninth century, and the cultural, academic expansions of the twelfth. The great number of manuscripts provided for the continuing availability of Augustine's works and ensured his wide influence on the development of Christian theology and philosophy, especially in the new universities that would arise in thirteenth-century Europe.[9]

The many copies of Augustine's books and sermons, together with the excerpts and selected passages in the medieval anthologies show the importance of textual criticism in evaluating the authenticity and accuracy of the many and varied manuscripts. This careful, scientific process of textual criticism has produced "critical editions" of Augustine's works that strive to identify textual discrepancies, explore questionable variations, and get as close as possible to his original wording. The oldest, printed critical Latin edition of all of Augustine's works was done by the Benedictine monks of St. Maur in France (1679–1700). Their work was reprinted by Jacques-Paul Migne in *Patrologia Latina* in mid-nineteenth-century Paris, and is known as the Migne Edition. The Migne Edition is still widely used among scholars and translators.[10]

### Fifth-Century Theological Controversy in Gaul

Prosper of Aquitaine, as we mentioned, was one of Augustine's correspondents.[11] Prosper, though not a cleric, championed Augustine's theology of grace against John Cassian (360–435) and other monks of Marseilles and Lérins in southern Gaul. Cassian and another monk Faustus (ca. 405–ca. 490), who later became bishop of Riez, found Augustine's theology of grace to be extreme, especially as elaborated in his writings from the 420s where he uses predestination to emphasize God's sovereignty. However, Cassian and Faustus also rejected Pelagius's teaching on salvation, which they thought put too much emphasis on human effort. Their so called "semi-Pelagianism" tried to find a middle way between Augustine and Pelagius.[12]

Prosper fought and taught against any compromise of Augustine's theology of grace, including and especially compromises being offered by monks. With his friend Hillary (ca. 403–99), who was bishop of Arles, Prosper traveled to Rome to secure the pope's support of Augustinian theology of grace against the more Pelagian leanings in Gallican monasticism.[13] However, even Prosper was uncomfortable with Augustine's teaching about predestination, and sought to balance it with his own emphasis on God's desire for universal salvation.[14] Thus, through his *Liber Sententiarum* and his activism, Prosper ensures that Augustine's theology of grace is extended and appreciated into the later fifth century.

## The Second Council of Orange (529) and Caesarius of Arles

The uneasy Gallican truce between Augustinian and the so-called semi-Pelagian theologies of grace broke out into another skirmish in the early sixth century. The monastery at Lérins remained a stronghold of resistance against what the monks considered the more extreme dimensions of Augustine's theology of grace and dismissal of free will. Though himself a former monk at Lerins, Caesarius (ca. 470–543), bishop of Arles, championed Augustine's teaching.

To that end he convened a church council at Orange in 529 to discuss and hopefully settle the matter.[15] Augustine's theology of grace was affirmed by the council, and Pelagian and semi-Pelagian teachings condemned. Following the lead of their Gallican predecessor Prosper of Aquitaine, Caesarius and the council members affirmed a wholly Augustinian understanding of grace, though without explicitly using or endorsing Augustine's idea of predestination. In fact, the canons of the council explicitly reject the idea of "reprobation," that is, the teaching that God predestines some souls to be damned and others to be saved. Augustine himself never asserts this idea of reprobation, or as it came to be called "double predestination." But the idea must have been circulating if the council decided to condemn it in its documents.[16]

Augustine's theology of predestination is difficult to understand—both for fifth-century monks and for many today. Predestination was Augustine's construct, drawing from Paul's Letter to the Romans, especially chapters 7 and 9. Augustine affirms that our salvation, our being drawn into a saving relationship with God is completely and totally the work of God. We have neither the resources of intellect nor the strength of will to turn toward God, since both intellect and will have been completely corrupted and fatally weakened by the original sin of Adam that all human beings inherit. If we make a turn to God, a *conversio*, it is only because God, in the infinity of divine wisdom and love, has decided from all eternity to extend to certain individuals the grace that initiates and sustains conversion. Thus some persons are predestined to be saved. This theological construct of predestination looms large in Augustine's later anti-Pelagian writings, but it is also found in his earlier works on grace, such as in his *Miscellany of Questions in Response to Simplician*, written in 396–97.

Augustine's predestination does not refer to God's *foreknowledge* of how we will live our lives. God does not decide to give us saving grace because the divine omniscience has already from eternity "watched" our life unfold and so reward us for good deeds. Predestination affirms grace and salvation to be completely God's initiative, irrespective of our deeds and of God's knowledge of them. As mentioned above, Augustinian predestination does not include reprobation. God does not actively choose to damn certain individuals from all eternity and save others. Because of original sin, all humanity is, since the expulsion of Adam and Eve from the garden, God-forsaken, a *massa damnata*, a *massa perditionis* (*Letter* 194.2.4). Damnation, in Augustine's view, is our inheritance from Adam and Eve. Divine mercy leads God to save certain persons from this lost state and so predestine them for salvation.

All this comes from Augustine's interpretation of Paul's Letter to the Romans, an interpretation that certainly spoke to Augustine's own experience of search and conversion.[17] Most of Augustine's critics and even many of his advocates have had some level of discomfort with his teaching of predestination. One of his foremost biographers and deep admirers Gerald Bonner writes, "Nothing is gained by attempting to defend the doctrine [of predestination], which remains a terrible one and more likely to arouse our awe than enlist our sympathy."[18] Perhaps the leading authority on the Augustinian topics of free will and predestination is James Wetzel of Villanova University. His work provides a solid contemporary examination of Augustine's deep insight and motive for this teaching. Wetzel claims that predestination is an essential part of Augustine's whole theology of grace and has to be somehow taken into account: "Without the doctrine of predestination, there is no Augustinian theology of grace."[19]

As we shall see, predestination returns to the forefront of theological history in the Reformation and the Council of Trent, extending beyond even what Augustine taught when Calvin espouses double predestination or the teaching of reprobation. At the middle of the sixth century, however, Caesarius had managed a conciliar compromise that strongly affirmed an Augustinian theology of grace and salvation, while avoiding the complexities and confusion surrounding predestination. Pope Boniface II approved the council's declaration in 531, thereby declaring Augustine's understanding of grace to be church teaching.[20]

In addition to his leadership at the Second Council of Orange, Caesarius spread Augustinian teaching in another way as well. He excerpted many passages from Augustine's sermons and interwove them into his own homilies. These homilies were widely circulated and ensured that Augustine's voice continued to echo in churches throughout sixth- and seventh-century southern Gaul.[21] Thus, with the help of Prosper of Aquitaine, Eugippius, and Caesarius of Arles, together with papal approval in the fifth and sixth centuries, Augustine's influence in the Early Middle Ages becomes pervasive. His interpretations of scripture remain normative, especially his readings of Genesis and Paul. His work *Teaching Christianity* becomes the textbook for the study of scripture and the practice of preaching and teaching the Bible.

However, Augustine's writings focus not only on Sacred Scripture and faith in the inspired Word of God. Philosophy and human reason also figured prominently in his search for truth. His affirmation of faith *and* reason inspires philosophers such as Boethius (480–526) and John Scotus Eriugena (ca. 810–ca. 877) to explore and extend the importance of critical thinking and philosophical method as part of the Christian heritage.[22] Among the Latin fathers of the church, Augustine is unique in his use of philosophy to seek understanding of his faith. The growing importance of philosophy in the Christian writers of the Early Middle Ages was due in great part to Augustine. Even in their introduction of Aristotle into Christian theology, Albert the Great and

Thomas Aquinas follow the Augustinian paradigm of engaging the thought of philosophers, and wedding faith and reason in the search for truth.

## The High Middle Ages (1100–1400)

The influential thinkers of the eleventh and twelfth centuries were schooled in various aspects of Augustine's thought, and they used his ideas as launching pads to develop their own. Anselm of Canterbury (1033–1109) owed his phrase "faith seeking understanding" to Augustine's emphasis on faith and reason and to his definition of faith as "thinking with assent" (*On the Predestination of the Saints* 2.5).[23] Anselm develops his ontological argument for the existence of God by building on Augustine's affirmation of the power of reason. Hugh of St. Victor (ca. 1096–1141) reaches back through John Scotus Eriugena to Augustine to spread a renewed interest in Neo-Platonism that flowered in the twelfth century.[24]

Augustine's continuing influence in subsequent centuries is assured by an important text of the theologian and bishop Peter Lombard (1100–60). This was his *Libri Quatuor Sententiarum* or *Four Books of Sentences*, published around 1150. Lombard cites Augustine extensively. This work becomes the standard textbook for the theology faculties at the major universities in Europe during the High Middle Ages and into the Reformation. Lombard's extensive reliance on Augustine ensured the Bishop of Hippo's dominant presence in the curricula of medieval universities and in the theological debates of the Middle Ages. All major scholars, up to and including the Reformers Luther and Calvin, address and comment on Lombard's theological themes and positions, thereby drawing all masters and students into conversation with "Father" Augustine.[25]

## The Place of Augustine in Scholasticism

Two significant developments in the twelfth and thirteenth centuries had a profound influence on the legacy of Augustine's writing and thinking. The first of these was the rise of the medieval universities of Europe.

From the early 1100s, the locus of education begins to shift from the monasteries and cathedral schools of Europe to newly founded "universities." These new schools evolved into institutions of learning somewhat separate from and independent of the clerical communities of canons regularly attached to a city's cathedral, and from communities of monks in one of the great European abbeys.[26] Reflecting the increase in trade, commerce, and communication in general that characterized this changing period of European history, the universities became centers of learning between and among which scholars traveled and ideas were exchanged. This ferment in thought affected the philosophical and theological legacy of Augustine.

Among the leading scholars, or "scholastics" as they are called, who held chairs at the new universities in the twelfth century was Peter Lombard. Peter, as we have mentioned, gave Augustine pride of place in his *Sentences*, which came to prominence as the paradigm for theological and philosophical writing and thinking for the next four centuries.[27] Subsequent scholastics earned their title and role as masters depending on how they agreed or disagreed with Lombard's interpretation of points of doctrine and with his interpretation of Augustine on such questions. In this way Lombard, greatly influenced by Augustine's thinking, had set the template for study and academic advancement.

However, in the thirteenth century, a significant change occurred in the theology taught and studied at the universities. Augustine's influence, and the lack of Greek or Latin copies of most of Aristotle's writings, meant that Plato and Neo-Platonism dominated Western Christian thought and study from the fifth to the twelfth centuries.[28] All that changed in the thirteenth century.

The writings and thought of Aristotle were rediscovered by the Europeans, thanks to translations of his works from Arabic into Greek and Latin by Islamic philosophers and philologists. Islamic culture and society had spread across North Africa and into the Iberian Peninsula during the kingdom of Al-Andalus, from the eighth to the fifteenth centuries. Islamic philosophers, especially Avicenna or Ibn Sina (ca. 980–1037) and Averroes or Ibn Rushd (1126–98) wrote commentaries on Aristotle.[29] Translations of their works and of Aristotelian texts made their way from Islamic Spain into the new European universities. One of the first scholastics to embrace Aristotelian philosophy was the Dominican friar Albertus Magnus or Albert the Great (ca. 1200–80).

Albert and his most famous student and Dominican confrere Thomas Aquinas (1225–74) began to reflect on the tenets of their Christian faith in light of philosophical language and categories they found in Aristotle.[30] This shift from Plato and Neo-Platonic philosophy to Aristotle was revolutionary. It is no surprise that it was met with suspicion and resistance. This new inclusion of Aristotelian thought in Christian theology was twice condemned by the archbishop of Paris, who had Thomas's teaching in mind.

Thomas himself read Aristotle and his Arab interpreters critically, allowing his faith to shed light on the ideas of "The Philosopher," as he called Aristotle. However, Thomas's teachings and writings began a lively dialogue and vigorous debate among those theologians who favored Aristotle and those who favored Augustinian Neo-Platonism. This dialogue and debate continued over the subsequent centuries as the European universities expanded and grew.[31]

### Founding of the Order of Hermits of Saint Augustine

The second development in the Middle Ages that profoundly affected how the thought of Augustine continued to grow in importance was the founding of the Order of Hermits of Saint Augustine. The twelfth and thirteenth centuries witnessed a widespread spiritual renewal in Europe. Laymen dropped out of society to live in small religious groups or communes. Francis of Assisi (1181–1226) and his early companions were an example of one such movement and group in the Italian region of Umbria. In 1210, Francis and his band of followers were recognized as a new religious order of wandering, preaching mendicants, a title which distinguished them from monks who stayed in their monasteries. In 1217, Dominic Guzman, a Spanish priest, founded another order of mendicant preachers that bore his name, the Dominicans.

In 1244, many autonomous communities of lay hermits living in small groups around Tuscany were also united into one new mendicant religious order. Pope Innocent IV brought the Tuscan Hermits together and gave them the *Rule of Life* that Augustine had written for his own and other communities of men and of women in fourth- through fifth-century North Africa. Thus they became the Order of Hermits of Saint Augustine. In 1256, the newly founded Order of St. Augustine was expanded by welcoming and including communities outside of Tuscany and Italy.[32]

Many members of this new order of Augustinian mendicant friars took their place alongside Dominican and Franciscan friars as students and masters or teachers in the universities of the thirteenth century. The Augustinian friars were not founded to be a united "school" of thought dedicated to the heritage of their nominal founder. There was no uniformity of thought among Augustinian scholars, that is, they were not expected to study only Augustine, or to present consistent or homogeneous interpretations of his writings. However, as time went on, more and more of the friars did promote his writings and dedicated themselves to ensuring that his works were preserved and his thoughts represented in the lively theological debates of the universities.

## The Augustinian School of the Thirteenth Century

The thirteenth century sees the emergence of what historians have labeled the "Augustinian School." As we have mentioned, in the writing and teaching of Albert the Great, Christian theology begins to turn from its exclusive allegiance to Neo-Platonism to new-found interest in Aristotle. This turn is completed in the writings of Thomas who builds his theology solidly on Aristotle, even while he continues to refer to Augustinian and Neo-Platonic concepts. Thomas and his disciples extend Augustine's emphasis on faith *and* reason, but they approach and analyze reason along Aristotelian lines.

As Thomas's Aristotelian approach gains ground, certain aspects of Augustine's thought begin to stand out by contrast. These include Augustine's emphasis on the will, and his understanding of grace as healing the will. Thomas emphasizes the priority of intellect. His approach becomes known as intellectualism. By contrast, the Augustinian tradition, following Augustine's doctrinal emphasis on will and grace, emphasizes the priority of will. This is referred to as voluntarism.[33] Certainly neither excludes the other: intellect and will both figure prominently in the Christian anthropologies of Thomism and Augustinianism. It is a matter of emphasis that involves subtle theological differences in how one understands virtue, habit, sin, free will, and the effects of grace.

The Augustinian School includes many Franciscan friars such as Bonaventure (1221–74) who emphasizes Augustine's theology of divine illumination, the powers of the soul, and the existence of *rationes seminales* that are implanted by God in his creatures and that lead to the development of species. On its side, Thomism preferred Aristotle's theory of knowledge that understands learning to originate in sense experience, that defines the various faculties of the soul, and that sees the great variety of created species not mentioned in Genesis to emerge from the innate potentiality of matter rather than from the idea of divinely implanted *rationes seminales* that Augustine had borrowed from the Skeptics.

Other Franciscans like John Duns Scotus (1265–1308) and Alexander Hales (1185–1245) have a clear preference for Augustine's Neo-Platonism. They understood themselves to be continuing the tradition of previous Augustinian thinkers like Anselm of Canterbury and Bernard of Clairvaux. These Franciscans often cast themselves as defending Christian orthodoxy amidst the incursion of the "new" thinking based on Aristotle. In addition there were also thirteenth-century Augustinian friars whose works championed an Augustinian, Neo-Platonic approach. These include Giles of Rome (1243–1316), who was actually a student of Thomas Aquinas in Paris, and James of Viterbo (1255–1308). Giles, who came to teach at Paris, argued for the superiority of the will, in light of Augustine's writings. James developed the implications of Augustine's political thought for the social challenges of the thirteenth century. Other Augustinian friars who wrote in defense of Augustine's position were Gregory of Rimini and Hugolino of Orvieto.[34]

Despite some clear differences between Thomistic intellectualism and Augustinian voluntarism, however, the Augustinian School of the thirteenth century is by no means an easily identifiable group of scholars that embraces a common understanding of Augustine's thought and a unified theological and philosophical system. Bonaventure, for example, studied and wrote extensively about Aristotle.[35] Giles's years of study under Thomas are evident in the extensive influence of Aquinas's thought on Giles's own theology.[36] And while developing a political theology for the thirteenth century, James of Viterbo not only comments on Augustine's *City of God*, he also borrows extensively from Aquinas's political thought.[37]

A good picture of the theological and philosophical positions held by the many masters of theology in the medieval universities does not draw hard, broad lines between and among them. It is more accurate to say that as Aristotle's thought is introduced into Christian theology by Albert, Thomas, and others, it comes into energetic dialogue with Augustine's older Neo-Platonic Christianity. In the active exchange of ideas that characterized the scholastics, each "school" of thought helped to elucidate the contributions and insights of the other. For our purposes, it is enough to say that even after the significant contributions of Thomas, Augustine's thought, while no longer the sole theological paradigm in the West, remains very important.

### A Neo-Augustinian School of the Fourteenth Century

The German Augustinian friar and scholar Adolar Zumkeller (1915–2011) argues persuasively for a "Neo-Augustinian School" in the fourteenth century.[38] This school or movement is identifiable by a particular issue championed by two of its early representatives, the Augustinian friar Gregory of Rimini (1300–58) who taught at Paris and in Italy, and the English cleric Thomas Bradwardine (1300–49) who taught at Oxford and who, for a short time, became archbishop of Canterbury. Responding to what they judged to be a new Pelagianism arising from theologies with Aristotelian emphases, they were responsible for a revival of Augustine's anti-Pelagian works.

Beginning with Gregory and Bradwardine, this movement exerts a strong influence on many Augustinian friars who were teaching across Europe at various universities. A common theology of grace begins to emerge within the late fourteenth-century Augustinian Order and to influence subsequent generations of friars. As an emerging school of thought, they emphasize will and love as the targets of divine grace. They also speak of affective knowledge as distinct from Aristotelian-Thomistic speculative knowledge.[39]

To develop Augustinian theology further, scholars of this Neo-Augustinian School began to identify and cite more of Augustine's texts beyond those few that had been popular for centuries. In 1354, the Augustinian friar Bartholomew of Urbino

(d. 1350) produced his *Milleloquium Sancti Augustini*, which was a collection of fifteen hundred passages from Augustine's writings. Bartholomew's work differs from the *florilegiae* and *sententiae* of earlier centuries. It evidences the more sophisticated exegetical rigor of late medieval scholarship and literary culture.[40] It also ensured a continuing presence of Augustine's ideas and a growing influence of his thought, especially in the German universities where many Augustinian friars and monks studied and taught— something of consequence in the fifteenth and sixteenth centuries, as we shall see. Augustine's ideas and the anti-Pelagian themes of the "Neo-Augustinian School" made a profound impression on a young Augustinian monk at the Erfurt monastery. His name was Martin Luther.[41]

The influence and place of Augustine throughout Europe's Middle Ages is a field that needs continuing study. Damasus Trapp advances a daring summary of that influence. He distinguishes between "Augustine" by which he means a working awareness of Augustine's writing and thought, which Thomas and his disciples certainly had, and "Augustinianism" by which he means a philosophical and theological predilection to privilege will, grace, and human experience while not omitting the study of intellect, nature, and the logic of propositions more characteristic of Thomism. He writes:

> Early scholasticism [tenth to twelfth centuries] had an Augustine and an Augustinianism of its own; Aristotelic Thomism [thirteenth century] had an Augustine but no Augustinianism; late scholasticism [thirteenth to fifteenth centuries] rediscovered Augustine within an Augustinianism of its own![42]

Amidst the spreading ardor of this Neo-Augustinian School of thought, the power and force of Augustine's anti-Pelagian thought and sentiment begins to brew during the fifteenth and sixteenth centuries. It boils over in the writings and preaching of

Luther. But in the calm before that firestorm, we find a cultured interlude, a rediscovery of and return to the centuries of Greek and Roman times. The Renaissance had its own, far different appreciation of Augustine.

## The Renaissance (1350–1550)

The Renaissance engenders yet another rediscovery of Augustine, and begets its own kind of Augustinianism, which we might call Augustinian humanism. Augustine's influence continues into the Renaissance as he becomes an inspiration for many thinkers and artists of the time. The fourteenth and fifteenth centuries brought a renewed interest in and revival of the literature, art, and architecture of the Greco-Roman period. This Renaissance, this rebirth of interest in the classics of antiquity occasioned another retrieval of Augustine who was, after all, the last great Latin writer and rhetorician. It was not so much his anti-Pelagian theology that interested Renaissance thinkers. Nor did the theological tomes of the Augustinian schools of the thirteenth, fourteenth, and fifteenth centuries excite them. It was their keen interest in two aspects of Augustine that drew them to his thoughts and texts, namely his attention to classical literature and how to read it, and his focus on human experience as the starting point for religion.

Renaissance figures such as Petrarch (1304–74), Boccaccio (1313–75), and Ficino (1433–99) in Italy; Nicholas of Cusa (1401–64) in Germany; and Thomas More (1478–1535) in England—to name but a few—found inspiration in Augustine's writings. Petrarch, for example, signals the turn from academic concentration on the heady logic of scholastic argument and logical propositions to an exploration of the human person who was the locus of religious experience. Petrarch found in Augustine's *Confessions* the journal of a soul in its quest for discovery of self and God. Petrarch carried a copy of *Confessions* on his person whenever he could. Augustine's journey of faith mirrored Petrarch's own experience and inspired him to further exploration of human experience.[43]

Both Petrarch and Boccaccio exemplified the Renaissance recovery of and return to an appreciation of the literary classics and philosophical ideas of Greco-Roman antiquity. In Augustine they found an ecclesial ally.[44] The great Bishop of Hippo, so revered by church theologians, was himself the last great skilled reader and interpreter of Latin classics. Renaissance humanists were drawn to works such as *City of God*, especially to the earlier books where he provides an eloquent review of Roman and Greek philosophy, literature, and history. There they found encouragement to explore the literature and philosophy of antiquity, as a way of plumbing the depths of human experience. And hadn't Augustine himself encouraged the study of the Liberal Arts for the betterment of the person, the interpretation of scripture, and the preaching of the Gospel in his influential work *Teaching Christianity*?[45]

Augustine's Neo-Platonism was also of great interest in the Renaissance. It inspired Marsilio Ficino, whose interpretation of Platonism was to remain influential down to the nineteenth century.[46] The German Renaissance humanist and bishop Nicholas of Cusa finds in Augustine's analogies for meditating on the Trinity an inspiration for his own deeply mystical humanism of the fifteenth century.[47] Nicholas titled his famous work *On Learned Ignorance* from Augustine's phrase *docta ignorantia* to express the profound philosophical-theological realization that to comprehend the nature of God is infinitely beyond our humanity capacities.[48]

Thomas More lectured on *City of God* in London in 1501. Erasmus of Rotterdam (1469–1536), the leading humanist of the sixteenth century, published his own edition of Augustine's complete works in Latin in 1528–29 at Basel.[49] In all, the Renaissance found in Augustine a "safe" hero to whom they could appeal in their spirited arguments with, or rejection of, the dry formulae of medieval scholastic theology and their strong preference for classical literature.[50]

Renaissance interest in classical texts, hermeneutics, and human experience, as opposed to scholastic practice of logical propositions and dogma led them to a retrieval of Augustine the Christian humanist of *Confessions*, who plumbs the depths of mind and heart to uncover the abiding mystery of the Holy One in the secret recesses of the person.

As they had in the medieval universities, members of the Order of Saint Augustine played a role in advancing the thought of their patron during the Renaissance. The Italian Augustinian Friar Diogini di Borgo San Sepolcro (ca. 1300–42) taught Boccaccio when the latter was a young student, and introduced him to the study of the humanities. Diogini, who studied at the University of Paris, also introduced Petrarch to the writings of Augustine and became his father confessor. Maffeo Vegio (1407–58) was a Milanese poet and humanist, who eventually joined the Order of Saint Augustine in Rome. He used Augustine extensively in his treatise on Christian education, *De educatione liberorum*.

The center of the order's involvement with the Renaissance was its community at *Santo Spirito* in Florence. The church itself, begun in 1444, is the work of the great Florentine Renaissance architect Filippo Brunelleschi (1377–1446), and is among the purest creations of early Renaissance architecture. Under the leadership of the Augustinian friar Luigi Marsigli (1342–94), *Santo Spirito* became the site of a Florentine "academy" of renaissance thinkers, artists, and architects. Petrarch was close to the friars at *Santo Spirito*, and Boccaccio bequeathed his library to the Augustinian community there. The young Michelangelo Buonaroti studied cadavers in the city morgue that was administered by the *Santo Spirito* community.

So Augustine's legacy in the West enriched the flowering of interest in antiquity, literature, architecture, and art that we call the Renaissance. Both his own writings, and the scholarship and activism of the mendicant friars that followed his *Rule of Life*, contributed significantly to the vitality and beauty of the fourteenth, fifteenth, and sixteenth centuries.

# 5
# LEGACY II
## Reformation to Today

## The Reformation

The excesses of Renaissance society, including the wealth and power of the church and its allies, resulted in many abuses. Reform was sorely needed.[1] Many of those who called for reform found inspiration and direction in the writings of Augustine. His influence once again comes to the forefront. Both Martin Luther (1483–1546) and John Calvin (1509–64) built their theological foundation on certain aspects of Augustine's theology.

The story of Luther is well known. On the basis of a vow made amidst a dangerous thunderstorm, the young man Luther joined the Augustinian monastery in Erfurt, Germany. As a young monk, Luther was tortured by an obsessive scrupulosity. He confessed his guilt often and excessively. He despaired of ever pleasing God and winning eternal life. He found his way out of this spiritual quagmire with the help of Augustine and an Augustinian.

His priest confessor at the monastery in Erfurt was the Augustinian monk and scholar Johannes von Staupitz (1460–1524).[2] The Neo-Augustinian school that developed in the fourteenth century continued into the fifteenth and sixteenth centuries. It significantly influenced theologians such as von Staupitz who studied and taught in Augustinian monasteries and colleges, especially in northern Europe. Von Staupitz introduced the young Luther to Augustine's theology of grace and his interpretation of St. Paul, sharing Augustine's insistence that our salvation does not depend on our good works, but on God's totally unmerited, pre-destined forgiveness. Von Staupitz also encouraged Luther to pur-sue further studies in theology and scripture in order to deepen his appreciation of the role of faith and grace in the spiritual life. Following von Staupitz's advice, Luther went on to study scripture and Augustine. In subsequent years, Augustine's theology of grace, based on his interpretation of Paul, and Luther's own study of scripture, especially Paul, had a profound personal effect on his life of faith.

However, in developing his own theological opinions, Luther selects certain aspects of Augustine's theology and excludes others. He emphasizes the Augustinian concepts of sin, justification by God's forgiving grace, and the predestination of the elect chosen to receive grace.[3] Luther ignores other aspects of Augustine's thought such as his understanding of the self in rela-tionship with God, the divinizing effects of grace on the person, and the mystical elements in many of Augustine's writings. Luther, like many other reformers who disdained philosophy, also ignores Augustine's Neo-Platonism, preferring instead his commentaries on scripture. In Augustinian terms, Luther emphasizes faith over reason, grace over works, forgiveness over sanctification, external justification over interior relationship, and scripture over the teaching authority of the church. So while Luther is certainly a theological heir to Augustine himself, and to the Neo-Augustinian school of the Late Middle Ages, he is also selective in his use of Augustine's ideas and writings.

Augustine was also a primary influence on the priest John Calvin. Though he was not an Augustinian monk like Luther, Calvin's self-directed theological studies led him into a thorough review of Augustine's writings, especially the anti-Pelagian works. In his magisterial tome *Institutes of the Christian Religion* (1536), Calvin references Augustine over eight hundred times, far more than he cites any other theological source. He credits Augustine for his conversion and for "opening the way" for him into reform theology.[4]

Like Luther, Calvin emphasizes Augustinian ideas of sin, grace, justification, and predestination. He also deemphasizes or ignores Augustine's teachings on sanctification, mysticism, illumination, and spiritual ascent as well as Augustine's use of Neo-Platonism. Calvin pushes the idea of predestination further than Luther. In his *Institutes*, Calvin retrieves from history the teaching of double-predestination or reprobation, that is, God's eternal choice of those saved and of those damned (*Institutes* III.21).[5] In developing his own theology of double predestination, Calvin stresses Augustine's idea that only certain human beings are preordained by God's will to be chosen from among the *massa damnata* of humanity for salvation; the rest of humanity is predestined to be damned.[6]

The reformers appealed to Augustine in their desire to reform aspects of a church that had grown corrupt and cynical. They also found in the story of Augustine's conversion and discovery of grace the encouragement and guidance for their own Christian faith, and that of their followers. In many ways Augustine's theology of grace was just the antidote needed to counter pastoral practices and ecclesial policies that encouraged a mechanical reliance on prayers and works that would have outraged even Pelagius. However, the pastoral balance and theological compromise achieved by Prosper of Aquataine and Caesarius of Arles a thousand years before the Reformation did not happen in the sixteenth century. In their debate with the monks of southern Gaul, Prosper and Caesarius had identified the heart of Augustine's theology of grace and maintained a pastoral balance that avoided possible misunderstandings of predestination. Such compromise did not happen amidst the fiery arguments and battles of the European Reformation.

## The Council of Trent

The Catholic response to the Reformers emerged from the deliberations of the Council of Trent (1545–63). The delegates, representing many theological schools—including those of the Reformers—debated how to respond to the theologies of Luther, Calvin, and others, and at the same time reform the Catholic Church. The Reformers had claimed Augustine as the source and inspiration for their theological agenda and challenge to the Church of Rome. The bishops and theologians of Trent also used Augustine's theology in their debates and documents.

One of the leading theologians at Trent was the Augustinian friar Girolamo Seripando.[7] Seripando had been prior general of the Augustinian Order, and in addition was a bishop and cardinal. He is considered the last great teacher of the Neo-Augustinian school. At Trent, Seripando was a papal legate and even presided over the council for a while. During the conciliar debates, he was a vocal advocate for the theology of Augustine and its medieval interpretations. Though the council did not accept all of his Augustinian positions, Seripando was responsible for Trent's affirmation of Augustine's theologies of sin and grace as well as its inclusion of the dimensions of Augustinian thought neglected by the Reformers, such as internal sanctification.

What emerges from Trent is a new reading of Augustine's teachings on original sin and justification.[8] The Reformers understood Augustine's teaching of original sin and its effects to have completely corrupted and fatally compromised free will. Concupiscence, pervading all of human experience was the continuing legacy of original sin throughout history. They stressed the absolute necessity of divine grace, encountered through Sacred Scripture, which was the sole agent of justification. Good works did not justify or save.

Trent agreed with the Reformers and with the Augustinian school that original sin had led to the loss of divine grace. However, the council held that free will, though weakened and wounded by original sin, was not thereby destroyed.[9] The council fathers defended free will against the Reformers' concept of a totally corrupted humanity. Grace calls us to faith and empowers us to respond to that call. It also empowers us to good works that are a sign of divine favor and further the work of the kingdom.[10] The council, in contrast to Reformation theology, emphasized the interiority of the divine presence and the transformative nature of grace.[11] Not only did original sin not destroy the trinitarian image of God in the human person; grace both heals and restores that image, inspiring interior holiness and elevating the believer to relationship with the divine.[12]

The council's Decree on Justification cites Augustine five times—more than any other theological source, except Scripture. His theology of grace, as affirmed at the Second Council of Orange, is repeated and adopted at Trent. The Decree on Justification also briefly mentions what it calls "the mystery" of predestination as a way of affirming grace and salvation as totally God's gift, and not the result of faith or works.[13] By emphasizing the Augustinian themes of interiority and divinization, Trent retrieves the spirituality of divine illumination characteristic of thirteenth-century Augustinian thinkers such as Bonaventure and Duns Scotus as well as the more mystical tendencies in Augustine's own theology of the inward spiritual ascent of the soul.

Thomistic theology had provided Trent with the ideas and language needed to affirm Augustine's theology of grace, while at the same time avoiding the pessimistic anthropology of Lutheran and Calvinist theologies. In this way, Trent, especially in its Decree on Justification, models an integration of Augustinian, Neo-Platonic thought and Thomistic-Aristotelian thought. Trent did not settle all theological argument about grace. Nor did it want to foreclose ongoing theological debate about justification and sanctification. But it did manage to call on the best of Augustinian theology, enrich it with Thomistic theology, and pass onto future generations a rich and balanced understanding of the relationship between God and humanity. Augustine himself would have been pleased.[14]

## Seventeenth to Twenty-First Centuries: Augustine in Modern Theology and Postmodern Thought

### The Modern Period: Descartes, Pascal, Jansenius

René Descartes (1596–1650) picks up the thread of Augustinian interiority.[15] Though he does not acknowledge any intellectual or spiritual debt to Augustine, Descartes initiates the modern or "post-medieval" period in Western philosophy by abandoning the scholastic Aristotelian-Thomistic starting points in nature and the senses, and exercising a turn to the subject. From the medieval philosophical notion of substance, he withdraws within to the experience of human consciousness. His *cogito ergo sum* seeks to establish a solid, immovable footing for the foundation of all of his philosophy.

Twelve centuries earlier, Augustine, seeking to refute the skepticism of the Second Academy of Athens, anticipates Descartes's *cogito* in *City of God* where he writes: "I am completely certain that I exist, and that I know that I exist, and that I love that I know this." And in the event that deception creeps into his assurance, Augustine continues in the same text: "I am deceived, therefore I am" (*City of God* XI.26).

But the similarity between Augustinian and Cartesian thought is short-lived.[16] Augustine's turn within leads to an encounter with the mystery of a divine to the self and a realization of the weak and wounded nature of human will. These basic realities of Augustinian interior life lead the soul to encounter its own subjectivity and that of other persons. For Descartes, the turn within leads to a canonization of reason that leaves the affective and volitional dimensions of the person and the ethics of social responsibility unintegrated.[17] Thus one might say that Cartesian philosophy is very Augustinian in its interiority, in its "turn within," but is distinctly un-Augustinian in its lack of subjectivity or personhood. For the latter we must turn to Descartes's contemporary Blaise Pascal.

Pascal (1623–62) is perhaps the most distinctly Augustinian thinker of the early modern period. His idea of the divided self reflects the influence of Augustine's teaching of the divided will and attendant moral struggles. His "reasons of the heart" is a powerful alternative to Descartes's solitary and solely rational pursuit of truth, and to the Neo-Scholastic rationalism that characterized Catholic teaching of the seventeenth century. Pascal combines interiority, subjectivity, and spirituality in ways that influence French philosophy and theology for subsequent centuries. One could even say that Augustine's inward turn to the subject and personhood, under the influence of fourth- and fifth-century Neo-Platonism, reemerges in the modern period through Pascal.[18]

Another important seventeenth-century Augustinian influence, with which Pascal was involved, was the thought of the priest and bishop Cornelius Jansenius. Jansenius (1585–1638) was a notable Catholic Dutch theologian and churchman. He was a scholar in the thought of Augustine and a professor at the University of Leuven. Jansenius was particularly interested in Augustine's anti-Pelagian writings. His posthumously published *Augustinus* was a summary of his thinking about Augustine's theology of grace and nature. It became very influential and very controversial.

Jansenius was keen to assert the anti-Pelagian strains in Augustine's thinking and writing. His concern was to balance what he considered to be questionable theological positions among the Jesuits of France, positions that he thought compromised the primacy of and radical human need for divine grace. The subsequent theological debates were subsumed into political battles and academic rivalries of the era, especially after Jansenius's untimely death in 1638 from plague.

The Benedictine nuns of the Abbey of Port-Royal, outside Paris, championed Jansenius's anti-Pelagian Augustinianism. The controversy escalated as the "Jansenists," with their tendencies toward Augustine's idea of predestination, and beyond Augustine to double predestination, were accused of Calvinism. For that they were punished by Rome, and Jansenism was dubbed heretical. The contemporary scholar Mathijs Lamberigts of the Catholic University of Leuven argues that Jansenius's positions on grace—and Augustine's—were greatly exaggerated and misunderstood in the political and religious controversies that followed his death and the publication of his *Augustinus*.[19] Nonetheless, the influence of Port-Royal on the spiritual, clerical, and ecclesiastical life of France was considerable. The Abbey and the school of spirituality it promoted reflected a severe brand of Augustinianism that influenced French Catholicism and religious life over subsequent centuries.

This severe spirituality of Jansenism spread beyond France across wider northern European Catholic circles. For example, Irish seminary students were not permitted to pursue their studies in Ireland, which at that time was occupied by a very anti-Catholic eighteenth- and nineteenth-century Britain. Consequently, many studied abroad in France where their training was deeply influenced by a severe Jansenist spirituality. This fact has had widespread consequences for Catholic life in Ireland, America, Canada, and Australia where Irish clergy predominated throughout the nineteenth and early twentieth centuries.

Pascal was a patron of Port-Royal, and his sister entered the community of nuns there. However, his own interpretation of Augustine was more humane and continued on through the influence of his literary masterpiece *Pensées*. So while connected with Port-Royal, Pascal's Augustinian emphasis was on divine immanence. The implications of his teaching lead to a more positive anthropology than is often drawn from Augustine's anti-Pelagian writings.

## Contemporary Christian Theology

Pascal's work opened the way to more scholarly interest in human subjectivity throughout the nineteenth and twentieth centuries. His writing about the experience of divine immanence and the centrality of subjectivity found a German counterpart and successor in the nineteenth-century Protestant theology of Friedrich Schleiermacher (1768–1834). Schleiermacher, considered the father of liberal Protestant theology, went through his own crisis of faith and emerged with the conviction that faith must be based on the believer's immanent experience of the divine indwelling. These themes are deeply Augustinian.[20] Though this "liberal" approach was to be countered by the more orthodox theology of Karl Barth (1886–1968) a century later, Schleiermacher's interiority continues to influence much of Protestant religious experience today. Within more conservative Protestant communions, it can dampen the lingering peals of predestination and reprobation that continue to echo down the years from Calvin's Reformation.

On the Catholic side, Maurice Blondel (1861–1941) and Karl Rahner (1904–84) continued to explore the "turn to the subject" practiced by Augustine, Pascal, and Schleiermacher. Blondel situates his philosophy within Neo-Platonism; and Rahner, within Thomistic-Aristotelianism. However, both rework these older philosophical and theological categories to construct their own theologies of immanence, drawing largely from Augustine's thought.[21] Rahner, a German Jesuit, develops a theology of grace as the Self-communication of God to the soul. His extensive writings represent the fullest attempt to retrieve Augustinian subjectivity and place it in dialogue with twentieth-century existentialism, particularly the philosophy of Martin Heidegger.[22]

In a similar theological approach, the Swiss Protestant theologian Paul Tillich (1886–1965) also develops an understanding of religion along Augustinian lines, identifying the inner experience of the Ground of our Being to be the presupposition of the source and context of the God question. Augustinian interiority and subjectivity has thus been a recurring thread of the fabric of Christian theology in the modern period.[23]

The Augustinian friar Michael Scanlon of Villanova University identifies what we might appropriately call the "heart" of contemporary theology built upon Augustine's theological project. It is his "personalism."[24] Augustine's personalism can be understood as his affirmation that each human being can encounter a personal, loving God in the depths of his soul and the vicissitudes of her life. Scanlon quotes Jean Guitton on what they both consider to be the core of Augustine's Christianity and theological anthropology: "We may say that St. Augustine is the first man in the West to have attained, in personal fashion, the experience the Jewish people had in a collective way."[25] Augustine understands the self as constituted by its encounter with God and the vivifying, transforming, and redeeming effects of divine grace amidst one's daily life.

Scanlon makes the case that this key idea of Augustinian personalism must be retrieved from other aspects of Augustine's thought that are not essential to it and that undercut its relevance for contemporary Christian theology and spirituality. Two of these nonessential parts of Augustine's thought are predestination, with its theological corollaries, and his dualistic understanding of history and eternity. Scanlon argues that predestination is not essential to an Augustinian theology of grace.[26] One can, he claims, affirm divine omnipotence and the radical human need for grace without resorting to predestination. This is basically what Rahner has accomplished in his retrieval of Augustinian interiority and his idea of the "supernatural existential" or God's universal Self-communication through human subjectivity.[27]

The second nonessential idea in Augustine's theology that needs to be bracketed in order to retrieve and reframe Augustinian personalism is the radical dualism between history and eternity. Augustine, especially in his writings on Genesis, managed to move beyond the Manichean dualism of matter and spirit that characterized his early years. However, Scanlon argues, he moved into a new kind of dualism: the dualism of history and eternity. In Augustine's understanding, our Christian pilgrimage leads us through the trials of time and the vicissitudes of history into the bliss of eternity and the beatific vision. The historical consciousness of our present day requires that we moderate or move beyond this second dualism in Augustine. We need a theology of history that locates the divine, redeeming presence in history as well as in eternity.[28] While on this pilgrimage toward God, *ad deum*, we nonetheless dedicate our time and efforts to become agents of divine grace that redeems history by slowly transforming social structures and patiently working for justice and peace.

Augustine himself sees the goal or purpose of divine grace, which works mysteriously in the soul, to be our personal salvation that is ultimately realized in eternity. Scanlon's retrieval of Augustinian theology for the present day promotes the relevance of Augustinian interiority and subjectivity for contemporary historical consciousness. Current Christian emphases on the works of justice and peace for the transformation of social structures, he argues, benefit from the sustaining experience of Augustinian interiority just as much as the latter is deepened and transformed by historical consciousness. While there are certainly examples of Augustine himself working for justice and peace, his characteristic emphasis is on the unchanging and unassailable happiness of heaven.[29] In the next chapter, we will look at various aspects of Augustine's thought that are being researched today. An operative question for this review is how much of that research might contribute to Scanlon's retrieval of the Augustinian tradition for contemporary historical consciousness.

### The Second Vatican Council (1962–65)

We have seen how Caesarius of Arles championed Augustine's theology of grace at the Second Council of Orange in the sixth century. In the sixteenth century, the Augustinian friar and bishop Seripando helped negotiate a more nuanced Augustinianism at

Trent. So, too, at the Second Vatican Council many theologians and bishops brought Augustine's ideas on grace, church, scripture, revelation, and evangelization to the discussions and debates of the participants.[30] Augustine's influence at Vatican II can be seen in the frequent citations of his writings in the Council's documents—more than twenty-five times.

Theologians such as Yves Congar and Henri de Lubac emphasized the importance of the early church fathers, including and especially Augustine, for the deliberations of the Council. Karl Rahner, as we have seen, used Augustine's understandings of the self and subjectivity to build his theology of grace. Rahner's theology was quite influential at Vatican II. Joseph Ratzinger also found in Augustine's theology, not only the subject for his doctoral dissertation, but also an inspiration for his ecclesiology or understanding of the church.[31] Both of these German theologians were present at the Council and in different ways influenced and enriched its proceedings.

Augustine's continuing influence in Catholic theology during and beyond Vatican II has been the subject of some debate. Massimo Faggioli, a church historian with expertise in Vatican II, identifies two opposing postconciliar interpretations of Vatican II.[32] One, which he calls "Augustinian" or "Neo-Augustinian," is more conservative and supports an ecclesiology of a smaller but purer and more authentic church amidst a sinful, secular world. The other, which he calls "Neo-Thomist," is more progressive, arguing for creative interactions between church and world. While Faggioli's analysis of the two conflicting interpretations is compelling, his use of "Neo-Augustinian" to describe one side can be challenged.

He ignores the positive influence of Augustinian personalism on the Council's deliberations, especially through Rahner's theology (Faggioli puts Rahner in the Thomistic camp). Vatican II further develops Trent's theology of grace and justification, which was already a creative integration of Augustinian and Thomistic thought. It does this through its retrieval of Augustinian subjectivity combined with an affirmation of the redemption of history through grace. Faggioli's categorization of the two postconciliar camps as Augustinian and Thomistic can cause confusion about their integration at Trent and Vatican II.[33]

What Faggioli describes as "Neo-Augustinian" sounds very much like a Donatist understanding of a purer church amidst a sinful, unredeemed world. Augustine's conviction, repeated throughout *City of God*, is that in human history it is difficult if not impossible to identify citizens of the City of God. They are not all within the church. In fact, the City of God is not coextensive with the church, nor is the City of Man coextensive with the world. "In truth, those two cities are interwoven and intermixed in this era and await separation at the last judgment" (*City of God* I.35). The theologians whom Faggioli identifies as "Neo-Augustinian," including Joseph Ratzinger, Henri de Lubac, Jean Danielou, Hans Urs van Balthasar, and Louis Bouyer, are better described as preferring a certain interpretation of Augustine, and one that does not always take into account Augustine's subtle integration of the two cities. As we have seen, Augustine's thought is so expansive that successive generations of Christians have used his ideas to argue many different sides of an issue.

Faggioli's "Neo-Augustinian" is an unredeemed, unretrieved interpretation of Augustine that ignores and forecloses other contemporary readings of Augustine, such as Rahner's or Scanlon's. Such categorization of Augustine overlooks contemporary research in the field of Augustine Studies, which reveals much more complexity in Augustine's thought.

What he calls "Neo-Thomist" is a Thomism that he judges to have moved beyond neo-Scholasticism to a "'re-interpreted Thomism,' counseling openness to the world."[34] In fact, the retrieval of both Augustinianism and Thomism is accomplished through integrating each system of thought by critiquing it through contemporary historical consciousness—which in many ways Vatican II did. So a survey of the post–Vatican II battle for meaning might better be described by one camp that is uncomfortable with the critique that historical consciousness brings to both Augustinian and Thomistic theology (the more conservative groups) and another that advocates for deepening that critique of all theological systems or schools.

In sum, Faggioli's otherwise very interesting and creative analysis does not adequately account for the complexity of Augustine's thought. It relies more on secondary or tertiary readings of Augustine's Christology, ecclesiology, and theology of grace in its choice and application of the "Neo-Augustinian" category or camp. Nonetheless, his use of the two defining categories is another example of Augustine's continuing influence. It is also evidence of the continuing theological debates that his thought has sparked over the centuries.

## Postmodern Thought

Over the past half century or so, Augustine's ideas have continued to intrigue philosophers and thinkers beyond the communities of Christian theologians.[35] Two related philosophical movements in the twentieth and twenty-first centuries have their own takes on Augustinian interiority and subjectivity. Postmodernism reminds us that both an Aristotelian philosophy of substance and a Neo-Platonic philosophy of consciousness—and any theologies drawing from them—are products of the social, political, and economic contexts out of which they arise. To some extent, then, postmodernism brackets the philosophical significance and limits the relevance of the insights that emerge from Augustinian thought. How can a fifth-century philosophy and anthropology, forged in the late antique encounter of Greco-Roman thought and biblical theology have any relevance for us today? Augustine's theology is a product of his unique time and place in history, no matter how intriguing that historical period may be. Or so goes some postmodernist critique.

In a similar way, linguistic analysis also forecloses theological language. This Anglo-American school of thought argues that metaphysical language of any type is slippery, imprecise, and ulti-mately meaningless. With its emphasis on clear, distinct, and measurable referents for words, linguistic analysis undercuts the whole interiority-subjectivity project of philosophers and theolo-gians. It sees the language of interiority as riddled with ambiguity and uncertainty, saying little or nothing.

Ludwig Wittgenstein (1889–1951), a leading figure in the Anglo-American school, begins his *Philosophical Investigations* by conversing with Augustine about words and their meanings. Wittgenstein, who considers Augustine a worthy philosophical partner, deconstructs the theory of language found in *Confessions* I.8.13.[36] Wittgenstein summarizes Augustine's position:

> The individual words in language name objects— sentences are combinations of such names. In this pic-ture of language we find the roots of the following idea: Every word has a meaning. This meaning is correlated with the word. It is the object for which the word stands.[37]

Wittgenstein then goes on to critique this understanding of language and offer a completely different approach. Subsequent commentators point out that Wittgenstein's critique of Augustine's theory of language misses much of Augustine's own subtle aware-ness of the ambiguity inherent in language.[38] Nonetheless, propo-nents of the Anglo-American school of analysis generally dismiss such philosophical and theological projects as Augustine's.

So it seems that little of Augustine's thought would survive such contemporary critiques as those offered by continental post-modernism and Anglo-America linguistic analysis. Yet propo-nents of both these philosophical schools continue to engage with Augustine. His ideas emerge with a kind of redeemed relevance from postmodernism and linguistic analysis, from each in a dif-ferent way. No less a champion of postmodernism than Jacques Derrida (1930–2004) turned his attention to Augustine in his later years. This French-Algerian philosopher, a Sephardic Jew, was born in Algeria, the same land that was Augustine's Roman North Africa.[39] Working with Michael Scanlon of Villanova University, and John Caputo of Syracuse and Villanova universities, Derrida and other contemporary philosophers have had extensive conversations about the relevance of Augustine's ideas for today.[40]

Caputo and Scanlon preface their collection of essays in *Augustine and Postmodernism: Confession and Circumfession*, with an introduction entitled "The Postmodern Augustine"—what they call "our slightly impish title." They draw attention to the Augustinian activity among leading scholars identified with contemporary continental philosophy: Derrida's personal journal "Circumfession," which he wrote as his mother lay dying across the sea in Nice, as Monica had in Ostia;[41] Jean-François Lyotard's *The Confession of St. Augustine*, which he was writing at the time of his death in 1997;[42] the publication in 1995 of Martin Heidegger's 1921 course on "Augustine and Neoplatonism";[43] the publication in 1996 of Hannah Arendt's doctoral dissertation on Augustine, *Love and Saint Augustine*;[44] Paul Ricoeur's *Time and Narrative* in which Augustine's thought played an important role;[45] and a reminder that Albert Camus's dissertation for his teaching license at the University of Algiers was on Neo-Platonism and included a chapter on Augustine.

From linguistic analysis' withering critique of any and all metaphysics—Platonic, Neo-Platonic, Aristotelian, or Thomistic—it would seem futile to hope for a retrieval of anything Augustinian. Yet even here, Augustine reemerges into twenty-first-century thought in an ironic twist. Wittengstein, as we have seen, opens his *Philosophical Investigations* in conversation with Augustine. Yet, Wittgenstein's dismissal of language that does not have specific, identifiable, quantifiable referents as useless or irrelevant has not been the final word in contemporary studies of the use of language.

From the latter half of the twentieth century and into the twenty-first, there has been in academe a renewed interest in rhet-

oric. Contemporary rhetoricians, exploring the nature of language, turn their attention to its social, political, economic power,
and to its basic function as a link between and among human
beings. In this pursuit they inevitably encounter Augustine, the
last great Roman rhetorician. While they may not be interested in
his theology of grace and original sin, or his ecclesiology, they are
interested in his powerful narrative in *Confessions*, in his analysis
of the aims of rhetoric in *Teaching Christianity*, or in his sweeping
review of ancient Greek and Roman philosophers, historians, and
rhetoricians in *City of God*.[46]

One can't help wonder if, like Augustine listening to
Ambrose those many years ago in Milan, these latest scholars who
read his works and study his words *about* words might make the
move Augustine himself thought so critical, that is, the move
beyond rhetoric to content. For Augustine, rhetoric and content
are in the end "inseparable" (*Confessions* V.14.24).

## Conclusion

Over the past four hundred years, since the time of the
Protestant Reformation and the Catholic Reformation at Trent,
and the beginning of modernism, themes from Augustine's rich
and varied intellectual heritage have continued to inform the writings of major thinkers, movements, and ecclesial communities.
Augustinian themes still color the unfolding tapestries of Western
civilization and intellectual history, from the bold, broad contrasts
of the Enlightenment through the more recent textured and subtle
hues of postmodernism. Augustinian threads of interiority, subjectivity, community, a radical need for divine grace, the wounded
human will, interpretation of text, and the role of authority are
still stretched across the looms of religion, culture, and philosophy. Leading thinkers continue to spin yarn from Augustine's
writings to create patterns of ethics, aesthetics, or metaphysics for
the utility they provide or the happiness they inspire.

Over the past sixteen hundred years, any thorough investigation into the intersection of the human and the divine; any exploration of the structures and dynamics of the human soul; or any quest for meaning, knowledge, and truth has been enriched by bringing Augustine into the conversation. He thought so deeply and wrote so extensively on such subjects that his perspective is difficult to ignore. Michael Scanlon suggests that Augustine's core insights are worth handing on to future generations. However, work must be done to retrieve those insights for contemporary explorations of historical consciousness and a twenty-first-century theology of the ongoing redemption of history.[47] In chapter 6, we will investigate the Augustinian texts and topics that are attracting the most study and attention today. There we may find hints at what retrievals of and new perspectives on his thought continuing research will offer, and what dimensions of his insights may come to new relevance.

# 6
# NEW DIRECTIONS IN
# RECENT RESEARCH

Over the past fifty to sixty years, there has been an exponential increase of scholarly work in the field of Augustine Studies. Books, journal articles, dissertations, essay collections, monographs and Web sites continue to multiply. The research covers topics such as Augustine's life and writings; late Roman North African language, society, religion, and culture; the structures, councils, and practices of the fourth- and fifth-century church; information on Augustine's theological and ecclesial predecessors, contemporaries, and successors; the continuing influence of Augustine on the church and Western thought; manuscript collections and studies; and, contemporary reviews and critiques of his ideas. Each year the influential journal *Revue des études augustiniennes et patristiques* publishes an extensive, annotated list of publications in the field. That annual list comprises about five hundred entries. In recent years, Laura Holt of the University of Notre Dame has written several very helpful reviews of new works in the field in *The Heythrop Journal.*[1]

From among this vast array of research, Hubertus Drobner identifies certain topics or themes that have received significant and sustained attention from scholars in recent decades and signal new directions in the field.[2] These include a new understanding of the role of Christ in Augustine's thought; renewed examination of his scriptural hermeneutics; more dynamic, developmental understandings of his ideas on love; revisiting his theologies of grace and predestination; and new perspectives on his writings about women, marriage, and virginity.

In this chapter, we will review these topics and themes by looking at what contemporary scholars have to say about them. However, we will preface our review of contemporary scholarship with a consideration of how changes in method have provided the fertile humus from which new insights and perspectives have grown. Understanding shifts in the methodology that guides contemporary research in Augustine Studies provides the context within which to appreciate developments in the field.

## Method in Augustine Studies

There are three discernible shifts in the method employed in Augustine Studies over recent decades. The first of these three shifts is from a dogmatic to a historical approach in the study of Augustine. We will call this a methodological attention to *context*. The second is a movement away from a detached, objective analysis of Augustine's ideas to a subjective, interactive, and expectant dialogue with his thought, which we will call a methodological openness to *conversion*. The third is from a dialectical scaffold that isolates concepts and contexts in presumed oppositional tension to a more integrative architecture that harmonizes them in ways that better reflect the reality in Augustine's own life and thought. We will call this third change in method a move toward *communion*. So these three changes or movements in method— careful consideration of context, conversational openness to conversion, and intentional integrative communion—characterize significant shifts in the contemporary field of Augustine Studies. We will consider each of these in turn.

## Consideration of Context: From a Dogmatic to a Historical Approach

The first of these three shifts, from a dogmatic to a historical approach in the study of Augustine's writings, is the most basic methodological change. As we shall see, it underlies the other two changes. An important article in 2004 by Allan Fitzgerald noted this change.[3] Reflecting on the history, contribution, and evolution of the journal *Revue des études augustiniennes et patristiques*, Fitzgerald notes how the study of Augustine has changed since World War II. The majority of projects by Augustine scholars prior to the mid-twentieth century were dedicated to and motivated by doctrinal issues and denominational stances. Augustine's works were studied and cited to support church teachings or to bolster a particular denominational interpretation of those teachings.

Such an approach can be traced all the way back to the *florilegia* and *sententiae* of the Early Middle Ages. You'll remember that these collections of passages by Augustine from across his writings were often done to highlight one or other of his teachings. The context of when, how, and why he wrote a particular book, letter, or sermon was not as important as his text. His words were understood and used to shape and solidify a particular doctrine of the church, such as the nature of divine grace, the effects of original sin, the weakness of human will, or the mystery of the Trinity. Sometimes these anthologies were produced, or subsequently used, in order to combat those who, in the opinion of the editor-compiler, dissented or doubted church teaching. Certainly, the soaring rhetoric and polemic style in some of Augustine's works provided encouragement for the subsequent apologetic use of his writings in the defense of orthodox doctrine.

The reformers of the sixteenth century often used Augustine's teachings on divine grace in their spirited critique of the Roman Church. In the Counter Reformation, Catholics appealed to Augustine in the defense of papal rights and prerogatives over and against Protestant theology.[4] Because Augustine was so influential in the development of Christian doctrine and in defining the terms in which that doctrine was expressed and taught, it is not surprising that generations of bishops and theologians appealed to Augustine's expressions of basic Christian teachings about grace, sin, and salvation in Christ. Doctrinal imperatives dominated the use of Augustinian texts well into the nineteenth and early twentieth centuries.

Thus Augustinian texts were employed in ways analogous to verses from scripture as "proof texts." Preachers and theologians throughout the history of the church used scriptural texts to explain and justify Christian teaching, or denominational differences about that teaching. However, during the nineteenth century, scholars who studied the Bible began to pay closer attention to the original contexts of biblical books and passages.[5] The reason a particular book of the Bible was written, the literary form employed by the author or authors, the community out of which a text emerged or for which it was composed, how the text itself may have evolved in oral transmission before it was written down: all these considerations began to change how biblical scholars went about their study of Sacred Scripture. Today historical, textual, and literary criticisms are important dimensions of method in Bible study. This revolution in scriptural studies has impacted every field of theology with its requirement to respect the context of biblical passages even as one engages the text with the goal of deepening and enriching theological insight.[6]

About a century after attention to method revolutionized the study of scripture, a similar shift occurred in Augustine Studies. First in post-World War II Europe, then in the United States after the Second Vatican Council, scholars begin to employ the tools of historical-critical methodology in the study of Augustinian texts and of Patristic texts in general.[7] The ecumenical movement is also important here. Historical-critical methodology was first applied to scripture by Protestant theologians, and later by Catholic scripture scholars. The growing ecumenical spirit among Patristic scholars in the mid-twentieth century ensured a wider and cooperative use of the method across denominational differences.

Just as context informs one's understanding of the text in the books of the Bible, so context is important in coming to wider, deeper appreciation of what fathers of the church, such as Augustine, wrote as they wrestled with the implications of their faith in Christ during the early centuries of Christian history. As happened in the study of scripture, so the study of Patristics became more and more interdisciplinary as scholars in history, linguistics, culture, literary criticism, classics, philology, and so forth helped each other to better understandings of and insights into Augustine, his theological predecessors, and his ecclesial successors.[8]

It is not an exaggeration to claim that, over the past fifty to sixty years, Augustine scholarship has moved beyond a kind of dogmatic reductionism that applied only one narrow lens to reading Augustine's words, to a careful, cooperative use of many methodological lenses in order to enjoy the wider vistas and broader horizons of the world in which Augustine lived and thought and wrote. The shift from a dogmatic to a historical approach has also led to more accurate translations and interpretations of his words.[9]

### Openness to Conversion: From Objective Analysis to Subjective Engagement

In *The Trinity*, Augustine describes the kind of reader he wishes to engage with his writings: "What I desire for all my works, of course, is not merely a kind reader but also a frank critic....The last thing I want is a reader who is my doting partisan, or a critic who is his own" (*The Trinity*, prologue). He was interested in the conversation that his books and sermons would inspire and the exchange in which both he and his readers would listen to and critique each other, remaining open to real change and development of ideas based on the deep listening that constitutes authentic dialogue. Not only *Confessions*, but all of Augustine's writings are confessional in that they emerge from his faith in God and in Christ, and from the continuing critique of his life and work in light of that faith. What Augustine hopes for, as an author whose works arise out of the crucible of faith, is that his readers use the occasion of reading his text to enter into a similar review and evaluation of their own life and thought from which they can themselves contribute to the ongoing dialogue of faith.[10]

He expressed his wish for this kind of dialogue to his contemporaries, and also to those who would read his works in subsequent generations. It is no longer sufficient simply to read and critique the writing of someone like Augustine in a way that objectifies him and prevents his subjectivity from engaging and critiquing the investigating scholar or reader. Contemporary hermeneutics, which prescribe critical attention to how we read texts from a culture or century not our own, notes that a full, engaging reading of that text is not complete when we have applied all the historical, critical, textual, and analytical tools at our disposal in analyzing the text in order to reach a better understanding of it. The second part of the hermeneutic process is to allow the historical text to critique us. How do the religious, cultural, social, political, and philosophical assumptions of the author stand in critique of our own contemporary assumptions? Are we canonizing our contemporary worldview in ways that diminish our capacity to receive and engage the thoughts of the author? In other words, do we have the same openness to self-critical evaluation that Augustine hopes he can sustain as an author in conversation with the ages?[11]

In Augustine Studies, a historical, critical analysis of his writing that goes beyond apologetic, doctrinal motivation, however significant a change in method, is still only part of the hermeneutic task. In Augustinian terms, the scholar is challenged to a "confessional" evaluation of his or her own deep assumptions, images, and convictions—what Gadamer calls one's "fore-meaning"—while studying those of Augustine as expressed in his writing.

In his chapter "Augustine's Secular City" in *Augustine and His Critics*, Robert Dodaro provides a working example of this confessional dynamic in his critique of William Connolly's book *The Augustinian Imperative: A Reflection on the Politics of Morality*.[12] While recognizing the valid points in Connolly's critique of Augustine, Dodaro argues that Connolly misses two important ideas. First, he does not do a thorough enough job in situating Augustine in the midst of the complex political, social, and religious world of fifth-century Roman North Africa. So Dodaro is arguing for a more thorough historical analysis. But Dodaro goes further. He cites a failure on Connolly's part to acknowledge the complexity and subtlety of confessional writing. Augustine's writing, says Dodaro, challenges his readers and critics to maintain "at least liminal awareness of the ways and extent to which its [the self's] core ideals, aspirations, attachments, fears, fantasies and motivations are constantly compromised by the plethora of social, cultural and, therefore, political forces from which the self can hardly be abstracted, even when it attempts through asceticism to flee social and political involvements entirely."[13] In this respect, Dodaro continues, each of us remains, for Augustine, "deceivers and deceived" (*Confessions* 4.1.1). Dodaro provides a deepening of Gadamer's idea of the "fore-meaning" we bring to the reading of a text by exposing the root of fore-meaning in the very ground of one's own sense of self.

In other words, method in contemporary Augustine Studies needs to be confessional in the sense that method itself comprises an openness to conversion, that is, an openness to changes and shifts in the assumptions and prejudices that support the structures of the self and its constitutive fore-meanings. Even as scholars deconstruct Augustine's language and ideas through historical, cultural, and textual analysis, they are advised to remain open to shifts in their own cultural, religious, and even disciplinary assumptions. The scholar, student, or critic of Augustine's text needs to work with "at least liminal awareness" (to quote Dodaro) of how his or her own culture, personal history, and assumptions affect, inform, and direct his or her engagement with Augustine's text and context. Contemporary hermeneutics affirms such awareness as a valuable aid in doing scholarship. In the study of Augustine, who introduced confessional writing into Western literature, confessional awareness, with concomitant conversion or openness to change in one's working assumptions, highlights the researcher's self-awareness as a component of method in contemporary Augustine Studies.

### Shift to Communion: Toward an Integrative Architecture in Method

In an important article in *Listening: Journal of Religion and Culture*, George Lawless offers a reading list of what he judges to be essential writings by Augustine for the novice in the field.[14] As he makes his recommendations of primary Augustinian texts, Lawless cautions the new reader of Augustine against a phenomenon that still characterizes Augustinian scholarship. This is the tendency to isolate different aspects of Augustine's thought from each other.

Such a tendency has been a methodological predisposition in Augustine Studies, according to Lawless. So, for example, Augustine's understanding of Christ can be studied without any significant appeal to his understanding of prayer. The two topics can be and more often than not are studied in isolation from each other.

Such methodological isolation is heir to dialectical tendencies that have characterized other aspects of philosophical and theological studies in recent centuries. These include the separation of Scripture and ecclesial tradition that characterized the sixteenth-century Reformation; the seventeenth- and eighteenth-century Enlightenment bifurcation of faith and reason; and, the establishment of theology as a "scientific" study in the nineteenth and early twentieth centuries that often separated theological study, be it Reform or neo-Scholastic, from lived Christian spirituality.

Lawless argues that the spirit and content of Augustine's writings contradict the dialectical methodology that isolates such concepts and contexts, often in oppositional tension. He asserts that the peculiar strength of Augustine is to "bridge the widening gap between the two spheres of spirituality and theology."[15] He continues:

> Augustine's readers are enabled to overcome the cog-
> nitive dissonance of recent centuries by examining
> first-hand the truly remarkable congruence which
> necessarily exists between theology and spirituality,
> doctrine and life, Scripture and tradition, text and the
> interpreting community.[16]

Attention to Augustine's integration of these various dimensions of Christian life and thinking demands a method-ological sensitivity to how one does or does not bring them into dialogue with each other in the course of one's own research and writing. This is a case of content informing method, of the message challenging the scholar to realign methodological presuppositions and widen investigative lenses so as not to impose post-Reformation, post-Enlightenment proclivities onto Augustine's text.

This methodological shift toward *communion*, as we might call it, needs to complement any deconstruction of Augustinian texts if one is to arrive at a fuller appreciation of both text and con-text. Methodological communion is actually an example of one kind of methodological conversion discussed in the previous sec-tion. This shift that Lawless calls for can be found in nascent form amidst the conversations and interdisciplinary scholarship that characterizes recent Augustinian research, symposia, and confer-ences.[17] However, it is not a methodological shift that is evident in all areas. As we will suggest later in this chapter, Augustine's Christology, that is, his theological understanding of the Incarna-tion, is often studied quite apart from any consideration of his own spirituality and relationship with his Lord Jesus as evidenced in his sermons and commentaries on the Psalms.

The shift toward communion is recommended by Hubertus Drobner in reflecting on current and future trends in Augustine

Studies. In his "Overview of Recent Scholarship" in Augustine Studies, Drobner cites the French Augustine scholar Pierre Marie Hombert.[18] He affirms Hombert's assertion that future research in Augustine Studies holds the most promise for new insight not so much in special, isolated research topics, but when the research and writing serves as "a meeting point of the theology of God's economy, Christology, soteriology, ecclesiology, theology of grace, and spirituality."[19]

In sum, the major shift in methodology in Augustine Studies has been from a doctrinal use of Augustine's writings to support one's own denominational theology to a more historical approach. This shift from dogmatic concern to historical context has two corollaries: a methodological openness to allow Augustine's own assumptions and times to critique our own, that is, an openness to intellectual conversion through hermeneutic honesty; and, the need for careful methodological reintegration of the various dimensions of Augustine's life and thought so we can understand him in his own context, that is, an integrative approach to Augustinian topics or communion.

## The Role of Christ

It may come as a surprise that Augustine wrote no theological treatise on Jesus Christ. Today the curricula of most graduate programs in theology require a course in Christology. In such courses, students delve into the Christological controversies of the fourth and fifth centuries, and study the Councils of Nicea, Constantinople, Ephesus, and Chalcedon. Augustine lived and preached right in the middle of these decades of Christian debate about the nature and identity of Jesus of Nazareth. Augustine was baptized in 387, six years after the First Council of Constantinople (381), which reaffirmed the teachings of Nicea (325). He died just one year before the Council of Ephesus (431), and twenty-one years before the Council of Chalcedon (451). Yet he wrote no tract on the Christological controversies that characterized the fourth and fifth centuries.

However, he certainly wrote about Christ. For example, Augustine preached against Arian understandings of Christ as not divine.[20] After the sack of Rome in August 410, refugees from Europe were flooding into North African cities such as Hippo. Some of these refugees brought with them Arian sympathies and Augustine had to address a heresy that previously had not been a pastoral issue in Numidia. It is clear in his homilies and in many other works that belief in the divinity of Christ was the foundation of Augustine's life and faith.

In Book X of *City of God*, he writes at length on the differences between Christian belief in the Incarnation and platonism, which had significantly influenced his religious development in Milan. In Book IV of *The Trinity*, he explains the role of Christ as the Mediator sent by the Father, equal to the Father, "this sacrament, this sacrifice, this high priest, this God, before he was sent and came, *made of woman…*" (*The Trinity* IV.2.11 [italics in NCP translation]).[21] For Augustine, there is no other mediator between the human and the divine than the divine Son of God, Jesus Christ.

The later division of Christian theology into dogmatic tracts or discrete subjects was not part of Augustine's thinking or writing. Consequently, scholars did not identify a specific "Christology" in Augustine's writings, and have not until recently devoted much time or space to Christ's place in Augustine's philosophy or theology. Preference has been given instead to his teachings about original sin, grace, free will, and so forth.

All this has begun to change in recent years. Humbertus Drobner believes that "it probably never entered Augustine's mind to make Christ an object of a sustained theological treatise, because he regarded him as the condition, the author and the method of all his thinking."[22] For Augustine, "Christ is not so much an object of his speculation, but the source and method for his theological thinking."[23] Or as Michael Cameron puts it, "Christ for Augustine was less a theological proposition and more a way of seeing."[24] The French Augustinian of the Assumption priest and Augustine scholar Goulven Madec (1930–2008) expressed it this way: "Christ our knowledge and our wisdom" was the "principle of coherence" in Augustine's thought.[25] Allan Fitzgerald has remarked that we do not need so much to discover or develop an "Augustinian Christology." Rather, Augustine scholars need to come to terms with Augustine's experience of Jesus Christ as the unifying thread of his lifelong reflection on the meaning of human existence.[26]

Two scholarly examinations of the role of Christ in Augustine's faith and in his theology have appeared over the past several decades. An important text by Swiss Benedictine monk and Patristic scholar Basil Studer *The Grace of Christ and the Grace of God in Augustine of Hippo: Christocentrism or Theocentrism?* appeared in English translation in 1997.[27] Reviewing both secondary sources and Augustine's own texts, Studer situates the question of Augustine's theology of Christ at the heart of his theology of grace. Also, an important encyclopedic summary of the role of Christ in Augustine's thought is the entry "Christus" in the *Augustinus-Lexikon* by Madec.[28] These two important works set the agenda for further studies on the centrality of Christ in Augustine's life and thought.

Among Augustine's own writings, perhaps the best entry into how he thought and what he believed about Jesus Christ are the commentaries he wrote on the 150 psalms in the Hebrew Bible. Augustine was the first to write a complete commentary on the psalms. His *Expositions of the Psalms* fills six volumes in the New City Press translations series.[29] Taken collectively, these commentaries comprise the longest of all of Augustine's works. Some of the commentaries are sermons or orations he delivered to a congregation or audience. A few are works he dictated in private so as to complete the collection. Some are long and involved; others short and direct. Reading through the commentaries, one encounters both Augustine's high literary style as well as his simpler homiletic approach. The dating of all this material shows that it represents more than twenty-five years of Augustine's thinking—and praying. He wrote his commentaries on Psalms 1 through 32 while still a priest. He then continued the project throughout his ministry as bishop, often adding additional comments to individual psalms. Indeed, this impressive body of work is a kind of journal that takes us through Augustine's own spiritual life, revealing the constant interpenetration of faith and reason, of praying and thinking that shaped and formed his theology.[30] And it is clear throughout his *Expositions of the Psalms* that Christ is at the heart of Augustine's faith and prayer.

Throughout the 150 psalms, the psalmist is speaking to, pleading with, complaining before, praising, or thanking God. Augustine asks the question: who is actually expressing all of these sentiments and thoughts? On one level it was King David, the traditional author of the psalms, speaking for himself or on behalf of the Hebrew people. But Augustine never settles for one level of interpretation of scripture.[31] Christians read all of the Hebrew Scriptures in light of their new covenant faith in Christ.[32] The entirety of Sacred Scripture is to be read and prayed in light of the mystery of Christ, the Son of God incarnate, crucified and risen from the dead. This is Augustine's basic principle of scriptural interpretation, and it is most vividly illustrated in his commentaries on the psalms. The one speaking and praying throughout the entire Psalter is Christ.

Yet isn't it also true that the faithful also pray the psalms, both privately in their homes and together in church during the liturgy? Augustine himself describes how important the psalms were to him from his conversion onward. So, is it the case that sometimes the texts of the psalms become the prayers of individual believers, sometimes the prayers of a congregation, and sometimes they represent the prayer of Jesus (as in "My God, why have you forsaken me?")? In the context of such questions, Augustine responds with his theology of the *Totus Christus*, the Whole Christ.[33] A central tenet of Christian faith is the union of believers with Christ. Drawing from St. Paul's theme of the Body of Christ,[34] Augustine affirms the organic, spiritual unity among Christ and his faithful. He understands this not as a metaphor or comparison. Union with Christ through baptism is a sacramental reality.[35] It is core to his theology of Christ. So the one who speaks the words of the psalm is Christ—sometimes as Head, sometimes as Body in its united members. But always the voice that reaches God is the voice of Christ.

A study of Augustine's interpretation and use of the psalms, then, opens a way into the deepest part of his theology; that is, his belief that all Christians are mysteriously united with Christ so as to become one with him forever. It is in this sense that his belief in Christ is his theological method. As a Christian, a priest, a bishop, a human being, Augustine thinks and writes and prays out of the depths of his baptismal union with the risen Christ. He understands himself and his congregation to be part of the *Totus Christus*. All of his ministry, preaching, and thinking arise from that union effected and consistently affirmed through the sacraments of the church.

The rise of interest in and study of Augustine's theology of *Totus Christus* over the past few decades is a good illustration of shifts in the method used in Augustine Studies. Augustine's theology of Christ, that is, his belief in the mystery of union with the risen Christ, interpenetrates all of his theological writing. Thus, his faith in Christ is itself the major principle inspiring what we have called the methodological shift to communion. Future study of Augustine's faith in Christ can help move Augustine Studies beyond a tendency to isolate different aspects of Augustine's thought from each other. Appreciation of his lived integration of theology and spirituality can become a methodological way into exploring the interrelationships among such concepts as "the theology of God's economy, Christology, soteriology, ecclesiology, theology of grace, and spirituality."[36]

# Augustine's Scriptural Hermeneutics

A study of Augustine's *Expositions of the Psalms* raises further questions about how Augustine read and interpreted Sacred Scripture. In addition to the Psalms, he also wrote extensive commentaries on other books of scripture: three commentaries on Genesis, two on the first seven books of the Old Testament (the Heptateuch), one on Job, two on Romans, two on the Gospels in general, one on Galatians, one on the Sermon on the Mount as well as his homilies on the Gospel of John and on the First Epistle of John.[37] Also, Books XI to XIII of *Confessions* are an extended commentary on the beginning of the first chapter of Genesis.[38] As we have seen, Augustine, like the other fathers of the church, also makes extensive use of both Old and New Testaments in his preaching and his doctrinal works. There has been an abundance of recent research on Augustine and his use of the scriptures. This research can be divided into two topic areas. One concerns the Latin text or manuscripts of the scriptures that he used—*what* he read; the other, how he interpreted, understood, and explained those texts—*how* he read it.

Unlike Jerome, Augustine knew no Hebrew, and his knowledge of Greek was limited.[39] Thus, his experience of the Old and New Testaments was primarily in and through Latin versions. As a young man studying Latin literature, he reports being repulsed by the poor quality of the Latin translation of the Bible that was in use in the fourth- and early fifth-century Roman Empire (*Confessions* III.5.9). This would have been the *Vetus Latina*, the "Old Latin" text, of which there were numerous variations.

In the mid 380s, Saint Jerome began working from both Hebrew and Greek manuscripts on a new and superior Latin text, which came to be called the Vulgate. Augustine knew of Jerome's work and even as a young priest in the early 390s had read drafts of some Old Testament books newly translated by Jerome.[40] However, throughout his ministry, most of Augustine's preaching and writing made use of the *Vetus Latina*. The French scholar Anne-Marie La Bonnardière produced a masterful compilation of Augustine's use of many of the books of scripture.[41] Citing all of Augustine's use of scriptural texts throughout his works is very difficult. Augustine quoted scripture from memory during his homilies and in his books. "He would often quote the same phrase differently at different times, not changing the meaning, but altering the word order or using synonyms to suit his rhetorical purposes or to emphasize a certain symbolism."[42] La Bonnardière's significant scholarship invites further research into the pervasive influence of Sacred Scripture in Augustine's writing, preaching, and prayer.

The second area of research on Augustine and scripture involves the study of his exegesis, or how he went about understanding and interpreting the texts. In this regard, Augustine understood his role as an interpreter of the sacred text to be part of his responsibility as preacher and teacher. His reading and wrestling with the scriptural message about Christ was the core of his service to the church. In his homilies, in his books, and in his letters, he strove to help Christians deepen their understanding of and commitment to Jesus Christ. His scriptural exegesis was an essential part of his ministry as priest and bishop.

For Augustine, the message, the content of all scripture—both Old and New Testaments—is the Word of God, now made flesh in Jesus of Nazareth. Thus all attempts to understand and interpret Sacred Scripture must be done in light of faith in Christ.[43] The Christian's faith in Christ is captured and expressed in the official creed of the church. Therefore, scriptural interpretation must always be practiced in dialogue with that creed and its component parts. This is the "canonical rule" (*canonica regula*) for exegesis as Augustine understood and practiced it.[44]

Faith in Christ, the Word of God and the Light of Truth, is central for reading and understanding scripture. This is Augustine's persistent message throughout the four books of *Teaching Christianity*. Recent research on Augustine's exegesis has explored and elaborated three ideas found in *Teaching Christianity*. The first is Augustine's use of the work of the Donatist theologian Tyconius for his scriptural exegesis. Tyconius was the first Latin author to set forth a system of rules for interpreting the Bible. In spite of Tyconius's Donatist connections, Augustine admired and made use of his rules for interpreting scripture.[45] In her book *The Book of Rules of Tyconius: Its Purpose and Inner Logic*, Pamela Bright attempts to present Tyconius's work in its own right, apart from Augustine's presentation and interpretation of it.[46]

Bright argues for the internal consistency and logic of the seven "mystical rules" that Tyconius discerns for reading scripture with the guidance of the Holy Spirit. In *The Apocalypse Commentary of Tyconius: A History of Its Reception and Influence*, Kenneth Steinhauser traces the influence of Tyconius's rules of exegesis both in Augustine's work and through subsequent Christian history.[47] These two books, and the wider interest in how Augustine understood and did scriptural exegesis, are good examples of the shift in method in Augustine Studies from a dogmatic approach to a consideration of historical and literary context.

A second area of current research into Augustine's use of scripture concerns his use of both literal and allegorical interpretations of scriptural texts. Augustine's understanding of a "literal" interpretation of scriptural text is not the same as what is commonly understood today as "literal" interpretation of scripture. His appreciation of human language was too sophisticated to accept any slavish adherence to text that argues for such things as six days of creation and five thousand years of our planet as "literally true." By literal he meant the primary, original, or historical meaning of the text in its original context. A figurative, spiritual, symbolic, or allegorical interpretation of a text is a legitimate reading, beyond the literal, that opens a text up to reveal its unfolding meanings in the emerging contexts of successive generations of readers.[48] He refers to this balancing of literal and allegorical interpretations of scripture in *City of God* where he writes, "I do not censure those who succeed in carving out a spiritual meaning from each and every event in the narrative, provided they always maintain its original basis in historical truth" (*City of God* XVII.3). So he emphasized the importance of being able to distinguish the literal sense of a passage from any possible figurative sense.

But when an allegorical or symbolic interpretation is indicated or possible, one needs more than the "canonical rule" in discerning the validity of such figurative meanings. Hence, as he strives to discern the meanings of scriptural passages in his books on Genesis and in *City of God*, he explores the nature of signs and symbols. This is a third topic related to Augustine's exegesis that is getting renewed attention. In Book XI of *Confessions*, as he is exploring the first chapter of Genesis, he prays for guidance in this process of symbolic interpretation of the text (XI.2.4). His book *The Teacher* is a long discourse on language and symbolism. And the relationship between signs (*signa*) and the things they signify (*res*) is carefully explored in Book I of *Teaching Christianity*.

Augustine's thoughts on signs are explored in a number of important investigations into his theory of language. David Dawson explores the theory of signs as elaborated in *Teaching Christianity* in his chapter "Sign Theory: Allegorical Reading and the Motions of the Soul in *De Doctrina Christiana*" in *De Doctrina Christiana: A Classic of Western Culture*.[49] John Rist also explores the topic in *Augustine: Ancient Thought Baptized*.[50] Robert Markus provides a review of the literature on this important topic in his *Signs and Meanings: Word and Text in Ancient Christianity*.[51] There is also the penetrating analysis *Augustine the Reader: Meditation, Self-Knowledge, and the Ethics of Interpretation* by Brian Stock.[52] Augustine's writing about symbolic or figurative interpretation is a challenging topic to explore, but one which shows how deeply he thought about the task and responsibility of scriptural interpretation. Future studies of his theory of symbols will be strengthened to the extent that the method employed in those studies examine Augustine's theory of sign and language within the context of his exegesis, and to the extent that they explore his exegesis in the context of his faith in Christ.

## Love of God and Love of Neighbor

Augustine has been called the "Doctor of Charity." He speaks often and passionately about *amor, caritas, delectio*—love. Passionate love of God, both Augustine's love for God and God's love for him, emerges in *Confessions* as a theme that reaches the height of its crescendo in Book X: "I love you, Lord, with no doubtful mind but with absolute certainty. You pierced my heart with your word, and I fell in love with you....But what am I loving when I love you?" (*Confessions* X.6.8).[53] In *Homilies on the Gospel of John* and *Homilies on the First Epistle of John*, Augustine writes and speaks eloquently about love of God and love of neighbor. Several scholars have turned their attention in recent decades to study the similarities and differences between our love for God and our love for neighbor.

In his article "The Double Face of Love in Augustine," Tarcisius Van Bavel, OSA, identifies and traces the development in Augustine's thinking on a growing identification of the three loves: love of God, of neighbor, and of self.[54] This identification of the three different loves as one reality develops in Augustine's thought, according to Van Bavel, because of a "daring inversion" we find in homily #7 in the *Homilies on the First Epistle of John* (around the year 407). In that homily on John's First Letter, Augustine makes a bold interpretation of the scriptural text by inverting two words. In 1 John 4:16 we read, "God is love." In the homily, Augustine claims "Love is God" (*Homily* 7.9). Van Bavel explores the implications of this hermeneutical turn in Augustine's thinking about love in the Johannine literature.

The Australian scholar Ray Canning, a student of Van Bavel, offers a tour de force through Augustine's thinking and writing about love. His book *The Unity of Love for God and Neighbour in St. Augustine* is an extensive, in-depth treatment on the subject from both historical and thematic perspectives.[55] Historically, Canning traces Augustine's writing on love from his conversion, through his early episcopal ministry, and into the long years of the

Pelagian controversy, showing the importance of context for the development of Augustine's thought. Thematically, Canning provides a panoramic overview of Augustine's language and categories for thinking about love.

He also marshals his significant research into primary texts from Augustine, and his command of a vast array of secondary texts in order to critique major twentieth-century European scholarship on Augustinian understandings of love. Canning's book is a foundational text for anyone interested in the topic of love in Augustine's thought. He concludes his treatment of Augustinian thinking on love with an extensive section on care for the "least" among us, as found in Jesus' parable of the Last Judgment in Matthew 25. For Augustine, love's ultimate task on earth is the pursuit of justice for the poor and the "least" among us, a theme so important to the Bishop of Hippo's exegesis of Matthew 25.[56]

Older studies of Augustine's ideas on love often focused on the distinction he made in the first book of *Teaching Christianity* between "enjoying" (*frui*) and "using" (*uti*).[57] This distinction concerns the difference between loving God the creator and loving different parts of God's creation. We love God as the only full and proper object of our love to be enjoyed in and for itself. We love other persons as creations of God, and that love is "useful" to us because it moves us along in our love of God. This earlier scholarship on Augustine's theology of love focused on this claim that only God, as the ultimate and only eternal good, was the proper object of our enjoyment and that human love was only a means to reach enjoyment of God.[58]

Scholars such as Van Bavel have argued that this distinction, and its implications for Augustine's idea of love, needs a much more sophisticated understanding of the context in which Augustine developed the *uti/frui* difference.[59] He shows how Augustine, even in his early ministry, modified this highly philosophical distinction in light of scripture.[60] Van Bavel's argument is that Augustine never uses this language again, and that the fullness of his ethics of love must include the significant development evident in his scriptural hermeneutics, especially with regard to the New Testament passages on love.[61]

## Grace

Contemporary research is also reconsidering another central Augustinian doctrine: grace. This reconsideration is characterized by two shifts in method. The first is a shift in context, that is, from a dogmatic to a historical approach to the study of Augustine. The second is a shift toward communion, namely, a methodology that integrates various dimensions of Augustine's thought in ways that better reflect the reality of how they harmonized in his own life.

The methodological shift in context is significant. Perhaps no other part of Augustine's theology is read and received more dogmatically than his writings on grace. No other section of his corpus is so thunderous in its doctrinal convictions and polemics as his anti-Pelagian writings. So studies that concentrate on historical analyses of these writings are an important development in the field. The leaders in this methodological shift include J. Patout Burns of Vanderbilt Divinity School. His seminal work *The Development of Augustine's Doctrine of Operative Grace* led the way for subsequent research that privileges consideration of the historical development of Augustine's thought about grace over theological commentaries that parse doctrinal distinctions.[62] The writings of Agostino Trapé, OSA, former Prior General of the Order of St. Augustine, and the work of Rebecca Weaver of the Union Presbyterian Seminary in Toronto are also important contributions to historical studies of how Augustine's theology of grace developed.[63]

This methodological shift from a dogmatic to a historical approach that contextualizes Augustine's writings on grace has been accompanied by a second shift that seeks to integrate various aspects of Augustine's thought. Specifically, recent research into the anti-Pelagian writings emphasizes the critical importance of the Christological dimension of Augustine's theology of grace.

We looked previously at the importance of Augustine's faith in Christ for understanding the whole of his thinking and writing. We considered contemporary research that claims that Christ, and Augustine's living faith in Christ, is fully appreciated for its influence on his thinking and writing only when we realize its central role in Augustine's own theological method. So it makes sense that recognition of the central place of Jesus Christ in Augustine's theology opens up new ways of reading and exploring the Pelagian controversy, which is such a significant part of Augustine's theological heritage.

The above-mentioned historical studies on grace by J. Patout Burns, Agostino Trapé, and Rebecca Weaver have indeed served to highlight the role of Christ in Augustine's thinking about grace. This connection has been developed in significant ways by Basil Studer, Joanne McWilliam, and Robert Dodaro, OSA.[64] What particularly emerges in these studies is the contrast between Augustine's understanding of Christ and that of Pelagius. Augustine's theology of grace depends heavily on his theology of the two natures in Christ, human and divine. We receive divine grace through the union of the two natures in Christ. God's grace enters our minds and hearts through our union with the humble humanity of Christ.

This suggests that at the heart of Augustine's critique of Pelagius's understanding of grace is a concern about Pelagius's understanding of Christ. Augustine's understanding of the profound union of the two natures in Christ thus anticipates the Christological teachings of the Council of Chalcedon in 451.[65] Future study of the Christology in Augustine's theology of grace can also open up reconsiderations of his understandings of free will and predestination, important dimensions of his anti-Pelagian writing.[66]

## Women, Sexuality, Marriage, and Virginity

Feminist theology in the second half of the twentieth century has focused on Augustine's writing about women, sexuality, marriage, and virginity. Writers such as Rosemary Radford Reuther and Elaine Pagels have examined his thought and language on these topics.[67] Some writers implicate him for the misogyny in subsequent Christian life and thought and indict him for the pessimistic understanding of sexuality that emerges from his theology of original sin and concupiscence.

Feminist writers and thinkers bring an important critical analysis to many issues in Christian theology and ecclesial practice. The field of Augustine Studies has and will continue to benefit from the new insights arising from scholars who stand on new ground and offer fresh perspectives on old questions. However, attention to method is as important in the study of Augustine's writings on these topics as it is in other areas.

As we saw at the beginning of this chapter, the field has been enriched by critical attention to the historical, social, and cultural contexts from which Augustine's texts emerged. With regard to his writings on women and sexuality, attention to context is especially necessary. There is a very wide gulf between the value we put on equality for all persons in the twenty-first-century Western world and the socioeconomic realities of the fifth-century Roman Empire. There is a chasm between our current understanding of human sexuality and that of the cultures and societies of which the early church was a part. Peter Brown writes that this gulf between present-day Christians and those of the Patristic period can "be bridged only by showing to that distant, Christian past, the same combination of wonder and respect that makes for fruitful travel in a foreign land."[68] Until we explore in depth the issues and assumptions about women and sexuality that were the received reality for early Christians and their pastors, we achieve only preliminary understanding and appreciation of what they said and wrote about gender relations and sexuality.

In his recently republished work *The Body and Society: Men, Women, and Sexual Renunciation in Early Christianity*, Peter Brown situates Augustine's understanding and thinking on these topics in the wider context of the first four centuries of the church.

Originally published in 1987, Brown's book surveyed the scholarship in the field at that time, and invited the reader into the great variety and complexity of understanding and practice around gender and sexuality in the Eastern and Western churches of the patristic period. His introduction to the twentieth anniversary edition of the book, published in 2007, is an important testimony to the importance of care in treading the fields of gender and sexuality in Patristics.[69]

There are two overviews of contemporary feminist critique of Augustine that provide some examples of methodological advances in the study of Augustine by feminist theologians. *Feminist Interpretations of Augustine*, edited by Judith Chelius Stark of Seton Hall, presents eleven essays by American scholars.[70] These essays look closely, not only at Augustine's thinking about the feminine, but also at his own relationships with women, including his mother Monica and his companion, the mother of Adeodatus. The attention to historical and social context recommended by Brown varies among the essays.

A second collection, *The Image of God: Gender Models In Judaeo-Christian Tradition,* was edited by the Norwegian scholar Kari Elizabeth Borresen.[71] This collection of ten essays by European and American women presents various perspectives on the history of the ambiguity and debate about the place of the feminine in creation and redemption. Borresen herself looks very closely at Augustine's use of scripture in his thinking about women and salvation. She argues that in his creative scriptural hermeneutics, Augustine strives to include women in the divine image.[72] To do so in the exegetical context of the fifth century, Augustine, she argues, desexualized both women and men to emphasize that in their common humanity (*homo* in Latin) they are God's image.[73] In this way she understands Augustine to have distanced himself from other fifth-century interpretations of Genesis 1:27 and 1 Corinthians 11:7 that explicitly exclude women from God's image in any way. So Borresen argues that Augustine, far from being a misogynist himself, performs these exegetical gymnastics in order to include women in the *imago dei*.[74] However, subsequent centuries missed this subtlety, and his desexualization of the embodied feminine got more notice than his inclusion of the feminine in the concept *homo*. The contemporary paradigm shift in theology to include the embodied feminine, along with the embodied masculine, as God's image is elaborated by Rosemary Radford Reuther's essay in this volume.[75]

Augustine's thinking about gender and sexuality had very practical, pastoral implications for his approach to marriage and virginity. Significant work in this area has been done in recent years by David Hunter of The University of Kentucky. His introduction and notes in the *Marriage and Virginity* volume in the New City Press translation is a valuable overview of the topic, which reflects Hunter's expertise in this dimension of early Christianity.[76] His 1994 article in *Augustinian Studies* provides another good summary of Hunter's rethinking and contextualizing of Augustine on topics related to sexuality.[77] He sees the Bishop of Hippo opposing those of his contemporaries (like Jerome) who denigrated marriage. By contrast, Augustine developed an argument for the three goods of marriage: offspring, fidelity, and sacrament of God's love.

Tarcisius Van Bavel applied his extensive work on Augustine's understanding of love to the study of gender and sexuality in the Bishop of Hippo's writings.[78] Van Bavel argues that one cannot isolate Augustine's remarks on women or sexuality from his theology of love and justice. Despite the limitations of his culture and its anthropology, Augustine affirmed the equality of men and women before God. In spite of the legal and social discrimination against women in late Roman antiquity, he considered women and men to share the same moral rights and responsibilities.

Van Bavel's approach in his study of the place of women in Augustine's thought is an example of what we have called communion in Augustine Studies, that is, a careful methodological reintegration of the various dimensions of Augustine's life and thought. Such an integrative approach explores the deep streams in his faith and his spirituality that run beneath and connect discrete aspects of his thought with each other. Future studies of gender and sexuality in Augustine stand to benefit from methodological shifts in context and communion, as much as from the ever-growing research on the social complexity and cultural diversity of Patristic Christianity.

These then are the areas of Augustine's thought receiving the most critical and creative attention in recent decades: the centrality of Christ in Augustine's thinking and to his theological method; his ways of interpreting, understanding, and teaching about scripture; his ideas on the love of God and of neighbor; his theology of grace; and, his writings on the roles of women and sexuality. All of these topics deserve further attention by new generations of Augustine scholars in coming decades as well.

# 7

# MEETING AUGUSTINE ANEW

*New Studies of His Life and*
*Other Resources*

## New Studies of His Life

Henry Chadwick, one of Augustine's great biographers, wrote, "He is one of the few men of antiquity about whom we know a great deal of personal detail....No figure of the ancient world is more accessible to us."[1] This is due in large part to Augustine's innate and richly cultivated narrative abilities. He studied rhetoric, and like other rhetoricians in late Roman antiquity, he knew how to craft a story, highlight telling details, and elicit a reader's or listener's affect. Augustine employs all of these rhetorical skills with great effect in *Confessions*.

One might presume that writing a biography of Augustine would be a simple matter. One need only consult *Confessions*; record what Augustine says about his life in the social, political, and religious context of late fourth- and early fifth-century Roman North Africa and Italy; and provide a chronological table or two. However the presumption here is that *Confessions* is autobiography. It is not. It is autobiographical, but not in any modern sense of the genre.[2] In the first nine books of his most popular work, Augustine does employ his considerable narrative and rhetorical skills as he tells us some stories about his earlier years, up to his conversion in 386 at age 32. In Book IX, he adds with touching detail the subsequent death of his mother Monica in 387. But all the crafted vignettes, personal details, and evocative stories in *Confessions* are at the rhetorical service of his main reason for writing this first-of-its-kind work. He invites his readers to see God's providence moving him gradually out of sin and error toward faith and Truth, as it is revealed in Christ and the scriptures. The autobiographical clips provided and scintillating scenes presented serve that one theological and catechetical aim.

So to write a biography of Augustine, an author must not only read *Confessions* carefully. She or he must also study the Bishop of Hippo's many letters that provide glimpses into his life as a priest and bishop, the sermons that reveal his relationships with the people he served for the second half of his life, and his many books that show how his thought grew and his life changed in response to pastoral responsibilities and the contingencies of ecclesial life. The vast and continually expanding academic studies of late Roman North African history, society, religion, and politics mean that we now know more about Augustine's time and place than anyone except his own contemporaries and immediate successors in the fifth century.[3]

A number of eminent scholars have exercised their knowledge of Augustine's writings and their expertise on his time and place in history to produce valuable biographies of the saint's life. This chapter provides an overview of the best biographies of Augustine written since the mid-twentieth century. However, before moving on to them, we will begin with the very first biography of Augustine, written a few years after his death.

### Possidius (Died ca. 437)

The first biographer of Augustine had the advantage of a personal relationship with him. Possidius had been a confrere in Augustine's monastery at Hippo and later became Bishop of

Calama, some fifty miles south of Hippo. They shared a lifelong friendship of almost forty years. When Augustine died in 430, the Vandal tribes were invading North Africa and vast social and religious change was afoot. Amidst all this ferment, Possidius wanted Catholic Christians to remember Augustine's great service to the church. So he chronicled Augustine's life, taking up the story where Augustine himself left off in his *Confessions*, that is, with his return to Africa after the death of Monica.

Possidius's *Vita Augustini* is an example of hagiography, a story written about the life of a holy person in order to edify and inspire readers, and to encourage them to imitate the saint's virtues. Possidius provides touching details from the life of his friend and fellow cleric. He emphasizes Augustine's work in the church as a minister of the Gospel, as well as his monastic witness to personal holiness and humility. Possidius also includes a valuable, if incomplete catalog (*indiculum*) of Augustine's works at the end of his biography, probably based on the volumes in the library at Hippo, and on Augustine's own review of his writings in his *Revisions*.

Scholars differ on how astute Possidius might have been regarding Augustine's genius as an original thinker whose writings were to have such a profound influence on theology and philosophy in subsequent centuries. Nonetheless, Possidius's account of Augustine's life as a bishop and monk is straightforward and not given to the sentimentality or preoccupation with miraculous occurrences typical of many hagiographies from the early Christian centuries and medieval times. In fact, it is a goldmine for corroborating dates and events in Augustine's ecclesial and literary efforts.

The insights provided by Possidius into Augustine's place in North African Church life are explored and amplified in two commentaries. The first is by Michele Cardinal Pellegrino, Archbishop of Turin from 1965 to 1977. His *The Life of Saint Augustine by Possidius* appeared in English in 1988.[4] It provides an excellent introduction to the work and helpful annotations on the text. *Possidius of Calama: A Study of the North African Episcopate in the Age of Augustine* by Erika Hermanowicz is a more recent, extensive treatment of the topic in English.[5] Her research into Possidius's own episcopal ministry, and into the situation of the wider North African Church, challenges the popular assumption that Augustine's theological ideas and ecclesial leadership always dominated North African Christianity. In fact, she proposes that on theological matters and ecclesiastical policy, Augustine's positions were often isolated and in the minority. She argues that Possidius wrote his *Vita Augustini* in order to secure his mentor's theological positions and legacy amidst the political upheaval and ecclesiastical diversity of a mid-fifth-century Latin Church in which Augustine had been but one among many different and often discordant voices who opposed the ecclesial reform he represented.

## Louis-Sebastien Le Nain de Tillemont (1637–98)

One more historical footnote before moving onto contemporary biographies of Augustine: After Possidius, throughout the Middle Ages, and into the Reformation, interest in Augustine was not biographical, apart from the spiritual aspects of Augustine's life as described in *Confessions*. It was more theological and dogmatic, drawing on Augustine's doctrinal writings as source texts for the Christian synthesis that emerged in the Middle Ages. However, in the seventeenth century, a French priest of the Jansenist Port-Royal Abbey produced a series of volumes on church history. In volume XIII of this work, he chronicles the life of Augustine. Tillemont was an early modern historian in the sense that he approached history through a critical and rigorous evaluation of the sources from the period he was writing about.[6] So Tillment produced the first "modern" biography of Augustine, which draws from source material that Tillemont painstakingly locates and identifies in Augustine's texts. It has been a valuable source for all subsequent biographers. Frederick Van Fleteren has done an annotated translation of Tillemont's seminal work on Augustine.[7] This recent translation will be of great interest to English-speaking scholars tracing the history of Augustinian biography.

## John J. O'Meara (1915–2003)

The first major twentieth-century English-language biography appeared in 1954. The Irish Latinist, philosopher, and theologian John J. O'Meara had written his Oxford thesis on Augustine's reading of Neo-Platonism, specifically the writings of Porphyry. That research formed the basis of his still influential and important *The Young Augustine*.[8]

In this account of the first part of Augustine's life, O'Meara introduces readers to the young North African in the context of his culture, education, career, and conversion to Christianity. Throughout the biography, O'Meara is particularly keen to refute the thesis of the early twentieth-century French patrologist Pierre Courcelle. Courcelle and others in France had argued that Augustine's conversion was basically a philosophical one to Neo-Platonism, and that Neo-Platonism remained a formative force and primary religious influence throughout Augustine's life.[9]

Certainly, Neo-Platonism was an important influence on Augustine's intellectual and spiritual development. However, from his own close reading of the Neo-Platonists and the intellectual circle of Christians in Milan, including Bishop Ambrose and the priest Simplicianus, who had significant influence on Augustine, O'Meara makes a compelling case that Augustine moved through Neo-Platonism to Christianity. He argues that Augustine's post-conversion religious life and mystical experiences were deeply rooted in the Bible and in Christian faith in the incarnate Christ. He reviews Augustine's works, especially his early preordination writings, to show that even before his priestly and episcopal ministry, Augustine's mind and heart had moved through but beyond Neo-Platonism and submitted to Christian teaching and belief.

Augustine retains some of the philosophical language and expressions of Neo-Platonism in his theological lexicon.[10] But

O'Meara's close analysis of Augustine's Latin shows how biblical language and scriptural spirituality come to dominate the young Augustine's theological writing and pastoral speaking.[11] While studies on the role of Neo-Platonism in Augustine's life and thought continue, O'Meara's thesis about the nature of Augustine's religion is generally recognized as more compelling than Courcelle's.[12]

O'Meara's expertise as a Latinist is evident in the introduction, which provides an overview of the *Confessions* as a literary work. He situates Augustine's Latin in its fourth- and fifth-century Roman North African context, and provides many details about daily life and education. He also helps the contemporary reader appreciate Latin rhetorical style, and its brilliant literary exercise by Augustine. This biography remains an important introduction to the saint's life, even as it engages in theological debate about the essence of his religious experience.[13]

### Peter Brown (b. 1935)

The next modern biography of Augustine also had its genesis in the patristic scholarship of England, though this time in Cambridge. The brilliant young Anglo-Irish scholar and historian Peter Brown completed his *Augustine of Hippo* in 1967 when he was only thirty-two.[14] It established his place as a leading historian of late antiquity, and in many ways opened a whole new chapter in contemporary Augustinian scholarship.

Brown's biography is beautifully written with grace and humor, and with delicate attention to detail that brings fourth- and fifth-century North Africa and Italy alive for the reader. He also writes with a historian's circumspection that brings the reader through the major personal changes and intellectual movements in Augustine's journey of life. As we have seen, O'Meara's biography strives to exorcise Courcelle's highly Neo-Platonic interpretation of Augustine's conversion. One hears throughout that biography the leitmotif of one theological controversy. By contrast, Brown writes as a sympathetic historian of late Roman antiquity with the goal of helping contemporary readers "to convey something of the course and quality of Augustine's life." While he does not avoid theological commentary, Brown does not emphasize it in his biography.[15]

He recounts Augustine's life in five periods: from birth to his success as Imperial *Rhetor* (354–85); from his conversion to his episcopal ordination (386–95); from his ordination to the invasion of Rome by Alaric (395–410); from the sack of Rome through the Donatist controversy and into the beginning of the Pelagian controversy (410–20); and, the last phase of his life dominated by his debates with the Pelagian partisan Julian, Bishop of Eclanum, Italy (420–30). For each period, Brown provides useful chronological tables that track both historical events in church and empire, as well as in Augustine's own life. His writings are also arranged in chronological order in these tables, along with suggested English translations.

Brown's biography is especially significant in that it was republished in 2000, more than thirty years after its appearance in 1967. This second edition has the great advantage of Brown's own continuous teaching, research, and writing as well as the vast amount of work done by many other scholars in Augustine Studies during the last three decades of the twentieth century, including many of Brown's former graduate students at Princeton. Like the older Bishop Augustine reviewing his own writings in his *Revisions*, Brown provides a critical assessment of his 1967 text (which is reprinted without changes) in light of the ever-growing field of Augustine scholarship. To the 1967 edition he adds a "Preface to the New Edition," and two new chapters: "New Evidence," and "New Directions."

In "New Evidence," he reviews the discovery of the Dolbeau sermons and the Divjak letters.[16] The chapter entitled "New Directions" provides an expert's valuable summary of the advances in the field from 1970 to 1999. Such topics include the chronology of the sermons, North African Christianity, the secular nature of late

Roman Antiquity, Manichean life, the Roman system of education, Bishop Ambrose, Christian Neo-Platonism, Donatism,
monasticism, and sex and marriage, among other topics.

Brown writes movingly about how the Divjak and Dolbeau
discoveries, along with the immense amount of Augustine scholarship in the last three decades of the twentieth century, changed
some of his presuppositions about Augustine. Brown revises his
estimation of the challenges that Augustine faced in his time and
place. Given Augustine's cultural context and ecclesial "competi-
tion," Brown finds the Bishop of Hippo more insightful, consistent, and compassionate than other clerics of his day. New
scholarship also reveals that Augustine's contemporaries did not
always defer to him or his ideas. Later canonization of his thought
by the church in subsequent centuries had obscured this fact from
Brown, and from Augustine scholars in general. Augustine's more
polemical tracts of his later years were not the triumphant trum-
peting of a victor. He was arguing, with great rhetorical affect, for
ideas that he believed essential to understanding of Christian
faith, but ideas which had by no means become central in Christian thinking of his day. An ever-expanding understanding of
Augustine's fifth-century context leads Brown to an increased
appreciation of Augustine's uniqueness as a fifth-century churchman. "His individuality continues to stand out, in decisive contrast to his contemporaries."[17]

Brown, like the subject of his biography, is himself a man
"who grows as he writes, and writes as he grows" (*Letter* 143.2).
Anyone who wishes to come to a deeper understanding of the
Bishop of Hippo should read Brown's biography as well as his
other books and articles.

### Gerald Bonner (b. 1926)

If in their biographies John O'Meara concentrates on the
role of Neo-Platonism in Augustine's conversion, and Peter Brown
on biography more than theology, Gerald Bonner crafted his *St.*

*Augustine of Hippo: Life and Controversies* to introduce the reader to the three main theological debates that Augustine engaged as priest and bishop: Manichaeism, Donatism, and Pelagianism.[18] He does this by interweaving the pastoral life and duties of Augustine with these three theological concerns.

Bonner encountered the thought of Augustine, suitably enough, in North Africa. As a young British soldier in World War II, he chanced upon a Latin copy of *Confessions* in a book store. When he returned to England, he made the study of Augustine a lifelong pursuit at the University of Durham. His is the first English language biography to make available the vast research on Augustine's theology produced throughout the first part of the twentieth century in patristic centers on the continent, especially at the *Institut d'Études Augustiniennes* in Paris. The Rev. Robert Russell, OSA, recognized early the importance of Bonner's approach. Russell's Augustinian Institute at Villanova University highlighted Bonner's work by inviting him to deliver the first annual Augustine Lecture at Villanova University in 1970 and by publishing his research in the journal *Augustinian Studies*.[19] Himself an Augustinian priest and distinguished Augustine scholar, Father Russell appreciated Bonner's insights into the fundamental connection between Augustine's theological concerns and his role as a minister of the Word and Sacrament.[20]

Bonner makes the compelling point that the course of Augustine's life as a thinker was channeled through the highlands and lowlands of the pastoral concerns that confronted him. Before his ordination, he began to write against the teachings of his former Manichean associates. After his ordination, it became imperative that he do so for the benefit of the faithful. As an intellectual convert to Christianity, the ecclesial dimensions of Donatism probably held little interest for him and his companions at the monastic retreat they established at Thagaste upon returning from Italy in 388. However, after his priestly ordination in 391, Augustine had to deal with very real pastoral questions provoked by Donatist Christians in Hippo. As bishop and preacher he also had to respond to the elements in Pelagius's thought that he believed undermined the very essence of Christian faith in Christ. Still later he confronted the Arian understanding of Christ.

Bonner's biography was republished in 1986. In his preface to the second edition, he reflects on the effect that Augustine scholarship since 1963 has had on his own thinking about the Bishop of Hippo. While Bonner's second edition does not have the extensive reviews provided in Brown's second edition, Bonner's work remains an invaluable introduction to the religious context of Augustine's theological treatises as they emerge in his pastoral role as bishop.[21]

### Henry Chadwick (1920–2008)

One of the most distinguished British academics of the twentieth century, Henry Chadwick was Regius Professor of Theology first at Oxford, then at Cambridge. An ordained Anglican priest, he was also Dean of Christ Church at Oxford. An eminent scholar in early church history, Chadwick was recognized for his expertise in Augustine Studies. His valuable translation of *Confessions* was noted in chapter 2.[22]

Two unique biographies come from Chadwick's pen. The first was published in 1986 for the Very Short Introductions series on major world authors and topics by Oxford University Press. *Augustine: A Very Short Introduction* is very short, indeed, less than 130 pages, with a limited topical index.[23] Given the editorial constraints, Chadwick decided to trace the intellectual influences on Augustine's life and writings, rather than the social, political, or other influences. He shows the formation of Augustine's mind by Cicero, Mani, Porphyry, Plotinus, and Christ.[24] He takes the reader on a fast and fascinating tour of Augustine's main ideas and the works in which they are expressed. It is a biography of the mind that quotes many memorable and moving lines from Augustine's works. Chadwick is careful to distinguish between Augustine's thought and later medieval interpretations thereof.

Based on a manuscript originally prepared in 1981 by Chadwick himself, *Augustine of Hippo: A Life* is a less dense and more leisurely biography.[25] It was published posthumously in 2009, thanks to editorial efforts by Chadwick's wife and colleagues who retrieved the manuscript and readied it for publication. A moving forward by Peter Brown emphasizes the importance of Chadwick's life's work and its value for Augustine Studies.

Drawing from his vast knowledge of classical literature, Chadwick highlights Augustine's allusions to that literature. He marshals his formidable command of detail about Roman antiquity to create an account of Augustine's life and thought brimming with information about that time and culture so very different from our own. To quote from Brown's foreword, Chadwick's biography is filled with "the tang of life."[26]

Like the other astute twentieth-century biographers of Augustine, Chadwick is aware of how much the Bishop of Hippo differed from the dogmatic demagogue that later historians and commentators often portray him to be. He was the pastor of a small Catholic community, the minority Christian Church in Hippo. Like other Catholic bishops in his time and place, he was often humiliated by representatives of the imperial government, or by the wealthier families of the day, even as he strove to defend the rights of the poor.[27] He knew how to speak loudly, forcibly, and often to represent the thought and protect the standing of his people and their faith amidst the competing religious, social, and political forces of fifth-century Roman North Africa. Yet even in his rhetorical assaults on those with whom he disagreed, Augustine emphasized the importance of mutual respect and receptiveness. *Audi partem alteram*—"Hear the other side!" he writes in *The Two Souls* (22).[28]

Chadwick ends his biography by letting Augustine have the last word. He quotes from one of Augustine's last books *The Gift of Perseverance*. Eschewing the role of clever sage and final authority, Augustine puts his own theological writings in the context of a journey of exploration, a pilgrimage of faith seeking understanding:[29] "I should wish no one to embrace all my teaching except in those matters in which he has seen that I have made no mistake....I have not followed myself in everything. I think that by God's mercy I have made progress in my writing, but not at all that I have reached perfection....A man is of good hope if the last day of his life finds him still improving" (*The Gift of Perseverance*, 21.55).

### Miles Hollingworth (b. 1981)

A native of South Africa, Miles Hollingworth studied at St. John's College, Durham where he continues as a research fellow. He has written two books on Augustine and both have received praise: *The Pilgrim City: St. Augustine of Hippo and his Innovation in Political Thought* (2010) and *Saint Augustine of Hippo: An Intellectual Biography* (2013).[30]

In some ways, Hollingworth's biography of Augustine is heir to Chadwick's *Augustine: A Very Short Introduction* in that both emphasize the intellectual influences and development in Augustine's life and writings. However, the editorial parameters put around Chadwick's short introduction did not constrict Hollingworth. So his new intellectual biography is more expansive. It is also deepened by the author's philosophical interest, enriched by his lyrical style, and distinguished by a capacity to name the ironies and complexities of human experience. Thus, Hollingworth provides a fresh and inviting new look into Augustine's role as an intellectual innovator and creative genius. Rowan Williams identifies Hollingworth as a new, inspiring Augustine scholar of the highest quality who promises to attract a new generation of young students into the field.

### Serge Lancel (1928–2005)

No twentieth-century biographer of Augustine spent more time on Augustine's own land as Serge Lancel. He was professor of ancient history at the University of Grenoble and a noted expert in philology and archeology. Over many years he supervised archeological digs in Algeria and Tunisia, including at Hippo (modern Annaba) and at Carthage (modern Tunis). He advanced the study of the prehistoric, ancient, and medieval history of the Maghreb, the territory where Augustine was born and grew up, and which he crisscrossed in his many pastoral journeys as a bishop.

Lancel wrote extensive, thoroughly researched, and definitive texts on ancient Carthage, on Hannibal and his expeditions against Rome, on the ancient history of what is today Algeria and Tunisia, and on Augustine. His *Saint Augustin* was published in French in 1999.[31] The English translation came out in 2002.[32] It is a tour de force of Augustine's life, thought, and place in the history of Roman North Africa and in the Christian Church of that time and place. Written for the educated reader who enjoys the exactitude of historical method and the subtle distinctions it affords, Lancel's book brings the daily life of Augustine's time and place alive in startling new ways.

The depth and breadth of Lancel's historical analysis of Augustine in his context brings the results of extensive late twentieth-century French scholarship on Roman North Africa to English-speaking audiences. This over five-hundred-page work combines close historical detail, philosophical and theological sophistication, and thorough understanding of Augustine's pastoral duties and ecclesial roles. Lancel creates for the reader the experience of receiving daily, detailed, informed reports from a well-educated journalist "on-the-scene." His vivid accounts of particular places, customs, and historical personages excite your senses and pull you onto the salty waterfront of Carthage where Monica discovers that her deceptive son had already sailed for Rome (55–56), into the sheltered, treed garden in Milan where Alypius witnesses Augustine's tearful conversion (95–98), across the fruitful plains and majestic mountains of Numidia where the diocese of Hippo required its bishop to travel (chapters 22 to 24), through the hot and stormy ecclesiastical conference of Carthage where Catholic and Donatist bishops eyed each other suspiciously and angled politically for Imperial approval (chapter 26), beyond the Basilica of Peace where Augustine preached in Hippo to his monastic study where he labored year after year by the light of African oil lamps on such works as *The Trinity* and *City of God* (chapters 30 and 31). These are just a sampling of the intimacy with the Bishop of Hippo's life and struggles into which Lancel's text invites the reader.

Lancel's vast knowledge of Augustine's world and his deep Mediterranean empathy for this son of North Africa make his *St. Augustin* a book worth many careful readings and thorough study. It is the most historically complete and theologically astute biography available in English.[33]

### Goulven Madec, AA (1930–2008)

Father Goulven Madec was an Augustinian of the Assumption who devoted his whole life to the study of the Bishop of Hippo. The breadth of his scholarship covered classics, philosophy, and theology. For forty years, he was a member of *L'Institut d'Études Augustiniennes* in Paris, and honorary professor at *L'Institut Catholique*. He was also a director of research at *Le centre national de la recherche scientifique* in Paris.

For the reader of French, his *Portrait de saint Augustin* is a compelling and accessible overview of Augustine.[34] In just over one hundred pages, he reviews Augustine's life and ministerial work, as well as the Bishop of Hippo's basic convictions of faith and philosophy. The text has the great benefit of Madec's own enormous scholarship and erudition, and the invaluable advantage of his long association with one of the most important centers of Augustine Studies since the mid-twentieth century. An English translation of Madec's *Portrait* would be a welcome contribution.

### Thomas Martin, OSA (1943–2009)

All the biographies mentioned so far presume, to varying degrees, some knowledge of Augustine, his life, times, and theology. The scholar will find them all rewarding, and the generalist, challenging. *Augustine of Hippo: Faithful Servant, Spiritual Leader* is more accessible to the first-time reader about Augustine. It was published in 2011, a new biography of Augustine from the combined effort of two contemporary Augustine scholars, as part of The Library of World Biography series by Prentice Hall.[35]

Both Thomas Martin, who passed away before the book was finished, and Allan Fitzgerald, who edited the posthumous publication, are recognized Augustine scholars. They are also members of the Order of Saint Augustine. Martin taught at Villanova University, as does Fitzgerald, who previously taught at the *Institutum Patristicum Augustinianum* in Rome. In addition, Fitzgerald edited the influential *Augustine Through the Ages: An Encyclopedia* and until 2012 the journal *Augustinian Studies*. Together they brought a wealth of knowledge to the task of producing a new biography of the saint, and their book draws selectively and effectively from the past fifty years of Augustine scholarship.

They also bring a unique, spiritual relationship to the Bishop of Hippo in that their lives as Augustinian friars model the ideal that Augustine himself set forth in the rule of life he wrote for the monks and nuns of his own time.[36] It is no surprise that the organizing themes of their biography are Augustine's faithful service to the church as priest and bishop, and his role as spiritual leader of Christians. They write to introduce Augustine, who is their confrere and "spiritual leader," to a contemporary audience of Christians and others. They do this by emphasizing Augustine's Christian spirituality, and specifically what we might call his humanism. Focusing on Augustine's idea of the "self," which in many ways he introduced into world literature, they explore the various stages of his life and ministry by inviting readers to imitate Augustine's own introspection and reflection on experience.[37]

To this end, each chapter includes and most conclude with a passage from Augustine's own writings (or from Possidius's *Life of Augustine*). These passages come from a wide variety of Augustine's books, sermons, and letters, which provide primary text affirmations for the biographers' commentary on his life. The authors weave theological commentary in ways that reveal the spiritual and intellectual foundations of Augustine's ecclesial service and communal leadership. Augustine's struggles with Manichaeism, Donatism, and Pelagianism are explored not only in their implications for his own faith but also for his role as an official teacher of that faith. This 150-page biography is a fine introduction to Augustine Studies for the generalist or for the graduate or undergraduate student.

### James J. O'Donnell (b. 1950)

There is also James O'Donnell's interesting *Augustine: A New Biography*.[38] O'Donnell, whose extensive and thorough three-volume study of *Confessions* we have already mentioned, more recently turned his attention and energy to a revisionist interpretation of Augustine's life. His hermeneutical approach is to read *Confessions* as well as other works of Augustine, in light of Augustine's skill as a Roman rhetorician. Thus, he argues, we know only so much of Augustine, namely, what Augustine wanted us to know—the repentant convert and saintly bishop.

O'Donnell claims to pull the rhetorical curtain aside to glimpse what he suggests is the "real" Augustine. This is the "zealot" (41) bishop who lives in a seaside villa-like accommodation amidst the upper class of Hippo, very much an "ostentatious snob" (41, 90), always "on the make" (89), with a "tendency to curry favor upwards" (90). Augustine, according to O'Donnell, remains a Manichean all his life in his heart of hearts, since this was "the one truly impassioned religious experience of his life" (47). As a bishop, Augustine aligned himself with state authority in ways that had previously been seen only in the Eastern half of the Empire (80–81). Augustine "invented" the Catholic Church in Africa, which was only a minority Christian sect (O'Donnell relabels Catholics as "Caecilianists," after Bishop Caecilian). Again, armed with his rhetorical skill, Augustine edged out the

Donatists, who, according to O'Donnell, were the larger and more legitimate North African Church.

O'Donnell himself writes with clever humor and winning style. However, he seems to sideline the extensive scholarship on many of the issues he raises. He ignores the work of many accomplished scholars and opts for alluring drama over careful complexity. For that reason, it is difficult to consider his biography as a work that seeks conversation with other scholars in the field. However, his provocative style—itself a rhetorical device—challenges even the serious scholar to rethink and reconsider accepted wisdom in the field. Augustine himself might have relished a debate or two with O'Donnell.

Frederick Van Fleteren's review of this controversial, "unauthorized" biography highlights its strengths and weaknesses.[39] Van Fleteren critiques "not O'Donnell's ability, but his judgment; not his intelligence, but his interpretation" and he sees the limitations of this biography to be rooted in O'Donnell's lack of a theological methodology. In a surprising way, O'Donnell himself seems wedded to the image that Augustine carefully crafted in *Confessions* of himself as snobbish, ostentatious, on the make, and climbing the socioeconomic ladder of empire. The one reality in Augustine's life that O'Donnell precludes is conversion.

### Gary Wills (b. 1934)

The American public intellectual and prolific author Gary Wills provides us with the very readable *Saint Augustine: A Life*, a volume in the Penguin Lives Biographies series.[40] The first-time inquirer into Augustine will find this biography quite accessible and friendly. Wills is much more sympathetic to Augustine than O'Donnell and devotes his energy to helping the reader enter Augustine's fourth- and fifth-century North African society. Wills does this in many ways by his attention to language. He devotes himself to finding English words that render Augustine's life and thought in the Anglo-Saxon idiom. Thus, he translates *Confes-*

sions as *The Testimony*, *Adeodatus* as *Godsend*, and *circumcelliones* (the Donatist partisans) as *hut people*. He also suggests shortened, Anglicized translations of some of Augustine's books.

George Lawless's review of Wills's biography is generally positive.[41] Though he expresses concerns about the difficulties and challenges in Wills's translation project, Lawless notes that Wills does an immense service in retrieving Augustine from the historical accretions of intervening centuries that prevent us from seeing Augustine in his own time and place. Wills's book is "historical revisionism at its finest" by an enormously talented nonspecialist.

## Journals and Institutes

Several journals provide field guides for tracking the rich and diverse contemporary scholarship on Augustine. These include *Revue des études augustiniennes et patristiques* (Paris, since 1955),[42] *Augustiniana* (Louvain, since 1951), *Augustinianum* (Rome, since 1961), *Augustinian Studies* (Villanova, since 1970), and the North American Patristic Society's *Journal of Early Christian Studies* (Abilene, since 1980).[43] Each year, in the second number of its annual issue, the *Revue des études augustiniennes et patristiques* includes a comprehensive list (*recension*) of all journal articles, encyclopedias, manuscript and textual studies, conference proceedings, translations, anthologies, books, and even dissertations and unpublished works from across the many historical, theological, philosophical, linguistic, and other disciplines in the wide field of Augustine Studies. Based on diligent searching by scholars at *L'Institut d'Études Augustiniennes* in Paris, it is the most extensive and accurate review of the latest work done by Augustine scholars around the world and in many languages. This can be a valuable resource for the English-speaking scholar who is somewhat comfortable with French and the other major European languages.

The Center for Augustinian Studies in Würzburg (*Zentrum für Augustinus-Forschung in Würzburg*), Germany, affiliated with the University of Würzburg, has been building a data base of secondary sources in the field. It offers access to its significant collection at its Web site www.augustinus.de. Only parts of the Web site are in English, so some knowledge of German is helpful.

For English speakers who wish to gain a knowledge of the many and varied writings and conversations among Augustine scholars today, the friendliest resource is undoubtedly the journal *Augustinian Studies*. Established in 1970 by Fr. Robert Russell, OSA, of Villanova University, and until 2012, under the able editorial guidance of Fr. Allan Fitzgerald, OSA, this journal continues to provide Augustine scholars, especially those in the English-speaking world, with a highly respected forum in which to present their own work and to respond to that of their colleagues.[44] By perusing each issue's list of articles, book reviews, books received as well as book review discussions, the interested reader enjoys a hospitable and accessible entry into current conversations in the contemporary world of Augustine Studies. Over the past forty years, the journal has presented the published text of the St. Augustine Lecture, delivered annually at Villanova University through its *Augustinian Institute*.

Another indispensable research tool for anyone interested in Augustine is *Augustine Through the Ages: An Encyclopedia*, edited by Fr. Allen Fitzgerald, OSA.[45] This work contains five hundred entries by almost 150 Augustine scholars who write succinct, comprehensive articles on topics for which they are recognized as eminent scholars. Each article also provides a valuable bibliography of major books or articles on the topic. Happily, a second edition is expected within a few years.

Fitzgerald's encyclopedia has a worthy successor in Karla Pollmann's *Oxford Guide to the Historical Reception of Augustine*.[46] Pollmann, of the University of St. Andrews, was Editor-in-Chief, and worked with general editor Willemien Otten, of the University of Chicago, and twenty co-editors. This collection presents the scholarship of more than four hundred international experts who document Augustine's influence and legacy in many academic, religious, and cultural fields. It will be indispensable for Augustine scholars going forward.

## Anthologies, Edited Collections of Essays, and Introductory Texts

The vast amount of Augustine's writings make approaching the field difficult. Where to start? There is a new generation of works that help readers gain an understanding of and access to Augustine's ideas. These books also make recent research in Augustine Studies available to new or occasional readers in the field. There are three types of these contemporary introductory texts to consider. They include anthologies, collections of essays, and general introductory texts to his life and thought.

### Anthologies

Anthologies can provide a manageable introduction to Augustine's thought as well as an invitation to go deeper and further as the reader's interest is piqued. By presenting selected texts, an anthology gives a sense of how someone like Augustine thought about particular topics or events. It also traces the major themes that are essential in Augustine's general corpus and the role that his writing has played in the development of the theological and philosophical traditions of the West.

Selections from a vast corpus such as Augustine's have appeared throughout history. As we mentioned in chapter 4, the *florilegia* and *sententiae* began to appear in the centuries following his death, inspired by the compiler's religious fervor and doctrinal interest. These were the early medieval equivalent of anthologies. Contemporary anthologies reflect the twentieth-century methodological shift to historical context. So they introduce the reader to

Augustine's writings, while at the same time they provide context by annotations and commentaries that bring the latest research by scholars to the chosen texts.

*Augustine in His Own Words* by William Harmless, SJ, is an excellent introduction to the Bishop of Hippo.[47] Harmless, a Jesuit priest, is a contemporary patristic scholar of note who teaches at Creighton University. He has written on Augustine and the catechumenate, as well as on monasticism in the early church.[48] Harmless arranges this selection from Augustine's writings both thematically and historically. He begins with passages from *Confessions*, then moves to selections that introduce us to Augustine as philosopher, bishop, preacher, and exegete. Other chapters introduce the reader to *City of God* and *The Trinity* as well as to Augustine's polemical works against the Manicheans, Donatists, and Pelagians.

Harmless's command of the contemporary research is evident in his introductions to and commentaries on the texts he chooses in each section. His work also brings the reader the advantage of the depth and breadth of his wider patristic scholarship. Particularly helpful is the chronology of the events in Augustine's life as well as of his major books. For translations of the selected passages, Harmless uses both the older (1948/1950) Catholic University of America The Fathers of the Church series as well as the New City Press *The Works of St. Augustine: A Translation for the 21st Century*. This book is a valuable text for both graduate and undergraduate courses in Augustine or patristic studies in general.

In 1984, Paulist Press published *Augustine of Hippo: Selected Writings* by Mary T. Clark as part of its extensive Classics of Western Spirituality, an important series under the leadership of legendary Paulist Press publisher, Fr. Kevin Lynch.[49] Sr. Mary Clark of Manhattanville College has been a leading American Catholic philosopher, civil rights activist, and Augustine scholar for almost seven decades. This anthology enjoys the great benefit of her many years of research and writing on Augustine, as well as her careful work to update existing English translations available in the mid 1980s.

Clark chooses passages that highlight Augustine's spirituality. She arranges her selections to begin with the middle books of *Confessions*, and then move through passages from *Expositions of the Psalms*, *Homilies on the Gospel of John*, *Homilies on the First Epistle of John*, *The Trinity*, *City of God*, the monastic *Rule*, and two letters. Her introduction is an excellent essay on Augustine's spirituality, written with the benefit of Clark's own spiritual life as a Religious Sister of the Sacred Heart as well as her discerning philosophical analysis and insight.

Because of its place in a series on Western spirituality, Clark's anthology is suited to courses or discussion groups that focus on Augustinian spirituality and theology of prayer, though it also serves as a good general introduction to Augustine. Her comments and notes enjoy the great benefit of her significant scholarly work over many years and her perspective on Augustine's role in the history of philosophy as well as on his life of faith.

An older, classical Augustinian anthology of many decades has been Vernon Bourke's *The Essential Augustine*.[50] Bourke (1907–98), who taught for many years at the University of St. Louis, was a leading Canadian-American Catholic philosopher and theologian with expertise in St. Thomas Aquinas and St. Augustine, particularly in their ethics.

Bourke's selections from Augustine as well as his arrangement and commentaries on the texts, reflect his extensive philosophical background. He traces established medieval philosophical and theological categories to their Christian origins in Augustine's writings. These include faith and reason; our capacity to understand God; the ontological levels of body, soul, and the divine; morality; grace; and political and historical philosophy as found in *City of God*. *The Essential Augustine* remains in print because of the quality of Bourke's scholarship and his penetrating insights into the history of Western philosophy, especially from the ancient to the medieval periods. The text is still a valuable resource for courses in the history of Christian philosophy. However, it does not enjoy the benefit of Augustinian scholarship of the past fifty years, nor the accessibility of more recent translations of Augustine's texts, such as the New City Press series.

A more modest recent addition to Augustinian anthologies is my own *Saint Augustine of Hippo: Selections from Confessions and Other Essential Writings, Annotated and Explained*.[51] This enchiridion of Augustine's writings is part of SkyLight Publications's Illuminations series. The purpose of this series is to bring the writings of spiritual masters from many religious and philosophical traditions over the ages to the contemporary general reader. The book organizes selections from Augustine according to major themes that reflect categories in his own thought as well as topics of interest to a contemporary reader. These include the journey of faith, human responsibility for sin, divine grace and free will, community and friendship in God, Jesus, the Holy Spirit, the church and sacraments, and contemporary moral issues.

Translations are mostly from the New City Press series, and the annotations and commentaries draw from recent Augustinian scholarship. The nature of the Illumination series makes this book very much an introductory anthology, suitable for secondary education, adult discussion programs, or perhaps introductory theology courses at the university level.

In addition to such anthologies, New City Press has chosen selections of Augustine's writings already published in the translation series and republished them in accessible one-volume collections dedicated to a particular topic. The volumes in this "Augustine Series—Selected Volumes" so far include *Selected Writings on Grace and Pelagianism*;[52] *Trilogy on Faith and Happiness*;[53] *The Monastic Rules*;[54] *Essential Sermons*;[55] and *Prayers from the Confessions*.[56] These are very helpful volumes to anyone wanting to research particular topics in Augustine's writings.

There are other topical collections of note that provide introductions to Augustine's thought on various subjects or from particular periods of his life.[57]

*Edited Collections of Essays*

Throughout this book, we have cited many edited volumes that collect recent scholarly research on Augustine. We highlight a few of them here.

John Doody of Villanova University and Kim Paffenroth of Iona College are editors of a series entitled "Augustine in Conversation: Tradition and Innovation" published since 2005 by Lexington Books. The goal of these collections of essays by contemporary scholars is to put Augustine's thinking on a particular topic in dialogue with various fields of study that might benefit from the categories, language, and insights of the Bishop of Hippo. The topics include history, liberal education, politics, world religions, literature, and politics.[58] Topics to come include psychology, science, apocalyptic, peace and justice, and the environment or ecology.

As with every collection of essays by a wide variety of scholars, reviews have been mixed, though generally favorable. It is to be expected that contributing authors, some of whom straddle different academic disciplines, have differing levels of expertise in Augustine Studies. Some contributors engage him on the terrain of a disciplinary content and method other than Patristics, which may inspire particular critique from a Patristics expert. Overall, however, this series extends invitations to thinkers in many fields to engage Augustine and discover the richness of his thought for contemporary explorations and interpretations of various topics. These essays critique Augustine's thinking in light of contemporary scholarship. They also allow Augustine's thinking to stand in critique of contemporary disciplinary presuppositions and assumptions. It is a valuable series that we can hope will continue well into the future, and perhaps include topics such as Islam and comparative theology.

Another valuable topical collection of secondary sources is *The Cambridge Companion to Augustine.*[59] This volume is part of the Cambridge Companions to Philosophy series. The editors, Eleonore Stump of St. Louis University and her mentor Norman

Kretzmann (1928–98) who taught medieval philosophy at Cornell, bring together the thinking of sixteen different philosophers and theologians to trace Augustine's influence on the history of Western philosophy. A new Cambridge Companion is forthcoming.

Topics covered include faith and reason, sin and evil, predestination, biblical interpretation, the divine nature, time and creation, the soul, free will, memory, cognition, skepticism, knowledge and illumination, philosophy of language, ethics, political philosophy, and Augustine's perduring influence in the medieval period and beyond. This collection represents some of the best contemporary philosophical debates about Augustinianism and its place in the history of Western thought.

More recently Mark Vessey has edited *A Companion to Augustine* for the Blackwell Companions to the Ancient World series.[60] This is a treasure trove of thirty-five essays by leading Augustine scholars. It also contains an extensive bibliography that will prove helpful for further research into the many areas of the field.

### Introductory Texts

For the teacher or pastor seeking to introduce classroom students or a study group to Augustine's life and thought, there are good resources. We mention just a few here.

James Wetzel's *Augustine: A Guide for the Perplexed* is born of this Villanova University professor's scholarship and teaching.[61] As part of the Continuum Guide for the Perplexed series, it presents a clear, concise, and accessible introduction to Augustine. Wetzel covers the general themes across Augustine's life and thinking, and provides a list of further readings for each chapter in his book. Some of these suggested readings would be far beyond the ken of most undergraduates. But, then again, part of the agenda of undergraduate studies is to accumulate a bibliography for the rest of one's life.

Wetzel's own scholarship has revolved around will and grace and predestination, and these receive ample coverage in his text.[62]

Wetzel privileges a philosophical reading of Augustine, situating him in the time and context of Ciceronian and Neo-Platonic Late Roman Antiquity. This is valuable and also appropriate for the Continuum series. However, Augustine's life of faith and service in the Christian Church, out of which so much of his thinking evolved, receives less attention in Wetzel's text. The reader, especially an undergraduate, might underestimate the faith dimension of Augustine's marriage of faith and reason.

Mary T. Clark's *Augustine of Hippo* is also from Continuum, a volume in their Outstanding Christian Thinkers series.[63] Clark's four decades of reading Augustine, her philosophical and theological command of the material, and her own life of faith as a religious sister make her text a good companion to Wetzel's more philosophical approach. She traces the main theological, philosophical, and existential themes that span Augustine's life with her typical forthrightness and clarity.

A chronology of Augustine's life and the historical events in the empire, along with a chronological list of his major writings provide the reader with a good sense of Augustine's context and the great breadth of his literary output. Her bibliography is solid, but a bit dated, without the advantage of Wetzel's more recent review of the literature.

Another introductory text to the Augustinian tradition is that of Thomas Martin, OSA, *Our Restless Heart: The Augustinian Tradition.*[64] This book is part of the Orbis Press Traditions of Christian Spirituality series and so concentrates on Augustine's influence on the history of Christian theology and spirituality. Martin presents the "restless heart" theme as the signature of Augustine's own journey of faith and of the spiritual heritage— Catholic and Protestant—that has grown up around Augustinian confessional writing, monastic traditions, and ecclesial reform. Martin's book touches upon Augustine's own life, but concentrates more on the effect he had on subsequent Christian history.

Serge Lancel wrote that "Augustinian bibliography is rich, even superabundant."[65] Hopefully this final chapter, and indeed this whole text has given you a sense of that richness and superabundance. As new generations of Augustine scholars, women and men, from many countries and continents deepen their knowledge of the Bishop of Hippo and of his times, we can expect new perspectives, new insights, and new resources to study the life and work of this man of late antiquity who has been a source of endless fascination for so many. Lancel, reflecting on his own study of Augustine advises this: "Let us ask ourselves rather what lesson we may draw from his life, quite apart from any strictly religious option. But that question has just been answered: because he set highly exacting standards on the honour of being a man in his own times, St. Augustine may perhaps be entitled to inspire our own."[66]

# CONCLUSION

Any attempt to answer the question "What are they saying about Augustine of Hippo" is an ongoing project. So much continues to be written every year about Augustine—so many books, scholarly articles, encyclopedic works, Web pages—that Possidius's claim about the extent of Augustine's writings can easily and analogously be applied to secondary sources: "So many are the scholarly works published, that any student would hardly have the energy to read and become acquainted with all of them."

The research and writing we have reviewed here represents some of the best contemporary scholarship on the life and thought of a son of North Africa and early African Christianity. In the year 2030, we will commemorate the sixteen-hundredth anniversary of his death. No doubt the coming decade leading up to that commemoration will inspire yet more scholarly conferences, debates, books, articles, and electronic resources—certainly enough to ensure Augustine's ideas a vibrating presence in the electronic "cloud" of information and databases that encircles our globe. Were he still writing and preaching among us today, no doubt he would have much to say about that "cloud," its potential for grace-endowed good as well as sin-induced evil, about the moral imperatives of our global village, the encounter of cultures and religions, and the vital issues around the sustainability of God's good creation.

Many dimensions of Augustine's thought provide valuable contributions to the growing conversations among world religions. His insights into the mystery of Christ, his sophisticated appreciation of the complexity of sacred texts, his convictions about the nature of divine grace, and his theology of prayer are important sources for interfaith and comparative theology. In these topics, Christians can find much to enrich their contributions to critical engagement with people from other religious traditions. That engagement has made continued research in Augustine Studies all the more imperative.

Any review of the abundant, continuing literature on Augustine cannot fail to remind the reader that this bishop of Berber descent, who died in a city under siege by Arian Vandals, whose Christian successors soon dispersed or disappeared under the westward expansion of Arabic Islam, whose writings were saved against all odds—this restless seeker of Truth—continues to excite imaginations and incite debates in every new generation. Hopefully this volume will help you to enter more deeply into the vision Augustine had of God and humanity, and with the aid of divine grace, take your own stand among the issues that he considered vital for human life and thought.

# APPENDIX

## The Complete Works of Saint Augustine:
## A Translation for the 21st Century

Augustinian Heritage Institute/New City Press
Series Editors: John E. Rotelle, OSA, and Boniface Ramsey

## Part I: Books

*Confessions.* Vol. I/1.
Introduction, translation, and notes by Maria Boulding, OSB.
Hyde Park, New York: New City Press, 1997, 2012.

*Revisions.* Vol. I/2.
Translation and notes by Boniface Ramsey, 2010.

*Dialogues I.* Vol. I/3.
Forthcoming.
This volume contains: *Dialectic, Grammar, Rhetoric, Answer to the Academics, The Happy Life, Order, Soliloquies,* and *The Immortality of the Soul.*

*Dialogues II*. Vol. I/4.
Forthcoming.
This volume contains: *The Magnitude of the Soul, Free Will, Music,* and *The Teacher*.

*The Trinity*. Vol. I/5.
Introduction, translation, and notes by Edmund Hill, OP, 1991.

*City of God, 1–10*. Vol. I/6.
Introduction and translation by William Babcock. Notes by Boniface Ramsey, 2012.

*City of God, 11–24*. Vol. I/7.
Introduction and translation by William Babcock. Notes by Boniface Ramsey, 2013.

*On Christian Belief*. Vol. I/8.
Translations by Edmund Hill, OP, Ray Kearney, Michael G. Campbell, and Bruce Harbert, edited by Boniface Ramsey. Introductions by Michael Fiedrowicz, 2005.
This volume contains: *True Religion, The Advantage of Believing, Faith and Creed, Faith in the Unseen, Demonic Divination, Faith and Works,* and *Enchiridion on Faith, Hope, and Charity*.

*Marriage and Virginity*. Vol. I/9.
Translation by Ray Kearney. Edited with introductions and notes by David Hunter, 1999.
This volume contains: *The Excellence of Marriage, Holy Virginity, The Excellence of Widowhood, Adulterous Marriages,* and *Continence*.

*Morality and Christian Asceticism*. Vol. I/10.
Forthcoming.
This volume contains: *Lying, Against Lying, The Work of Monks,*

*The Care To Be Taken of the Dead, The Christian Combat, The Instruction of Beginners, The Advantage of Fasting,* and *Patience.*

*Teaching Christianity.* Vol. I/11.
Introduction, translation, and notes by Edmund Hill, OP, 1996.

*Responses to Miscellaneous Questions.* Vol. I/12.
Translation by Boniface Ramsey, 2008.
This volume contains: *Miscellany of Eighty-three Questions, Miscellany of Questions in Response to Simplician,* and *Eight Questions of Dulcitius.*

*On Genesis.* Vol. I/13.
Translation and notes by Edmund Hill, OP, edited by John E. Rotelle, OSA. Introductions by Michael Fiedrowicz, 2002.
This volume contains: *On Genesis: Refutation Against the Manichees, Unfinished Literal Commentary on Genesis,* and *The Literal Meaning of Genesis.*

*The Old Testament.* Vol. I/14.
Forthcoming.
This volume contains: *Observations on the Heptateuch, Questions on the Heptateuch, Eight Questions of the Old Testament, Notes on Job,* and *Answer to the Jews.*

*The New Testament I/II.* Vol. I/15–16.
Forthcoming.
These volumes contain: *Agreement among the Evangelists, Questions on the Gospels, Seventeen Questions on Matthew,* and *The Lord's Sermon on the Mount.*

*The New Testament III.* Vol. I/17.
Forthcoming.
This volume contains: *Mirror of Scripture: "Who Does Not Know?," Exposition on the Letter to the Galatians, Exposition on*

*Certain Questions in the Letter to the Romans*, and *Unfinished Commentary on the Letter to the Romans.*

*Arianism and Other Heresies.* Vol. I/18.
Introduction, translation, and notes by Roland J. Teske, SJ, 1995.
This volume contains: *Heresies, Memorandum to Augustine, To Orosius in Refutation of the Priscilliansts and Origenists, Arian Sermon, Answer to an Arian Sermon, Debate with Maximinus, Answer to Maximinus,* and *Answer to an Enemy of the Law and the Prophets.*

*The Manichean Debate.* Vol. I/19.
Translation and notes by Roland J. Teske, SJ, edited by Boniface Ramsey, 2006.
This volume contains: *The Catholic Way of Life and the Manichean Way of Life; The Two Souls; A Debate with Fortunatus, a Manichean; Answer to Adimantus, a Disciple of Mani; Answer to the Letter of Mani known as the Foundation; Answer to Felix, a Manichean; The Nature of the Good;* and *Answer to Secundinus, a Manichean.*

*Answer to Faustus, a Manichean.* Vol. I/20.
Introduction, translation, and notes by Roland J. Teske, SJ, 2007.

*The Donatist Controversy I.* Vol. I/21.
Forthcoming.
This volume contains: *Psalm Against the Donatist Party, Baptism, A Letter to Catholics On the Donatist Sect (the Unity of the Church), Answer to the Letter of Parmenian,* and *Answer to the Writings of Petilian.*

*The Donatist Controversy II.* Vol. I/22.
Forthcoming.
This volume contains: *Answer to Cresconius; Answer to Gaudentius, a Donatist Bishop; The One Baptism in Answer to Petilian;*

*Summary of the Conference with the Donatists; To the Donatists after the Conference; Proceedings with Emeritus;* and *Sermon to the People of the Church of Caesarea.*

*Answer to the Pelagians.* Vol. I/23.
Introduction, translation, and notes by Roland J. Teske, SJ, 1997.
This volume contains: *The Punishment and Forgiveness of Sins and the Baptism of Little Ones, The Spirit and the Letter, Nature and Grace, The Perfection of Human Righteousness, The Deeds of Pelagius, The Grace of Christ and Original Sin,* and *The Nature and Origin of the Human Soul.*

*Answer to the Pelagians II.* Vol. I/24.
Introduction, translation, and notes by Roland J. Teske, SJ, 1998.
This volume contains: *Marriage and Desire, Answer to the Two Letters of the Pelagians,* and *Answer to Julian.*

*Answer to the Pelagians III.* Vol. I/25.
Introduction, translation, and notes by Roland J. Teske, SJ, 1999.
This volume contains the *Unfinished Work in Answer to Julian.*

*Answer to the Pelagians IV.* Vol. I/26.
Introduction, translation, and notes by Roland J. Teske, SJ, 1999.
This volume contains: *Grace and Free Choice, Rebuke and Grace, The Predestination of the Saints, The Gift of Perseverance,* and selected letters.

## Part II: Letters

*Letters, 1–99.* Vol. II/1.
Translation and notes by Roland J. Teske, SJ, edited by John E. Rotelle, 2001.

*Letters, 100–155.* Vol. II/2.
Translation and notes by Roland J. Teske, SJ, edited by Boniface Ramsey, 2003.

*Letters, 156–210.* Vol. II/3.
Translation and notes by Roland J. Teske, SJ, edited by Boniface Ramsey, 2004.

*Letters, 211–270.* Vol. II/4.
Translation and notes by Roland J. Teske, SJ, edited by Boniface Ramsey, 2005.

## Part III: Sermons

*Sermons, (1–19) on the Old Testament.* Vol. III/1.
Introduction by Cardinal Michele Pellegrino (translated by Matthew J. O'Conell). Translation and notes by Edmund Hill, OP, 1990.

*Sermons, (20–50) on the Old Testament.* Vol. III/2.
Translation and notes by Edmund Hill, OP, 1990.

*Sermons, (51–94) on the Old Testament.* Vol. III/3.
Translation and notes by Edmund Hill, OP, 1991.

*Sermons, (94A–147A) on the Old Testament.* Vol. III/4.
Translation and notes by Edmund Hill, OP, 1992.

*Sermons, (148–183) on the New Testament.* Vol. III/5.
Translation and notes by Edmund Hill, OP, 1992.

*Sermons, (184–229Z) on the Liturgical Seasons.* Vol. III/6.
Translation and notes by Edmund Hill, OP, 1993.

*Sermons, (230–272B) on the Liturgical Seasons.* Vol. III/7.
Translation and notes by Edmund Hill, OP, 1993.

*Sermons, (273–305A) on the Saints.* Vol. III/8.
Translation and notes by Edmund Hill, OP, 1994.

*Sermons, (306–340A) on the Saints.* Vol. III/9.
Translation and notes by Edmund Hill, OP, 1994.

*Sermons, (341–400) on Various Subjects.* Vol. III/10.
Translation and notes by Edmund Hill, OP, 1995.

*Sermons, various* (newly discovered). Vol. III/11.
Translation and notes by Edmund Hill, OP, 1997.

*Homilies on the Gospel of John (1–40).* Vol. III/12.
Translation by Edmund Hill, OP, edited and annotated introduction by Allan Fitzgerald, OSA, 2009.

*Homilies on the Gospel of John (41–124).* Vol. III/13.
Forthcoming.

*Homilies on the First Epistle of John.* Vol. III/14.
Translation and notes by Boniface Ramsey, edited by Daniel E. Doyle, OSA, and Thomas Martin, OSA, 2008.

*Expositions of the Psalms, 1–32.* Vol. III/15.
Translation and notes by Maria Boulding, OSB, edited by John E. Rotelle. General introduction by Michael Fiedrowicz, 2000.

*Expositions of the Psalms, 33–50.* Vol. III/16.
Translation and notes by Maria Boulding, OSB, edited by John E. Rotelle, 2000.

*Expositions of the Psalms, 51–72.* Vol. III/17.
Translation and notes by Maria Boulding, OSB, edited by John E.
Rotelle, 2001.

*Expositions of the Psalms, 73–98.* Vol. III/18.
Translation and notes by Maria Boulding, OSB, edited by John E.
Rotelle, 2002.

*Expositions of the Psalms, 99–120.* Vol. III/19.
Translation and notes by Maria Boulding, OSB, edited by Boniface
Ramsey, 2003.

*Expositions of the Psalms, 121–150.* Vol. III/20.
Translation and notes by Maria Boulding, OSB, edited by Boniface
Ramsey, 2004.

# LISTS OF AUGUSTINE'S WORKS

*Augustine Through the Ages: An Encyclopedia* provides two complete lists of Augustine's writings. Both lists are in Latin alphabetic order. The first list includes common abbreviations of titles, the full Latin titles, English titles, Latin editions of the texts, and English translations, including the New City Press *Works of Saint Augustine*. The second list provides dates of composition and brief explanations of the purpose and context of the work, and other information.

In *St. Augustine* (London: SCP Press, 2002), Serge Lancel provides a chronological list of Augustine's major writings (p. 533). In *Augustine of Hippo: A Biography* (Los Angeles: University of California Press, 2000/1967), Peter Brown includes Augustine's major works in the chronological tables of Augustine's life.

# NOTES

## Introduction

1. See Joseph Ratzinger/Pope Benedict XVI, *Popolo e Casa di Dio in Sant'Agostino* (Milano: Jaca Book SpA, 1978/2005); also, *Volk und Haus Gottes in Augustins Lehre von der Kirche* (München: Karl Zink Verlag, 1954); Pope Benedict XVI, *The Fathers* (Huntington, IN: Our Sunday Visitor, 2008) provides an excellent summary of Augustine's theology and its place in Benedict's thought; Joseph Lam C. Quy, OSA, *Theologische Verwandtschaft: Augustinus von Hippo und Joseph Ratzinger/Papst Benedikt XVI* (Würzburg: Echter, 2009); Rowan Williams, "Good for Nothing?" *Augustinian Studies* 25 (1994): 9–24; Rowan Williams, "Insubstantial Evil," in *Augustine and His Critics*, ed. Robert Dodaro, OSA, and George Lawless, OSA (New York/London: Routledge, 2000). Benedict quotes Augustine in all of his encyclicals. Rowan Williams served on the advisory board of the journal *Augustinian Studies*.

2. Members of the Order of St. Augustine (OSA), of the Augustinians of the Assumption (AA), and of the Augustinian Recollects (OAR), along with many Jesuits (SJ) and Dominican Friars (OP), as well as women from various religious communities have contributed much to the study of the Bishop of Hippo.

3. See Frederick Van Fleteren, ed., *Martin Heidegger's Interpretations of Augustine: Sein und Zeit und Ewigkeit* (Lewiston, ME: The Edwin Mellen Press, 2005); and, Hannah Arendt, *Love and Saint Augustine*, ed. Joanna Vecchiarelli Scott and Judith Chelius Stark (University of Chicago Press, 1929/1996).

4. See John D. Caputo and Michael J. Scanlon, OSA, eds., *Augustine and Postmodernism: Confession and Circumfession*, Indiana Series in the Philosophy of Religion (Bloomington, IN: Indiana University Press, 2005). This valuable series of essays surveys Augustine's influence on Heidegger, Lyotard, Arendt, and Ricoeur. See also F. J. Thonnard, "*Saint Augustin et les grand courants de la philosophie contemporaine*," *Revue des études augustiniennes* 1 (1955): 68–80. Thonnard notes Augustinian influence on Heidegger, Jaspers, Kierkegaard, Scheler, and others.

5. The field is called "Augustinian Studies" or "Augustine Studies." I will use the latter.

6. "Even at table he found more delight in reading and conversation than in eating and drinking" (*The Life of Saint Augustine* [XXII.6]). Possidius, *The Life of Saint Augustine*, The Augustine Series, trans. Michele Cardinal Pellegrino, ed. John E. Rotelle, OSA (Villanova, PA: Augustinian Press: 1988).

7. Quotations from the works of Augustine will be noted in the text, rather than in endnotes, and are from the New City Press series *The Works of Saint Augustine: A Translation for the 21st Century*.

8. "Reliance on fellow scholars and a continuing dialogue among many, varied participants may, in fact, be the most enduring legacy that can be hoped for in these postmodern times of historical scholarship." Allan D. Fitzgerald, OSA, "Tracing the passage from a doctrinal to an historical approach to the study of Augustine," *Revue des études augustiniennes et patristiques* 50 (2004): 301.

9. Possidius, *Life*.

10. Peter L. Brown, *Augustine of Hippo* (Los Angeles: University of California Press, 1967/2000), vii.

11. Brown, *Augustine of Hippo*, 447.

## 1. Life: Meeting Augustine

1. Thomas A. Martin, OSA, *Augustine of Hippo: Faithful Servant, Spiritual Leader*, ed. Allan D. Fitzgerald, OSA (New York: Prentice Hall, 2011), 13–14.

2. Augustine recounts how he loved the travels and tribulations of Virgil's *Aeneas*, but disliked reading Homer's stories because he struggled with the Greek language (*Confessions* I.14.23).

3. Peter Brown, *Augustine of Hippo* (Los Angeles: University of California Press, 1967/2000), 54.

4. Though it grates against our modern sensibilities, it was common practice to replace a concubine with a woman considered in society to be a more suitable spouse as a young man made his way up the social, economic ladder of the Empire. Augustine's woman was not an asset to his career, since she was not of his social class. See Serge Lancel, *St. Augustine*, trans. Antonia Neville (London: SCM Press, 2002), 271–305.

5. Robert Dodaro, OSA, "Augustine's Secular City," in *Augustine and His Critics—Essays in Honour of Gerald Bonner*, ed. Robert Dodaro, OSA, and George Lawless, OSA (London: Routledge, 2000), 248.

6. Lancel, *St. Augustine*, 46.

7. "This lust is not some kind of alien nature, as the ravings of the Manichees would have it. It's our debility, it's our vice. It won't be detached from us and exist somewhere else, but it will be cured and not exist anywhere at all" (*Sermon* 151.3).

8. Brown, *Augustine of Hippo*, 50.

9. See Nicholas J. Baker-Brian, *Manicheism: An Ancient Faith Rediscovered* (London: T&T Clark, 2011) for a new study of the religion.

10. Augustine would not have had Jerome's Vulgate translation of the Bible available to him at this point in his life. Jerome worked on his translation from 382 to 405. In 372–73, when the young Augustine took up the scriptures in Carthage to study them, he would have been reading one of many so-called "Old Roman" or "Old African" Latin translations, which were "frequently clumsy and always rustic Latin" (Lancel, *St. Augustine*, 31).

11. Augustine wrote two books on lying: *Lying* (394–95) and *Against Lying* (420).

12. After the death of Plato, the Academy or school of philosophy in Athens increasingly advanced various forms of skepticism, which advises a reluctance to assert any teaching as true or to affirm human ability to know truth.

13. For a recent interesting analysis of Augustine's relationship with the Manichean community, see Jason BeDuhn, "What Augustine (May Have) Learned from the Manicheans," *Augustinian Studies* 43:1/2 (2012): 35–48.

14. Augustine's tutoring in Christian thought was more at the direction of one of Ambrose's priests, Simplicianus. This elderly, wise

man had a profound influence on Augustine's conversion. See *Confessions* VIII.1.1—2.2.3.

15. Probably the *Enneads* of Plotinus, translated by Marius Victorinus (Lancel, *St. Augustine*, 84).

16. Augustine discussed Neo-Platonist philosophy with the priest Simplicianus as the latter instructed him in the Catholic faith (*Confessions* VIII.2.3).

17. Augustine mentions the death of Adeodatus in *Confessions* IX.6.14 and that he dedicated his book *The Teacher* to his son.

18. "You rescue us from our wretched meanderings and establish us on your way; you console us and bid us, 'run: I will carry you, I will lead you and I will bring you home'" (*Confessions* VI.16.26).

19. Brown, *Augustine of Hippo*, 132–33.

20. Aware of how attractive a candidate he would be to a city or town without a bishop, Augustine avoided any place where that was the situation. Since Hippo already had a bishop, he thought it safe to go there. Years later, on an anniversary of his ordination, he recalled: "I came to this city to see a friend, whom I thought I could gain for God, to join us in the monastery. It seemed safe enough, because the place had a bishop. I was caught, I was made a priest, and by this grade I eventually came to the episcopate" (*Sermon* 355.2). See also, Possidius' *Life of Augustine* IV.

21. Lancel, *St. Augustine*, 150, 174.

22. Those who "handed over" the sacred books were called *traditores*.

23. The work of Maureen Tilley at Fordham provides a recent, excellent overview of Donatism: Maureen A. Tilley, trans. and ed., *Donatist Martyr Stories: The Church in Conflict in Roman North Africa*, Translated Texts for Historians, vol. 24 (Liverpool: Liverpool University Press, 1997). See also Peter Brown, "Religious Dissent in the Later Roman Empire: the Case of North Africa," in *Religion and Society in the Age of St. Augustine* (Eugene, OR: Wipf & Stock, 1972/2007), 237–59. An older classic work on Donatism that still provides insight and detail is W. H. C. Frend, *The Donatist Church: A Movement of Protest in Roman North Africa* (Oxford: Clarendon Press, 1952/1972).

24. Serge Lancel, *St. Augustine*, 167ff. See also C. Lepelley, "Circumcelliones," in *Augustinus-Lexikon I*, ed. Cornelius Mayer, OSA (Basel: Schwabe & Co. AG, 1986–94), 246–52.

25. Possidius tells us that on one occasion when Augustine was traveling back to Hippo, probably in 403, a group of circumcellions were lying in wait. But Augustine, by mistake, took a longer route and so avoided the ambush (*Life* XII.1—2). Augustine also mentions such an event in his *Enchiridion on Faith, Hope and Charity* 17.

26. For a close look at the pastoral and practical dimensions of the Donatist-Catholic conflict, see Maureen A. Tilley, "Family and Financial Conflict in the Donatist Controversy: Augustine's Pastoral Problem," *Augustinian Studies* 43 (2012): 49–64.

27. The published acts of the conference show that there were about 600 bishops from across central and western North Africa, evenly divided among Catholics and Donatists. See Lancel, *St. Augustine*, 246.

28. See chapter 3, pages 52–57.

29. Twice in *Confessions* X.29.40; and again in X.31.45.

30. Lancel suggests that the eyewitness may have been Augustine's friend Evodius, Bishop of Uzalis, or possibly Paulinus of Nola, who would become Augustine's correspondent (Lancel, *St. Augustine*, 326).

31. For a recent translation and reconsideration of Pelagius's work, see Pelagius, *Pelagius's Commentary on St Paul's Epistle to the Romans*, Oxford Early Christian Studies, trans. Theodore de Bruyn (Oxford: Clarenden Press, 1993/2002).

32. See chapter 3, pages 58–59.

33. Henry Chadwick, *Augustine of Hippo—A Life* (Oxford: Oxford University Press, 2009), 65–67.

34. Possidius describes Augustine's pastoral ministry as "laborious days and nights filled with toil" (Possidius, *Life*, XXIV.11), or, as Lancel beautifully translates it: "working by day, and waking by night" (Lancel, *St. Augustine*, 214–15).

## 2. Writings I: Major Books

1. Thomas Martin, OSA, *Augustine of Hippo—Faithful Servant, Spiritual Leader*, ed. Allan Fitzgerald, OSA (New York: Prentice Hall, 2011), viii. By comparison, the authors note, we have 884,647 words from Shakespeare.

2. See William Harmless, SJ, "A Love Supreme: Augustine's 'Jazz' of Theology," *Augustinian Studies* 43 (2012): 149–77 for the engaging analogy of jazz to appreciate Augustine's theological writing style.

3. See Paula Fredriksen, "The *Confessions* as Autobiography," in *A Companion to Augustine*, ed. Mark Vessey (Oxford: Wiley-Blackwell, 2012), 87–98; and Catherine Conybeare, "Reading the *Confessions*," in Vessey, *A Companion to Augustine*, 99–110.

4. Hubertus Drobner, "Studying Augustine: an overview of recent research," in *Augustine and His Critics*, ed. Robert Dodaro, OSA, and George Lawless, OSA (London: Routledge, 2000), 20.

5. Lancel gives a brilliant overview of the intellectual process of composing and the physical labor of writing in late Antiquity (Serge Lancel, *St. Augustine*, trans. Antonia Neville [London: SCM Press, 2002], 213–18). Producing even one *liber* or book of a work was an expensive and laborious matter.

6. Drobner, "Studying Augustine," 20.

7. Kim Paffenroth and Robert Kennedy, eds., *A Reader's Companion to Augustine's Confessions* (Louisville, KY: Westminster John Knox Press, 2003).

8. Joseph C. Schnaubelt, OSA, and Frederick Van Fleteren, eds., *Collectanea Augustiniana* (New York: Peter Lang, 1990).

9. There is also John M. Quinn, OSA, *A Companion to the Confessions of St. Augustine* (New York: Peter Lang, 2002). This is an extensive commentary on the text from the pen of a thorough philosopher. Quinn's frame of reference is ancient Greek philosophy (e.g., the Neo-Platonism that influenced Augustine) and the medieval Christian philosophic-theological synthesis for which Augustine's thought was so formative.

10. Margaret R. Miles, *Desire and Delight: A New Reading of Augustine's Confessions* (New York: Crossroad, 1992; Eugene, OR: Wipf & Stock Publishers, 2006).

11. Miles, *Desire and Delight*, 64.

12. William Mallard, *Language and Love: Introducing Augustine's Religious Thought Through the Confessions Story* (University Park, PA: Pennsylvania State University Press, 1994).

13. See, for example, Augustine, *Confessions*, trans. Gary Wills (New York: Penguin Classics, 2008); and, Shirwood Hirt, trans., *Love*

*Song: A Fresh Translation of Augustine's Confessions* (New York: Harper and Row, 1971).

14. Jaroslav Pelikan, *The Mystery of Continuity: Time and History, Memory and Eternity, in the Thought of St. Augustine* (Charlottesville: University of Virginia Press, 1986). The first four chapters are from Pelikan's Richard Lectures at the University of Virginia. The remaining chapters are from his Hale Lectures at Seabury-Western Theological Seminary.

15. Roland J. Teske, SJ, *Paradoxes of Time in Saint Augustine* (Milwaukee: Marquette University Press, 1996).

16. James J. O'Donnell, *Augustine: Confessions*, 3 vols. (Oxford: Oxford University Press, 1992).

17. Ibid., 1:xxxiii.

18. Ibid., 1:xl.

19. Ibid., 1:li.

20. *Confessions*, trans. Maria Boulding, OSB, *The Works of Saint Augustine: A Translation for the 21st Century* (Hyde Park: New City Press, 1997; study ed., 2012).

21. Augustine, *Confessions*, trans. Henry Chadwick (Oxford: Oxford University Press, 1991/2009).

22. Augustine, *Confessions*, trans. R. S. Pine-Coffin (New York: Penguin, 1961).

23. Augustine, *Confessions*, trans. Frank J. Sheed (New York: Hackett, 1993/2006; New York: Sheed and Ward, 1943/1970).

24. For example, the cultured pagan Volusian of Carthage. See Chadwick, *Augustine of Hippo: A Life* (Oxford: Clarendon, 2009), 128–29; and Peter Brown, *Augustine of Hippo* (Los Angeles: University of California Press, 1967/2000), 298.

25. This is the same Marcellinus who represented Emperor Honorius at the conference of Carthage in 411 that adjudicated the schism between Catholics and Donatists in Africa. To Augustine's great regret, Marcellinus and his brother were executed by the empire on a trumped-up charge of sedition, propagated by the Donatists.

26. Augustine disputes at length with the Roman philosopher and historian Varro, and with the Platonists.

27. Augustine expresses the basic theme of *City of God* in a homily he delivered around the year 410: "The times are evil, the times are troubled, that's what people say. Let us live good lives, and the times are good.

We ourselves are the times; whatever we are like, that's what the times are like" (*Sermon* 80.8).

28. Marrou delivered the St. Augustine Lecture at Villanova University in 1965: "The Resurrection and Saint Augustine's Theology of Human Value" (Villanova, PA: The Augustinian Institute, Villanova University Press 1966). See also his *Theologie de l'histoire* (Paris: Le Seuil, 1968).

29. Dorothy F. Donnelly and Mark A. Sherman, eds., *Augustine's De Civitate Dei: An Annotated Bibliography of Modern Criticism, 1960–1990* (New York: Peter Lang, 1991).

30. Mark Vessey, Karla Pollmann, Allan D. Fitzgerald, OSA, eds., *History, Apocalypse, and the Secular Imagination: New Essays on Augustine's City of God* (Bowling Green, Ohio: Bowling Green State University, Philosophy Documentation Center, 1999).

31. Hubertus R. Drobner mentions several other compendiums of recent research on the *City of God*: Drobner, "Studying Augustine," 21–22.

32. Peter L. Brown, *Augustine of Hippo: A Biography* (Los Angeles: University of California Press, 1967/2000).

33. Peter Brown, *Religion and Society in the Age of Saint Augustine* (London: Faber and Faber, 1972; Eugene, OR: Wipf & Stock Publishers, 2007).

34. See also Peter Brown, *Power and Persuasion in Late Antiquity: Towards a Christian Empire* (Madison, WI: University of Wisconsin Press, 1992). Brown widens the lens through which to view the complexities of social class, imperial politics, and history of the empire in the two centuries after Constantine.

35. Robert A. Markus, *Saeculum: History and Society in the Theology of St. Augustine* (Cambridge: Cambridge University Press, 1970/1988). The 1988 version is a revised edition, with a new introduction.

36. Robert A. Markus, *The End of Ancient Christianity* (Cambridge: Cambridge University Press, 1991); *Sacred and Secular: Studies on Augustine and Latin Christianity* (Aldershot: Variorum, 1994).

37. See also John M. Rist, *Augustine: Ancient Thought Baptized* (Cambridge: Cambridge University Press, 1996).

38. Robert Dodaro, OSA, *Christ and the Just Society in the Thought of Augustine* (Cambridge: Cambridge University Press, 2008). See also Dodaro, "Eloquent Lies, Just Wars and the Politics of Persua-

sion: Reading Augustine's *City of God* in a 'Postmodern' World," *Augustinian Studies* 25 (1994): 77–137.

39. Dodaro, *Christ and the Just Society*, 1.

40. See chapter 6, pages 116–18.

41. Gerard O'Daly, *Augustine's City of God: A Reader's Guide* (Oxford: Oxford University Press, 1999/2004).

42. Ibid., v.

43. James Wetzel, ed., *Augustine's City of God: A Critical Guide*, Cambridge Critical Guides (Cambridge: Cambridge University Press, 2012).

44. Dorothy F. Donnelly, ed., *The City of God: A Collection of Critical Essays* (New York: Peter Lang, 1995).

45. Augustine, *The City of God*, The Works of Saint Augustine II/6, trans. William Babcock, ed. Boniface Ramsey (Hyde Park: New City Press, 2013).

46. Arabella Milbank, *Marginalia*, Journal of the Medieval Reading Group at the University of Cambridge, 16:2011–12. See www.marginalia.co.uk/journal/13cambridge/.

47. Augustine, *City of God*, trans. Marcus Dods, et al. (New York: Hendrickson, 2009).

48. Augustine, *City of God*, trans. Henry Bettenson (New York: Penguin, 1972/1984/2003).

49. Augustine, *The City of God against the Pagans*, ed. and trans. R. W. Dyson (Cambridge, Cambridge University Press: 1998).

50. See also George Lawless, "Augustine of Hippo: an Annotated Reading List," *Listening: Journal of Religion and Culture* 26 (Fall) 1991: 176–78.

51. "At present I do not want to give my attention even to the books of *The Trinity*, which I have had in hand for a long time and have not yet completed, for they involve much work and I think that they can be understood only by a few. Hence, the projects press upon us more insistently that we hope will be beneficial for more people" (*Letter* 169.1.1).

52. Mary T. Clark, "*De Trinitate*" in *The Cambridge Companion to Augustine*, ed. Eleonore Stump and Norman Kretzmann (Cambridge: Cambridge University Press, 2001), 91–102.

53. With regard to Augustine's review of scriptural texts in light of his Catholic faith in the Trinity, see Jaroslav Pelikan, "*Canonica regula*: The Trinitarian Hermeneutics of Augustine," in *Collectanea Augustini-*

*ana: Augustine: "Second Founder of the Faith,"* ed. Joseph C. Schnaubelt, OSA, and Frederick Van Fleteren (New York: Peter Lang, 1990), 329–43.

54. *Cambridge Companion to Augustine*, 99.

55. John Cavadini, "The Structure and Intention of Augustine's *De Trinitate*," *Augustinian Studies* 23 (1992): 103–23.

56. Cavadini's article moves the arguments about the Neo-Platonic strains in Augustine's trinitarian theology to a new level by his elucidation of the apologetic edge of the text of *The Trinity*. See also Lewis O. Ayres, *Augustine and the Trinity* (Cambridge: Cambridge University Press, 2010). Ayres argues against exaggerating the Neo-Platonic themes in Augustine's trinitarian theology. Cavadini strengthens Ayres's argument. See also Lewis Ayres, "Where Does the Trinity Appear: Apologetics and 'Philosophical' Readings of the *De Trinitate*," *Augustinian Studies* 43 (2012): 109–26; and, John Cavadini, "Trinity and Apologetics in the Theology of St. Augustine," *Modern Theology* 29 (2013): 48–82. Another valuable study is Michel Barnes, "Re-Reading Augustine's Theology of the Trinity," in *The Trinity: An Interdisciplinary Symposium on the Trinity*, ed. Stephen T. Davies, Daniel Kendall, and Gerard Collins (New York: Oxford University Press, 1999), 145–76.

57. See chapter 6, pages 116–18.

58. It was unusual at that time in the Western part of the Roman Empire for a priest to preach. See Brown, *Augustine of Hippo*, 140; and Possidius, *The Life of Saint Augustine*, V.3. Valerius's succession planning included having Augustine begin to preach even while the old bishop was still the ordinary of the diocese. Why not let the former imperial *rhetor* employ his skill on behalf of the church, especially since the Greek Valerius spoke heavily accented Latin?

59. "What has Athens to do with Jerusalem?" Tertullian exclaims, "or the Academy with the Church?" in Tertullian, *De praescriptione* VII.9, *Tertulliani Opera*, Corpus Christianorum Series Latina I (Turnhout, Belgium: Brepols, 1954). Notice, however, that Tertullian, in fact, resorts to Athens in framing a rhetorical question, to which his ironic and presumptive response is "nothing." Augustine took a different approach.

60. See Pamela Bright, *The Book of Rules of Tyconius: Its Purpose and Inner Logic* (South Bend, IN: University of Notre Dame Press, 2009). Augustine admired the scriptural hermeneutics of Tyconius. The latter got into some trouble with his Donatist associates because of his approach to scripture.

61. Chadwick, *Augustine of Hippo*, 86, points out that Augustine reprioritizes the purposes of rhetoric as defined by Cicero. The Roman senator and philosopher taught that rhetoric is employed to instruct, to please, and to move or inspire. Augustine reorders the goals of Christian rhetoric in this way: to instruct, to move or inspire, and then to please, if pleasing made the Word more sweet and attractive to the listeners.

62. *Teaching Christianity* was first printed in 1463–65, just twenty years after Gutenberg invented the printing press. See Hubertus Drobner, "Studying Augustine: An Overview of Recent Research" in *Augustine and His Critics—Essays in Honour of Gerald Bonner*, ed. Robert Dodaro, OSA, and George Lawless, OSA (London: Routledge, 2000), 248. See also Chadwick, *Augustine of Hippo*, 82; and Richard Leo Enos, *The Rhetoric of Saint Augustine of Hippo: De Doctrina Christiana and the Search for a Distinctly Christian Rhetoric* (Waco, TX: Baylor University Press, 2008), 318. The first printing of *Confessions* was completed by 1470; and *City of God*, by 1467. The first complete printed edition of Augustine's collected works was published at Basel, Switzerland, in 1506. The oldest manuscript of *Teaching Christianity* may date from the fifth century and the time of Augustine himself—even perhaps from his own library. It is preserved in St. Petersburg.

63. *Saint Augustine: On Christian Teaching*, trans. R. P. H. Green, Oxford World's Classics (Oxford: Oxford University Press, 1997, 1999, 2008).

64. *Teaching Christianity*, trans. Edmund Hill, OP, *Works of Saint Augustine: A Translation for the 21st Century* (Hyde Park: New City Press, 1996).

65. See Roland Teske's remarks on both Green's and Hill's translations in his review in *Journal of Early Christian Studies* 5.3 (1997): 460–62.

66. Duane W. H. Arnold and Pamela Bright, eds., *De doctrina christiana: A Classic of Western Culture*, Christianity and Judaism in Antiquity, 9 (Notre Dame: University of Notre Dame Press, 1995).

67. Edward D. English, ed., *Reading and Wisdom: The De Doctrina Christiana in the Middle Ages* (Notre Dame: University of Notre Dame Press, 1994).

68. He goes on: "I uttered words of my own, interspersed with yours!…those words I uttered were the intimate expression of my mind, as I conversed with myself and addressed myself in your presence" (*Con-*

*fessions* IX.4.8). Augustine's own testimony in *Confessions* recommends his *Expositions of the Psalms* as an immensely important part in understanding his thought and spiritual life.

69. The New City Press series contains six volumes of *Expositions*.

70. For a compelling overview of Augustine's spirituality and Christology as revealed in *Expositions*, see Jean-Louis Chretien's introduction to the French translation of *Ennarationes in Psalmos/Les Commentaires Des Psaumes*, in *Oeuvres de saint augustin*, ed. M. Dulaey (Paris: L'Institut d'Études Augustiniennes, 2009), i–iii. For a complementary explanation of the contexts and techniques of *Expositions*, see Michael Fiedrowicz's introduction in Augustine, *Expositions of the Psalms*, The Works of Saint Augustine III/15, trans. Maria Boulding, OSB, ed. John Rotelle, OSA (Hyde Park: New City Press, 2000). Boulding, who also translated *Confessions* for this series, was a Benedictine hermitess. Her own intense spiritual life complements her background in classics to enrich her deep appreciation of Augustine's writings.

71. *Confessions* itself has been described as an "amplified psalter." See Michael Fiedrowicz's introduction in *Expositions*, 13.

72. Michael Fiedrowicz, *Psalmus Vox Totius Christi: Studien zu Augustins "Ennarrationes in Psalmos"* (Freiburg: Herder, 1997).

73. Augustine, *Expositions of the Psalms*, 13–66. Michael Fiedrowicz makes the very interesting and challenging claim that the three most important works of Augustine are *Confessions*, *City of God*, and *Expositions of the Psalms*.

74. The writings of Augustine that do not contain constant references to the psalms are his more philosophical tracts, e.g., *Answer to the Academics*, *Soliloquies*, *The Magnitude of the Soul*, *Free Will*, *The Nature and Origin of the Human Soul*, and *The Teacher*.

75. For analyses of the content, style, and physical situation of Augustine's preaching, see the introduction by Cardinal Michele Pellegrino in Augustine, *Sermons*, The Works of Saint Augustine III/1, trans. Edmund Hill, OP, ed. John E. Rotelle, OSA (Hyde Park: New City Press, 1990), 13–137; the introduction by Daniel E. Doyle, OSA, in *Saint Augustine: Essential Sermons*, The Works of Saint Augustine, trans. Edmund Hill, OP, ed. Daniel E. Doyle, OSA, and Boniface Ramsey (Hyde Park: New City Press, 2007), 9–22; and, Brown, *Augustine of Hippo*, 240–55.

76. The *Associazione Storico e Culturale di S. Agostino* in Cassago Brianza sponsors and publishes research on St. Augustine and on archeological exploration related to Cassago's claim to be the ancient Cassiciacum. See http://www.cassiciaco.it/.

77. See Catherine Conybeare, *The Irrational Augustine* (Oxford: Oxford University Press, 2006) for a thorough and insightful exegesis of the Cassiciacum Dialogues. She provides fresh, new insight into Monica's surprising role in Part Two: Women Doing Philosophy, 61–138. Conybeare's penetrating and close textual analysis makes her entire book worth several readings.

78. Even here, at the beginning of his Christian life of faith, Augustine affirms the integration of faith and reason.

79. Conybeare, *The Irrational Augustine*, 27–35.

80. Conybeare's argument is that these elements have been overlooked in past analyses of the dialogues.

81. Note Augustine's own language: "The more one uses and cites God's own words from scripture, the less room there is 'for the breath of pride' in one's compositions" (*Confessions* IX.4.8).

82. Pierre Courcelle, *Recherches sur les Confessions de saint Augustin* (Paris: E. DeBoccard, 1950/1968).

83. See, for example, the work of John O'Meara, examined in chapter 6, pages 139–40.

84. For a valuable overview of *The Teacher* in French, see Goulven Maldec, "*Analyse du 'De Magistro*,'" *Revue des études augustiniennes* 21 (1975): 63–71.

## 3. *Writings II: Theological Controversies, Sermons and Letters, and* Revisions

1. See Gerald Bonner, *St. Augustine of Hippo: Life and Controversies* (Norwich, England: The Canterbury Press, 1986; London: SMC Press, Ltd, 1963) for a classic investigation of Augustine's arguments against the Manicheans, Donatists, and Pelagians.

2. For excellent overviews and summaries of Augustine's anti-Manichean ideas and writings, see Roland Teske's introductions and notes in *The Manichean Debate*, ed. Boniface Ramsey, *The Works of Saint Augustine: A Translation for the 21st Century* I/19 (Hyde Park: New City

Press, 2006); and in *Answer To Faustus a Manichean*, ed. Boniface Ramsey, *The Works of Saint Augustine: A Translation for the 21st Century* I/20 (Hyde Park: New City Press, 2007). See also Michael Fiedrowicz's introductions and notes on *On Genesis: Refutation against the Manichees*, ed. John E. Rotelle, OSA, *The Works of Saint Augustine: A Translation for the 21st Century* I/13 (Hyde Park: New City Press, 2002); and in *On Christian Belief*, ed. Boniface Ramsey, *The Works of Saint Augustine: A Translation for the 21st Century* I/8 (Hyde Park: New City Press, 2005).

3. For more overviews of Augustine and Manichaeism, see Kevin J. Coyle, "Saint Augustine's Manichean Legacy," *Augustinian Studies* 34 (2003): 1–22; also, Johannes Van Oort, Otto Wermelinger, and Gregor Wurst, eds., *Augustine and Manichaeism in the Latin West: Proceedings of the Fribourg–Utrecht International Symposium of the International Association for Mission Studies, Nag Hammadi and Manichean Studies* (Leiden: Brill, 2001).

4. See chapter 1, page 7, for how his stay in Milan and the influence of Ambrose introduced Augustine to a figurative or spiritual way of reading scripture.

5. See Fiedrowicz, *On Genesis: Refutation against the Manichees*, 29, n. 15.

6. In his *Revisions* I.15.16, Augustine comments on and elaborates his definitions of *will* and *sin* in *The Two Souls*. The Pelagian writer Julian of Eclanum cited these definitions and used them against Augustine. How could infants suffer from original sin if they do not yet have free will, he asked? Augustine responds to that question in his *Unfinished Work in Answer to Julian*, especially Book V.

7. Jason Beduhn argues that Augustine never ceased being Manichean in his thought. See his controversial *Augustine's Manichean Dilemma, Vol. 1: Conversion and Apostasy, 373–388 CE* (Philadelphia: University of Pennsylvania Press, 2009); and, *Augustine's Manichean Dilemma, Vol. 2: Making a Catholic Self, 388–401 CE* (Philadelphia: University of Pennsylvania Press, 2013).

8. See Nicholas J. Baker-Brian, *Manichaeism: An Ancient Faith Rediscovered* (London: T&T Clark, 2011), and Samuel Live, *Manichaeism in the Later Roman Empire and Medieval China* (Manchester: University of Manchester, 1983; 2nd ed. Tubigen: Mohr, 1992).

9. Translations of the Anti-Donatist works are due to be published in the New City Press series, volume I/21 sometime in 2014.

10. The Maximianists were a sect that had broken with the Donatists in 393 and that were subsequently persecuted by the main Donatist party led by Primian, Donatist bishop of Carthage. Primian did not require rebaptism of the Maximianists upon reconciliation.

11. On this theme, see also *Homilies on the Gospel of John 5:6* where Augustine writes "Baptism, you see, is characterized by the one in whose authority it is conferred, not by the one through whose ministry it is conferred." Augustine's sacramental theology of Baptism drew from the thought of Optatus, Bishop of Milevis. See Alexander Evers, *Church, Cities, and People: A Study of the Plebs in the Church and Cities of Roman Africa in Late Antiquity* (Leuven: Peeters, 2010), the chapter on Optatus.

12. *Letter* 105.5.16.

13. For a splendid survey of the Donatist issue and the conference of Carthage, see Jane E. Merdinger, *Rome and the African Church in the Time of Augustine* (New Haven: Yale University Press, 1997).

14. Among the most important of these letters in which Augustine addresses the Donatist problem from a pastoral point of view are *Letters* 43–44, 76, 87–88, 100, 105, 108, 129, 133–34.

15. For a different perspective on Augustine's goals, see Brent Shaw, *Sacred Violence: African Christians and Sectarian Hatred in the Age of Augustine* (Cambridge: Cambridge University Press, 2011).

16. Serge Lancel, *St. Augustine*, trans. Antonia Neville (London: SCM Press, 2002), 271–305. For a close study of the economic forces, see Leslie Dossey, *Peasant and Empire in Christian North Africa* (Berkeley: University of California Press, 2010).

17. Lancel, a foremost authority on Roman North Africa and the Donatist controversy ends his treatment of Donatism with: "Augustine was not the father of Augustinianisms, nor was he responsible for Torquemada" (*St. Augustine*, 304). See also Peter Brown's "St. Augustine's Attitude to Religious Coercion," in his *Religion and Society in the Age of Saint Augustine* (Eugene, OR: Wipf and Stock, 2007), 237–59.

18. A classic though now dated treatment of the social, political, and economic aspects of Donatism is W. H. C. Frend, *The Donatist Church: A Movement of Protest In Roman North Africa* (Oxford: Oxford University Press, 1951/2003). A more recent study is Mark A. Handley, "Disputing the end of African Christianity," in A. N. Merrills, ed., *Vandals, Romans, and Berbers: New Perspectives on Late Antique North Africa* (Aldershot: Ashgate, 2004), 291–310.

19. Frend, *The Donatist Church*, 2.

20. New research into Donatism continues; for example *The Uniquely African Controversy: Studies on Donatist Christianity*, Matthew Alan Gaumer, Anthony Dupont, and Mathijs Lamberigts, eds. (Leuven: Peeters, forthcoming).

21. The New City Press volumes (I/23 and I/24) containing the Anti-Pelagian works are translated by Roland J. Teske, SJ, whose introductions and notes provide valuable explanations and commentaries.

22. See Carol Harrison, *Re-thinking Augustine's Early Works: An Argument for Continuity* (Oxford: Oxford University Press, 2005). Harrison stresses the continuity in the development of Augustine's theology of grace over the years.

23. These words of Augustine have been simplified over the years into the phrase attributed to him: *Roma locuta est; causa finita est*— Rome has spoken; the case is closed. The relationship between the North African episcopacy and the Roman episcopacy in the fifth century was a complex one. See Merdinger, *Rome and the African Church in the Time of Augustine*, chapters 7—9; Frend, *The Donatist Church*, 297.

24. For example, the Second Council of Orange (529) affirmed Augustine's theology of grace, without accepting his ideas on predestination. See chapter 4, pages 77–80.

25. For another look at Pelagius's thought, see Brinley Roderick Rees, *Pelagius: Life and Letters* (Rochester, NY: Boydell, 2004); and Mathijs Lamberigts, "Pelagius and Pelagians," in *The Oxford Handbook of Early Christian Studies*, ed. Susan Ashbrook Harvey and David G. Hunter (Oxford: Oxford University Press, 2008), 258–79.

26. *Pelagius's Commentary on St Paul's Epistle to the Romans*, trans. Theodore de Bruyn, Oxford Early Christian Studies (Oxford: Clarenden Press, 1993/2003).

27. The Gallic monks John Cassian (360–435) and Faustus of Riez (405–90) are most often associated with semi-Pelagian positions. See A. M. C. Casiday, *Tradition and Theology in St. John Cassian*, Oxford Early Christian Study Series (Oxford: Oxford University Press, 2007).

28. For a thorough treatment of Caesarius, see William Klingshirn, *Caesarius of Arles: Life Testament, Letters* (Liverpool: Liverpool University Press, 1994).

29. See *Sermons* 117, 126, 135, 139–40, 183, 229N, 341, and 330.

30. See *Homilies on the Gospel of John* 18, 20, 26; *Expositions of the Psalms* 52.6.

31. Augustine also responded to other Christological heresies such as Apollonarianism (Christ did not have a human mind or soul) and to many other heresies. See his *Heresies*, written in 428 or 429, in which he provides an extensive list of eighty-eight different Christian heresies from the time of the New Testament onward.

32. Peter Brown, *Augustine of Hippo: A Biography* (Los Angeles, University of California Press, 1967/2000), 444.

33. Cardinal Michele Pellegrino provides a valuable introduction to the manner in which Augustine prepared, delivered, and preserved his liturgical homilies. See Augustine, *Sermons*, The Works of Saint Augustine III/1, trans. Edmund Hill, ed. John Rotelle, OSA (Hyde Park: New City Press, 1990). For further information on the nature of the sermons, see Augustine, *Essential Sermons*, The Works of Saint Augustine, trans. Edmund Hill, OP, ed. Daniel E. Doyle, OSA, and Boniface Ramsey (Hyde Park: New City Press, 2007).

34. The eleven volumes present the sermons not chronologically, but by general topic area: sermons on the Old Testament, the New Testament, the Saints, the Liturgical Seasons, and various topics, and the twenty-six sermons newly discovered by Francois Dolbeau in 1990.

35. Augustine, *Sermons*, The Works of Saint Augustine III/1, trans. Edmund Hill, OP, ed. John E. Rotelle, OSA (Hyde Park: New City Press, 1990), 164 (translator's note).

36. Hill cites Augustine's comments in *On Christian Instruction* on how to preach and teach.

37. In Augustine's day, the congregation stood throughout the liturgical celebration, including the homily, while the bishop preached seated in his *cathedra*, the chair of his episcopal office.

38. As of this date, only *Homilies* 1 to 40 on John's Gospel have been translated for the New City Press translation series (vol. III/12), while translations of all ten homilies on John's First Letter are complete (vol. III/14). The two titles *Sermons* and *Homilies* are equivalent. The NCP editors decided to use *sermons* to approximate the Latin *sermones*, which is the title used in the manuscript tradition. *Homilies* is used to translate *tractates* or tractates, found in the manuscript tradition for Augustine's Johannine commentaries.

39. D. J. Milweski, "Augustine's 124 Tractates on the Gospel of John: the *Status Quaestionis* and the State of Neglect," *Augustinian Studies* 33/1 (2002): 61–77.

40. François Dolbeau, *Vingt-six sermons au people* (Paris: Études augustiniennes, 1996).

41. Isabella Schiller, Dorothea Weber, and Clemens Weidmann, *Zeitschrift für Klassische Philologie und Patristik und Lateinische Tradition, Wiener Studien*, vol. 121 (2008): *Sermones Erfurt* 1, 5, and 6; vol. 122 (2009): *Sermones Erfurt* 2, 3, and 4. These letters have not yet been translated into English in the New City Press series.

42. Jennifer Ebbeler, *Disciplining Christians: Correction and Community in Augustine's Letters*, Oxford Studies in Late Antiquity (Oxford: Oxford University Press, 2012).

43. Catherine Conybeare, "Spaces Between Letters: Augustine's Correspondence with Women," in *Voices in Dialogue: Reading Women in the Middle Ages*, ed. Linda Olsen and Kathryn Kerby-Fulton (South Bend, IN: University of Notre Dame Press, 2005), 57–72.

44. Mark Vessey, "Reponse to Catherine Conybeare: Women of Letters?" in *Voices in Dialogue: Reading Women in the Middle Ages*, 73–96.

45. Joanne McWilliam, "Augustine's Letters to Women," in *Feminist Interpretations of Augustine*, ed. Judith Chelius Stark, Re-reading the Canon Series (University Park, PA: Penn State University Press, 2007), 189–202. McWilliam provides brief commentaries on letters 92, 99, 124–26, 130, 147, 150, 188, 208, 210–11, and 263.

46. E. Ann Matter, "*De cura feminarum*: Augustine the Bishop, North African Women, and the Development of a Theology of Female Nature," *Feminist Interpretations of Augustine*, 203–214.

47. Brown, *Augustine of Hippo*, 446.

48. Ibid.

49. Ibid.

50. Ibid., 470.

51. Ibid., 492.

52. *The Works of Saint Augustine: A Translation for the 21st Century* translates *Retractationes* as *Revisions*.

53. When Augustine was writing *Revisions*, he never got to a review of his sermons or letters. Upon finishing the review of his books, he turned to the fray of the Pelagian controversy and to a response to

Julian of Eclanum's latest attack. So the sermons are not as easily chronicled as the rest of his works. See A. M. La Bonnardière, "*Recherches de chronologie augustiniennes,*" *Revue des études augustiniennes* 10 (1965): 165–77.

54. No less an authority on the political, social, and religious history of North Africa than Serge Lancel gives his analysis of the fate of Augustine's own library in Hippo: "Yet there is no lack of indications that allow us to propose—without proof, but with strong probability—that the very complete knowledge of Augustine's works to be found in Italy in the second half of the fifth century did not come from copies of these writings that had been circulated overseas only partially before the bishop's death, but was due to their transportation to Rome in their entirety and their inclusion in the collection of the apostolic library in the middle of the fifth century, under conditions and by means of which, it is true, remain mysterious, if not miraculous" (Lancel, *Saint Augustine*, 476).

55. For theories about the fate of Augustine's remains, see Harold S. Stone, "Cult of Augustine's Body," in *Augustine Through the Ages, An Encyclopedia*, ed. Allan D. Fitzgerald, OSA (Grand Rapids, MI: Wm. B. Eerdmans, 1999), 256–59. For thorough research about the state of the North African Church and of Augustine's monastic disciples after the Vandal and Arab invasions, see Luis Marin de San Martin, OSA, *The Augustinians: Origins and Spirituality*, trans. Brian Lowery, OSA (Rome: Curia Generale Agostiniana, 2013), 43–73.

56. Kenneth B. Steinhauser, "Manuscripts," in *Augustine Through the Ages, An Encyclopedia*, ed. Allan D. Fitzgerald, OSA (Grand Rapids, MI: Wm. B. Eerdmans, 1999), 525–33.

### 4. Legacy I: Middle Ages and Renaissance

1. Alfred North Whitehead wrote that all of philosophy is but "a series of footnotes to Plato." See Whitehead, *Process and Reality*, (New York: Free Press, 1987), 39. Michael Scanlon suggests a parallel: all of theology is "a long footnote to Augustine." See Michael J. Scanlon, OSA, "The Augustinian Tradition: A Retrieval," *Augustinian Studies* 20 (1989): 62.

2. Scanlon, "The Augustinian Tradition: A Retrieval," 61.

3. Willemien Otten and Karla Pollmann, eds., *Oxford Guide to the Historical Reception of Augustine* (New York: Oxford University

Press, USA, 2013). See Pollmann's general introduction, "The Proteanism of Authority: The reception of Augustine from his death to the present," in OGHRA, 1:3–14.

4. This explains how toward the end of his life he was able to write *Revisions*, the careful review of all his books. It is very possible that Possidius's *Indiculum* or Index of Augustine's books was a catalogue of the bishop's writings kept in the monastery library at Hippo. See Erika Hermanowicz, *Possidius of Calma: A Study of the North African Episcopate in the Age of Augustine* (Oxford: Oxford University Press, 2008), 56–65.

5. Sometimes the process of copying and distributing manuscripts got beyond his control, as when copies of *The Trinity* were distributed before he had finished work on the text (*Letter* 174).

6. Serge Lancel, *St. Augustine*, trans. Antonia Neville (London: SCM Press, 2002), 476. For a new and thorough study of the ecclesial situation in North Africa after the Vandal and Arab invasions, see Luis Marin de San Martin, OSA, trans. Brian Lowery, OSA, *The Augustinians: Origin and Spirituality* (Roma: Curia Generale Agostiniana, 2013).

7. M. F. W. Stone, "Augustine and medieval philosophy," in *The Cambridge Companion to Augustine*, ed. Eleonore Stump and Norman Kretzmann (Cambridge: Cambridge University Press, 2001), 255–56.

8. P. F. Gehl, "An Augustinian Catechism in Fourteenth Century Tuscany: Prosper's Epigrammatica," *Augustinian Studies* 19 (1985): 93–110. The *Epigrammatica*, distinct from his *Sententiae*, is a collection of Augustinian *floralegia* compiled by Prosper.

9. See Kenneth B. Steinhauser, "Manuscripts," in *Augustine Through the Ages, An Encyclopedia*, ed. Allan D. Fitzgerald, OSA (Grand Rapids, MI: Wm. B. Eerdmans, 1999), 525–33 for an overview of the manuscript tradition.

10. Migne's *Patrologia Latina* edition of Augustine's writings is readily available at www.augustinus.it, a Web project of the Italian Augustinian Friars at Tolentino.

11. See *Letter* 225, which Prosper wrote to Augustine in 428 or 429. About the same time a layman in Gaul by the name of Hillary also wrote to Augustine about Pelagian sympathies in the monasteries of Gaul. In their letters to Augustine, both men comment on the controversy over Augustine's ideas about predestination. These letters were more than likely the motivation for Augustine to write two of his last books *The Predestination of the Saints* and *The Gift of Perseverance*.

12. The designation "semi-Pelagian" was first applied to the thinking of John Cassian and Faustus of Riez in the late sixteenth century amidst the theologies and controversies of the Reformation and Counter Reformation. Contemporary scholars are wary of the designation. Cassian and Faustus were in no way supportive of what came to be identified as Pelagian theology. See R. A. Markus, "The Legacy of Pelagius: Orthodoxy, Heresy, and Conciliation," in *The Making of Orthodoxy: Essays in Honour of Henry Chadwick*, ed. R. D. Williams (Cambridge: Cambridge University Press, 1989), 214–34.

13. This Hillary is different from the layman by the same name who had written to Augustine.

14. See R. W. Mathison, "For Specialists Only: the Reception of Augustine and His Theology in Fifth Century Gaul," in *Collecteana Augustiniana, Vol. 2: Augustine, Presbyter Factus Sum*, ed. J. T. Lienhard, E. C. Muller, and R. J. Teske (New York: Peter Lang, 1993). Prosper later became secretary to Pope Leo the Great and continued to write and preach about the theme of God's will for universal salvation.

15. This was the Second Council to be held at Orange. The First Council of Orange (441) had dealt with ecclesial discipline and the strengthening of the church in Gaul. In so doing, it strengthened the reputation and influence of the monastery at Lerins.

16. This condemnation of reprobation appears in the summary or concluding paragraphs, after the list of twenty-five canons of the council.

17. It is interesting to note that *Confessions* is written just after Augustine finishes his *Response to Simplician* in which he first elaborates his theology of grace. *Confessions* is Augustine's personal case study of his experience of totally unmerited divine grace.

18. Gerald Bonner, *Augustine of Hippo: Life and Controversies* (London: SCM Press, 1963; Norwich: Canterbury Press, 1986), 392. See also Gerald Bonner, "Augustine and Pelagianism," *Augustinian Studies* 24 (1993): 27–47, for Bonner's slightly more sympathetic reading of predestination.

19. See James Wetzel, "Snares of Truth: Augustine on free will and predestination," in *Augustine and His Critics: Essays in Honour of Gerald Bonner*, ed. Robert Dodaro, OSA, and George Lawless, OSA (London: Routledge, 2000), 124–41, esp. 125; also, Wetzel, "Predestination, Pelagianism, and Foreknowledge," in Eleonore Stump and Norman Kretzmann, eds. *The Cambridge Companion to Augustine* (Cambridge:

Cambridge University Press, 2001), 49–58; and, Wetzel, *Augustine and the Limits of Virtue* (Cambridge: Cambridge University Press, 1992). See also Eleonore Stump, "Augustine on free will," in *The Cambridge Companion*, 124–47.

20. See W. E. Klingshirn, *Caesarius of Arles: The Making of a Christian Community in Late Antique Gaul* (Cambridge: Cambridge University Press, 1994).

21. In his *Life of St. Augustine*, Possidius tells us that the epitaph on Augustine's tomb, which he himself had approved, read "Traveler, would you know how a poet, dead, lives on? When you read, I speak, and your voice is mine" (*Life of St. Augustine*, 31.8). In Caesarius's sermons, which took whole passages from Augustine's own sermons, the Bishop of Hippo's voice continues speaking through the Bishop of Arles and the many other clerics who made use of Caesarius's homiletic texts.

22. Norman Kretzmann, "Faith Seeks, Understanding Finds: Augustine's Charter for Christian Philosophy," in *Christian Philosophy*, ed. T. P. Flint (South Bend: University of Notre Dame Press, 1990), 1–36.

23. In his *Proslogion*, Anselm writes: "I long to understand in some degree your truth, which my heart believes and loves. For I do not seek to understand that I may believe, that I believe in order to understand. For this also I believe, that unless I believed, I should not understand" (chap. I). Note that Anselm does not offer the phrase *fides quaerens intellectum* as a definition of *theology* as such, since he would not have used that word. It is rather a description of what he saw happening in faith at study. Anselm's "faith seeking understanding" also echoes Augustine's comments on the relationship between faith and understanding in *Homilies on the First Epistle of John* 29.6 (on John 7:14–18).

24. Stone, "Augustine and medieval philosophy," 254–55.

25. For insights into Medieval receptions and appraisals of Augustine's ideas, see Willemien Otten, "Between Praise and Appraisal: Medieval Guidelines for the Assessment of Augustine's Intellectual Legacy," *Augustinian Studies* 43 (2012): 201–18.

26. The first of the new universities was at Bologna in 1088. The university at Paris coalesces from various monastic schools in 1119. See Walter Ruegg, "Forward. The University as a European Institution," in *A History of the University in Europe: Volume 1, Universities in the Middle Ages*, gen. ed. Walter Ruegg and ed. Hilde De Ridder-Symoens (Cambridge: Cambridge University Press, 1992/2003), xix–xxi.

27. The four books of Lombard's *Sententiae* were devoted to God, humanity, Christ, and the sacraments and eschatology. This division, itself influenced by the major themes in Augustine's writings, outlined the curriculum for the study of theology in the universities of the time.

28. The West had remained familiar with Aristotle's work on logic, upon which Boethius had commented, and with his categories, which Augustine had studied when he was in Carthage (*Confessions* IV.16.28). But this was a rather limited awareness of Aristotle's total corpus.

29. See Richard Rubenstein, *Aristotle's Children: How Christians, Muslims, and Jews Rediscovered Ancient Wisdom and Illuminated the Middle Ages* (New York: Houghton-Mifflin-Harcourt, 2003). Rubenstein writes in a popular, accessible style. His bibliography provides valuable resources for this period in history.

30. For a very accessible introduction to the thought of St. Thomas, see Francis Selman, *Aquinas 101: A Basic Introduction to the Thought of Saint Thomas Aquinas*, Christian Classics-Notre Dame, Indiana (South Bend, IN: Ave Maria Press, 2007).

31. It continues still. See the section on the Second Vatican Council and differing "Augustinian" and "Thomistic" interpretations of its teachings in chapter 5, pages 101–4.

32. For a new, reliable source on the Order of St. Augustine, see Luis Marin de San Martin, OSA, trans. Brian Lowery, OSA, *The Augustinians: Origin and Spirituality* (Roma: Curia Generale Agostiniana, 2013). For the history of the Rule of St. Augustine, see George Lawless, OSA, *Augustine of Hippo and His Monastic Rule* (New York: Oxford University Press, USA, 1990); Adolar Zumkeller, OSA, *Augustine's Rule: A Commentary* (Villanova, PA: Augustinian Press, 1987); and, Sr. Agatha Mary, SBP and Gerald Bonner, trans., Gerald Bonner, ed., *The Monastic Rules of Augustine: A Commentary*, The Augustine Series (Hyde Park, NY: New City Press, 2004). Throughout the Early Middle Ages, many of the canons, that is, the priests and deacons who were part of the bishop's household and his cathedral's liturgy adopted the Rule of Saint Augustine for their common life. The order known at the Canons Regular of Saint Augustine was well established by the twelfth century and so predates the mendicant order of Augustinian Friars.

33. Voluntarism is a very broad philosophical concept that is used to characterize the thought of many thinkers over the centuries. How-

ever, its origins are in the different emphases between Augustine and Thomas on the will and intellect.

34. For the most complete list and description of medieval Augustinian scholars who were members of the Augustinian Order, see Adolar Zumkeller, OSA, and John E. Rotelle, OSA, ed., *Theology and History of the Augustinian Order in the Middle Ages*, The Augustinian Series (Villanova, PA: Augustinian Press, 1996).

35. Stone, "Augustine and medieval philosophy," 256–57. Stone mentions that Bonaventure was familiar with the works of Avicenna and Averoes as well as with Aristotle.

36. "Introduction" to Giles of Rome, in *Theorems on Existence and Essence, Medieval Philosophical Texts in Translation*, 7, trans. M. V. Murray (Milwaukee: Marquette University Press, 1973).

37. M. Wilks, *The Problem of Sovereignty in the Later Middle Ages* (Cambridge: Cambridge University Press, 1964).

38. Adolar Zumkeller, OSA, "*Die Augustinerschule des Mittelalters: Vertreter und philosophische-theologische Lehre,*" *Analecta Augustiniania* (1964) 27: 167–262. Also, Zumkeller and Rotelle, ed., *Theology and History of the Augustinian Order in the Middle Ages*.

39. Augustinian theologians generally "advocated a primacy of the will, a primacy of grace, and a primacy of love. The will and not the intellect, was the basis of the innate human desire to see God. In addition, the Augustinian theologians were unified in defining theology as "affective knowledge" (*scientia/notita affectiva*), as distinct from "speculative knowledge." In E. L. Saak, "Scholaticism, Late," in *Augustine Through the Ages, An Encyclopedia*, ed. Allan D. Fitzgerald, OSA (Grand Rapids, MI: Eerdmans, 1999), 754–59.

40. Stone, "Augustine and medieval philosophy," 261.

41. Though the Order of Saint Augustine was founded in 1244 as part of the mendicant movement, reforms of the order arose in subsequent centuries. Thus certain religious houses of Augustinians were of stricter observance, and were called monasteries and the brothers were called monks, distinguishing them from the more active communities of friars. The Augustinian monastery in Erfurt was part of the German federation of strict observance.

42. Damasus Trapp, "*Adnotationes,*" *Augustinianum* 5 (1965): 150. I am indebted to Stone, "Augustine and medieval philosophy," 263 for citing this helpful quote.

43. A valuable overview of Augustine's influence on the early Renaissance is P. O. Kristeller, "Augustine and the Early Renaissance," in *Studies in Renaissance Thought and Letters* (Rome: Edizioni di Storia e Letteratura, 1956). See also William Bouwsman, "Two Faces of Humanism: Stoicism and Augustinianism in Renaissance Thought," in *A Usable Past: Essays in European Cultural History* (Berkeley: University of California Press, 1990), 45. A stoic approach to humanism starts from the cosmos; an Augustinian approach starts from the human being.

44. See Carol Everhart Quillen, *Rereading the Renaissance: Petrarch, Augustine, and the Language of Humanism, Recentiores*: Later Latin Texts and Context (Ann Arbor, MI: University of Michigan Press, 1998).

45. Carol Everhart Quillen, "Plundering the Egyptians: Petrarch and Augustine's *De Doctrina Christiana*," in *Reading and Wisdom: The 'De doctrina christiana' of Augustine in the Middle Ages*, ed. Edward D. English (South Bend, IN: University of Notre Dame Press, 1995), 153–71.

46. Kristeller, "Augustine and the Early Renaissance," 369ff.

47. H. Lawrence Bond, "Mystical Theology," in *Introducing Nicholas of Cusa: A Guide to a Renaissance Man*, ed. Christopher M. Bellitto, Thomas M. Izbicki, and Gerald Christianson (Mahwah, NJ: Paulist Press, 2004), 218–19. See also Philip Carey, *Augustine's Invention of the Inner Self: the Legacy of a Christian Platonist* (Oxford: Oxford University Press, 2000) for a compelling study of Augustine's philosophical and spiritual notion of the self that any Renaissance humanist such as Nicholas would find most agreeable.

48. John Monfasani, "Humanism," in *Augustine Through the Ages: An Encyclopedia*, ed. Allan D. Fitzgerald, OSA (Grand Rapids, MI: Wm. B. Eerdmans, 1999), 714–15. See Augustine's *Sermon* 52: "So what are we to say about God? If you have fully grasped what you want to say, it isn't God. If you have been able to comprehend it, you have comprehended something else instead of God" (52.16).

49. John Monfasani, "Humanism," 715. Monfasani notes that Erasmus took exception to Augustine's strong anti-Pelagian theology and its emphasis on the weakness of the human will. From a literary point of view Erasmus preferred Jerome, the great linguist of Christian Antiquity.

50. Carol Quillen, "Renaissance to the Enlightenment," in *Augustine Through the Ages: An Encyclopedia*, ed. Allan D. Fitzgerald, OSA (Grand Rapids, MI: Wm. B. Eerdmans, 1999), 718.

## 5. Legacy II: Reformation to Today

1. One thinks of the calls for reform by the Dominican Friar of Florence Girolamo Savonarola, who challenged his fellow citizens to bring their Renaissance "vanities" of art, jewelry, and other valuable artifacts to the regular bonfires he lit around the city. Savanarola himself eventually suffered the same fiery fate of those "vanities."

2. See D. C. Steinmetz, *Misericordia Dei: The Theology of Johannes von Staupitz in Its Late Medieval Setting* (Leiden: Brill, 1968).

3. In his *De Servo Arbitrio*, Luther expounds his own teaching on predestination, adopting Augustine's approach, emphasizing that we are saved exclusively by the grace of Christ, not by divine foreknowledge or decision.

4. J. Fitzer, "The Augustinian Roots of Calvin's Eucharistic Theology," *Augustinian Studies* 7 (1976): 69–98, esp. 69–72; also, A. N. S. Lane, "Calvin's Use of the Fathers and the Medievals," *Calvin Theological Journal* 16 (1981): 149–205.

5. This teaching of double predestination or reprobation was, as we saw in chapter 4, explicitly rejected by the Second Council of Orange.

6. For two other Augustinian texts on this theme, see *The Nature and Origin of the Human Soul* (4.16.11) and *Homilies on the Gospel of John* (48.4).

7. Vittorino Grossi, OSA, "*La giustificatione secondo Girolamo Seripando nel contesto dei dibattiti tridentini,*" *Analecta Augustiniana* 41 (1978): 5–24; "*L'auctoritas di Agostino nella dottrina del 'peccatum originis' da Cartagine* (418) *a Trento* (1546)," *Augustinianum* 31 (1991): 329–60.

8. Vittorino Grossi, "Trent, Council of," *Augustine Through the Ages: An Encyclopedia*, ed. Allan D. Fitzgerald, OSA (Grand Rapids, MI: Wm. B. Eerdmans, 1999), 843–45.

9. Council of Trent, "Decree on Justification," chap. 1 in *Decrees of the Ecumenical Councils*, ed. Norman P. Tanner, SJ (Georgetown: Georgetown University Press, 1990), 671.

10. Council of Trent, "Decree on Justification", chaps. 7 and 9, 673–74.

11. Though Trent does not cite this particular quote from Augustine, his words on the Trinity capture Trent's meaning: "Let me remem-

ber you, know you, and love you. Increase these gifts in me until you have reformed me completely" (*The Trinity* 14.17.23).

12. Council of Trent, "Decree on Justification", chap. 7, 673.

13. Ibid., chap. 12, 676.

14. "Philip Schaff once mused that had Augustine lived in the sixteenth century, 'he might have gone half way with the Reformers,' but that, in the end, because of his concern for the unity of the visible church and, we may add, for the philosophical, mystical, and speculative themes not adopted by the Protestant theology, he 'would have become the leader of an evangelical school...with the Roman Church.'" Cited in Richard A. Muller, "Reformation, Augustinianism in the," in Fitzgerald, *Augustine Through the Ages*, 707. Original citation in Philip Schaff, *History of the Christian Church*, vol. 8, *Modern Christianity: the Swiss Reformation*, 3rd ed. (Grand Rapids, MI: Wm. B. Eerdmans Publishing 1910/1979), 541.

15. Gareth B. Matthews, "Post-medieval Augustinianism," in *The Cambridge Companion to Augustine*, ed. Eleonore Stump and Norman Kretzmann (Cambridge: Cambridge University Press, 2001), 267–79.

16. For a treatment of Augustinianism in Descartes, see Stephen Menn, *Descartes and Augustine* (Cambridge: Cambridge University Press, 1998), 130–208.

17. For an extensive psychological and neurological critique of Cartesian thought, see Antonio Dimasio, *Descartes' Error* (New York: Putman, 1994/2005).

18. The brilliance of Pascal is reflected in his comfort with the inner life as well as his mathematical and scientific writings. In that sense his whole intellectual project combines the subjectivity of the Neo-Platonic Augustinian synthesis with the scientific objectivity of the Aristotelian-Thomistic synthesis.

19. M. Lamberigts and L. Kenis, eds., *L'augustinisme a l'ancienne Faculte de theologie de Louvain*, *BETL 111* (Louvain: University of Louvain, 1994); Mathijs Lamberigts, "Jansenius," in Fitzgerald, *Augustine Through the Ages*, 459–60.

20. Giovanni Morreto, "Schleiermacher und Augustinus," in *Internationaler Schleiermacher Kongress* (Berlin: W. de Gruyter, 1984), 365–80.

21. Jules Ruy Chaix, "Maurice Blondel et saint Augustin," *Revue des ètudes augustiniennes* 11: 55–84; Aime Forest, "L'augustinisme de

Maurice Blondel," *Sciences ecclesiastiques*, 14 (1962), 175–93; Michael Scanlon, OSA, "Karl Rahner: A Neo-Augustinian Thomist," *The Thomist* 43 (1979), 178–85.

22. Michael Scanlon, "The Augustinian Tradition: A Retrieval," *Augustinian Studies* 20 (1989): 61–92. See also Fredercik Van Fleteren, ed., *Martin Heidegger's Interpretations of Augustine: Sein und Zeit und Ewigkeit* (Lewiston, ME: The Edwin Mellen Press, 2005.) Sean J. McGrath also explores Augustine's influence on Heidegger in "Alternative Confessions, Conflicting Faiths: A Review of *The Influence of Augustine on Heidegger*," *American Catholic Philosophical Quarterly*, 82, #2, (2008), 317–35, in which he provides a helpful review of Craig de Paulo, ed., *The Influence of Augustine on Heidegger* (Lewiston, NY: Edwin Mellen Press, 2006).

23. See Michael Scanlon, OSA, "Theology, Modern," in Fitzgerald, *Augustine Through the Ages*, 825–26 for a succinct, compelling overview of the subject.

24. See Scanlon, "The Augustinian Tradition: A Retrieval," and "Theology, Modern."

25. Jean Guitton, *The Modernity of St. Augustine* (Baltimore: Helicon Press, 1959), 81, quoted in Scanlon, "The Augustinian Tradition: a Retrieval," 82.

26. Scanlon, "The Augustinian Tradition: a Retrieval," 72: "In no way, however, is pessimistic predestinationism essential to the notion of prevenient grace." Scanlon's opinion here differs from that of Wetzel, who believes that predestination is essential to an Augustinian understanding of grace.

27. Karl Rahner, *Foundations of Christian Faith* (New York: Seabury Press, 1978), 116–37.

28. See Scanlon, "The Augustinian Tradition: a Retrieval," 80–86.

29. For example, in *Letter* 10*.2.3, Augustine describes how when he was out of town his people back home in Hippo redeemed—literally bought back—women and children who had been captured for slavery by pirates. He applauds their work and meets with survivors of this trauma upon his return to Hippo. For an excellent summary of Augustine's ethical teachings, see Donald X. Burt, OSA, *Friendship and Society: An Introduction to Augustine's Practical Philosophy* (Grand Rapids, MI: Wm. B. Eerdmans, 1999). See also Secretariat for Justice and Peace, Curia Generalizia Agostiniana, "Augustine as 'Father of Christian Politi-

cal Activism,'" (Rome: Pubblicazioni Agostiniane, 2004). This publication of the Order of Saint Augustine elaborates the thesis that contemporary Christian theologies of justice and peace, that is, for the redemption of history, can be traced to various aspects of Augustine's thought.

30. John J. Hugo, "St. Augustine at Vatican II," *The Homiletic and Pastoral Review* 67 (1966): 765–72; Mariano Martin Ortega, "The Augustinian Charism and Vatican II" in *Augustinian Spirituality and the Charism of the Augustinians* (Villanova, PA: Augustinian Press, 1995), 140–53.

31. Joseph Ratzinger, *Popolo e Casa di Dio in Sant'Agostino* (Milano; Jaca Book SpA, 1978/2005); also, *Volk und Haus Gottes in Augustins Lehre von der Kirche* (München: Karl Zink Verlag, 1954).

32. Massimo Faggioli, *Vatican II: The Battle for Meaning* (Mahwah, NJ: Paulist Press, 2012), 66–90.

33. In his defense, Faggioli touches on this integration, but only lightly. See Faggioli, *Vatican II: The Battle for Meaning*, 89–90.

34. Faggioli, *Vatican II the Battle for Meaning*, 75, quoting Ormond Rush, *Still Interpreting Vatican II: Some Hermeneutical Principles* (Mahwah, NJ: Paulist Press, 2004), 16.

35. For an overview of Augustinian themes among the writings of contemporary philosophers, see Francois-Joseph Thonnard, "*Saint Augustine et les grands courants de la philosophie contemporaine,*" *Revue des études augustiniennes* 1 (1955): 68–80.

36. "When people called an object by some name, and while saying the word pointed to that thing, I watched and remembered that they used that sound when they wanted to indicate that thing. Their intention was clear, for they used bodily gestures, those natural words which are common to all races, such as facial expressions or glances of the eyes or movements of other parts of the body, or a tone of voice that suggested some particular attitude to things they sought and wished to hold on to, or rejected and shunned altogether. In this way I gradually built up a collection of words, observing them as they were used in the proper places in different sentences and hearing them frequently. I came to understand which things they signified, and by schooling my own mouth to utter them I declared my wishes by using the same signs" (*Confessions* I.8.13).

37. Ludwig Wittgenstein, *Philosophical Investigations*, trans. GEM Anscombe, ed. P.M.S. Hacker, Joachim Schulte; Hacker, Schulte (Oxford: Blackwell, 1951, 1958, 2001, 2009), 5, §1.

38. For a presentation and critique of Wittgenstein's take on Augustine, see Patrick Bearsley, "Augustine and Wittgenstein on Language," *Philosophy* 58 (1983): 229–36.

39. Derrida himself notes the parallels between his life and Augustine's, including the important role that their mothers played in their lives. See Jacques Derrida, "Composing Circumfession," in *Augustine and Postmodernism: Confession and Circumfession*, ed. John D. Caputo and Michael J. Scanlon, OSA, Indiana Series in the Philosophy of Religion (Bloomington, IN: Indiana University Press, 2005), 19–27.

40. See Caputo and Scanlon, *Augustine and Postmodernism* for an overview of these contemporary conversations.

41. Jacques Derrida and trans. Geoffrey Bennington, *Jacques Derrida*, Religion and Postmodernism Series, ed. Mark C. Taylor (Chicago: University of Chicago Press, 1999).

42. Jean-François Lyotard, *The Confession of St. Augustine*, trans. Richard Beardsworth, Cultural Memory in the Present (Stanford, CA: Stanford University Press, 2000).

43. Martin Heidegger, *The Phenomenology of Religious Life*, trans. Jennifer Anna Gosetti-Ferencei and Matthias Fritsch (Bloomington, IN: Indiana University Press, 1995/2004); Theodore Kisiel, *The Genesis of Heidegger's Being and Time* (Berkeley: University of California Press, 1995), 192–219.

44. Hannah Arendt, *Love and Saint Augustine*, ed. Joanna Vechiarelli Scott and Judith Chelius Stark (Chicago: University of Chicago Press, 1996). See also Peter Burnell, "Is the Augustinian Heaven Inhuman? The Arguments of Martin Heidegger and Hannah Arendt," *Augustinian Studies* 30:2 (1999): 283–92.

45. Paul Ricoeur, *Time and Narrative*, vol. 1, trans., Kathleen McLaughlin and David Pelauer (Chicago: University of Chicago Press, 1984/1990); vol. 2 (1985); vol. 3, trans. Kathleen Blamey and David Pelauer (1988/1990).

46. For an overview of Augustine and a twentieth-century study of rhetoric, see Kenneth Burke, *The Rhetoric of Religion: Studies in Logology* (Los Angeles: University of California Press, 1961/1970).

47. See Scanlon, "The Augustinian Tradition: A Retrieval," 89–92.

## 6. New Directions in Recent Research

1. See Laura Holt, "Augustine in Review," *The Heythrop Journal* 46 (2005): 199–207; "A Survey of Recent Work on Augustine," *The Heythrop Journal* 49 (2007): 292–308; "What Are They For? Reading Recent Books on Augustine," *The Heythrop Journal* 54 (2013): 101–19.

2. Hubertus R. Drobner, "Studying Augustine: An Overview of Recent Research," in *Augustine and His Critics*, ed. Robert Dodaro, OSA, and George Lawless, OSA (London: Routledge, 2000), 18–34.

3. Allan D. Fitzgerald, OSA, "Tracing the Passage from a Doctrinal to an Historical Approach to the Study of Augustine," *Revue des études augustiniennes et patristiques*, 50 (2004): 295–310.

4. For example, Girolamo Seripando, OSA (1493–1563), an influential theologian at the Council of Trent. See chapter 5.

5. For a careful study of the rise of Biblical Studies, see Michael C. Legaspi, *The Death of Scripture and the Rise of Biblical Studies*, Oxford Studies in Historical Theology (Oxford: Oxford University Press, 2010).

6. For a new study of Augustine's exegesis, see Michael Cameron, *Christ Meets Me Everywhere: Augustine's Early Figurative Exegesis*, Oxford Studies in Historical Theology (Oxford: Oxford University Press, 2012). Augustine himself encouraged prayerful study of Sacred Scripture in seeking the meaning of a text. In Books XI, XII, and XIII of *Confessions*, which are an extended commentary on the first chapter of Genesis, Augustine alludes to the possibility and importance of a multiplicity of meanings in the text: those of the human author, of the reader, and of the divine author. The reader should be open to all these meanings and seek them out by attention to the authors—human and divine—of the text (*Confessions* XII.18.27—32.43). In *Teaching Christianity*, Augustine makes the argument that the Liberal Arts should be pursued in order to come to deeper understandings of the books of scripture by studying the natural world and social settings in which scriptural authors wrote. Augustine's exegesis is not the same as contemporary scriptural exegeses, but his sensitivity to the many layers of meaning in the text is a methodological precursor to contemporary exegesis.

7. Fitzgerald, "Tracing the Passage," 297.

8. For a review of the development of method in Patristics, see Charles Kannengiesser, "Fifty Years of Patristics," *Theological Studies* 50/4 (1989): 633–56.

9. See Peter Brown, *Augustine of Hippo*, 484, 488, 495, 502–3.

10. As Cameron points out, Augustine uses passages from scripture to interpret the meanings of the events in his own life and invites his readers to make similar use of those passages to discover the meanings of their own experience. See Cameron, *Christ Meets Me Everywhere*, 15–16.

11. Gadamer warns the reader of historical texts to be "aware of one's own bias, so that the text can present itself in all its otherness and thus assert its own truth against one's own fore-meanings." Hans-Georg Gadamer, *Wahrheit und Methode. Grundzuge einer philosophischen Hermeneutick* (Tübingen, 1960, 1986) *Gesammelte Werke, Volume 1*, 269, as found in Jean Grondin, *Introduction to Philosophical Hermeneutics*, trans. Joel Weinsheimer, Yale Studies in Hermeneutics (New Haven, CT: Yale University Press, 1996). See Grondin, pages 32–38 on Augustine's important place in the history of philosophical hermeneutics.

12. Robert Dodaro, OSA, "Augustine's Secular City," in Dodaro and Lawless, *Augustine and His Critics*, 231–59. William Connolly, *The Augustinian Imperative: A Reflection on the Politics of Morality* (Newbury Park, CA: Sage Publications, 1993).

13. Dodaro, "Augustine's Secular City," 250.

14. George Lawless, OSA, "Augustine of Hippo: An Annotated Reading List," *Listening: Journal of Religion and Culture* 26 (Fall 1991): 173–88.

15. Ibid., 176.

16. Ibid.

17. Robert Markus, in remarking on the growing interdisciplinary nature of Augustine Studies, and Patristic Studies in general, wrote that Augustine scholars from many disciplines now focus on "intersecting, overlapping interests in which all these could converge, even coalesce." (Robert A. Markus, "Evolving Disciplinary Contexts for the Study of Augustine, 1950–2000: Some Personal Reflections," *Augustinian Studies* 32/2 [2001]: 189–200). However, Lawless is suggesting that this convergence or coalescence has a way to go, particularly in the arena of theological studies on Augustine.

18. Hubertus R. Drobner, "Studying Augustine: An Overview of Recent Research," in *Augustine and His Critics*, 30.

19. Pierre Marie Hombert, *Gloria gratiae. Se glorifier en Dieu, principe et fin de la theologie augustinienne de la grace, Collection des études augustiniennes* (Paris: Institut d'Études augustiniennes, 1996), 488.

20. See, for example, *Sermon* 189.3,4, preached on Christmas around 410–12.

21. It is also interesting to note that the Western Christian affirmation that the Holy Spirit proceeds from the Father and the Son (*filioque*), unacceptable to Eastern Christians, is found in *The Trinity* IV.5.29 where Augustine is affirming the equality of the three persons: "Nor, by the way, can we say that the Holy Spirit does not proceed from the Son as well; it is not without point that the same Spirit is called the Spirit of the Father and of the Son." Augustine further develops this idea of the double procession in *The Trinity* V.15.

22. Hubertus R. Drobner, "Studying Augustine," 29.

23. Ibid.

24. Michael Cameron, *Christ Meets Me Everywhere*, 12.

25. Goulven Madec, "*Christus scientia et sapientia nostra: Le principe de coherence de la doctrine augustinienne*," *Recherches Augustiniennes* 10 (1975): 77–85.

26. See Fitzgerald's chapter on the role of Christ in Augustine's thought in the forthcoming *Cambridge Companion to Augustine*, 2nd ed., ed. David Vincent Meconi and Eleonore Stump (Cambridge: Cambridge University Press, 2014).

27. Basil Studer, OSB, *The Grace of Christ and the Grace of God in Augustine of Hippo: Christocentrism or Theocentrism?*, trans. Michael O'Connell (New York: Michael Glazier, 1997).

28. Goulven Madec, AA, "*Christus*" in *Augustinus-Lexikon*, vol. 1, ed. Cornelius P. Mayer, OSA, and Erich Feldmann (Basel: Schwabe, 1987), cc. 845–908.

29. Volumes III/15 to III/20.

30. In *Confessions* IX.8, writing about his postconversion and prebaptismal retreat at Cassiciacum, he says: "How loudly I began to cry out to you in those psalms, how I was inflamed by them with love for you and fired to recite them to the whole world, were I able, as a remedy against human pride!"

31. We will look shortly at contemporary studies of Augustine's scriptural hermeneutics.

32. This reinterpretation of Hebrew Scripture by Christians leads to the question of supersessionism, or the replacement of the "old covenant" by the Christian "new covenant." See C. C. Peckhold, "Theo-Semiotics and Augustine's Hermeneutical Jew: Or, What's a Little Super-

sessionism Among Friends?," *Augustinian Studies* 37/1 (2006): 27–42. For an extensive and probing analysis of Augustine's relationship with the Jewish faith and community see Paula Fredrikson, *Augustine and the Jews: A Christian Defense of Jews and Judaism* (New Haven: Yale University Press, 2008/2010). See also the reviews of Fredrikson's book by Sabrina Inowlocki, Phillip Cary, and Elena Procario-Foley in *Augustinian Studies* 40:2 (2009): 279–99.

33. See Tarcisius Van Bavel, OSA, *Christians in the World* (New York: Catholic Book Publishing Company, 1980), chap. 7: "Pauline and Patristic Teaching on the Body of Christ"; also, Hubertus Drobner, "Psalm 21 in Augustine's *Sermones ad populum: Catecheses on Christus totus and rules of interpretation*," *Augustinian Studies* 37/2 (2006): 145–69.

34. Romans 12; Corinthians 10, 12.

35. Van Bavel asserts that Augustine develops the Pauline metaphor of the Body of Christ further than any other Patristic writer, and that this Body of Christ/Total Christ theology falls fallow after Augustine. Van Bavel, *Christians in the World*, 80–81.

36. Pierre Marie Hombert, "*Gloria gratiae*," 488.

37. *On Genesis Against the Manicheans* (388–90), *Unfinished Literal Commentary on Genesis* (393–94), *The Literal Meaning of Genesis* (401–15), *Observations on the Heptateuch* (419), *Questions on the Heptateuch* (419), *Notes on Job* (399), *Unfinished Commentary on the Letter to the Romans* (394–95), *Exposition on Certain Questions in the Letter to the Romans* (394), *Exposition on the Letter to the Galatians* (394–95), *Questions on the Gospels* (399–400), *Agreement among of the Evangelists* (399–400), *The Sermon on the Mount* (393–96), *Homilies on the Gospel of John* (406–21), and *Homilies on the First Epistle of John* (406–7); there is also the late *The Mirror of Scripture* (427).

38. In these three books of *Confessions*, Augustine writes about 8,000 words on the first seventeen words of Genesis! These books of *Confessions* might be best understood and read as a grounding of his experience in the scriptures about creation, more than an actual "commentary" on Genesis 1.

39. Lancel says that Augustine probably had a decent reading knowledge of Greek, with a dictionary. But his ability to read and perhaps speak some Greek was limited, especially considering his mastery of Latin literature and rhetoric. See Lancel, *St. Augustine*, 16.

40. Drobner, "Studying Augustine," 24.

41. Anne-Marie La Bonnardière, *Saint Augustin et la Bible, Bible de tous les temps* (Paris: Beauchense, 1986). See also her *Biblia Augustiniana*, 7 fascicles (Paris: Études augustiniennes, 1960–75) for the impressive compilation of her extensive work on Augustine's use of the Bible. La Bonnardière's work is continued by James W. Wiles, *A Scripture Index to the Work of St. Augustine in English Translation* (Lanham, MD: University Press of America, 1995).

42. Drobner, "Studying Augustine," 24. Add to this the fact that there were, in addition to the *Vetus Latina*, an "endless variety" of variations on specific Latin texts as Augustine himself writes in *Teaching Christianity* II.11.16, and one gets a sense of the magnitude of La Bonnardière's accomplishment.

43. *Teaching Christianity* I.11—21. As we have already noted, Michael Cameron emphasizes the centrality of Christ in Augustine's reading and interpreting the Bible. In *Christ Meets Me Everywhere*, Cameron explores Augustine's exegesis and the role of Christ in his exegesis, in the writing on scripture he did from his conversion in 386 up to the year 400.

44. See *The Trinity* II. I. 2. In the first seven books of *The Trinity*, Augustine brings passages of Sacred Scripture into dialogue with the Catholic teaching of the Trinity. He argues how canonical doctrine helps the reader of Sacred Scripture to interpret and so understand the deeper meanings of the texts in light of Catholic faith in the equality of Father, Son, and Holy Spirit. See Jaroslav Pelikan, "*Canonica Regula*: The Trinitarian Hermeneutics of Augustine" in *Collectanea Augustiniana*, ed. Joseph C. Schnaubelt, OSA, and Frederick Van Fleteren (New York: Peter Lang, 1990), 329–43.

45. He presents and to an extent critiques Tyconius's rules in Book III of *Teaching Christianity*. Augustine makes full use of Tyconius's rules in his *Expositions on the Psalms*.

46. Pamela Bright, *The Book of Rules of Tyconius: Its Purpose and Inner Logic* (Notre Dame, IN: University of Notre Dame Press, 1989/2009).

47. Kenneth B. Steinhauser, *The Apocalypse Commentary of Tyconius: A History of Its Reception and Influence*, European University Studies, series xxiii, Theology, vol. 301 (Frankfurt: Peter Lang, 1987).

48. *Teaching Christianity* III.5.9. See also Augustine, *The Literal Meaning of Genesis* XII.1.1—2.5. In Augustine's many writings on the Book of Genesis, he struggles with and explores the process of understanding the literal (or historical or proper) sense of the text, while at the same time allowing allegorical (or figurative, symbolic, or hidden) interpretations to emerge.

49. David Dawson, "Sign Theory, Allegorical Reading, and the Motions of the Soul in *De Doctrina Christiana*," in *De Doctrina Christiana: A Classic of Western Culture*, ed. Duane W. H. Arnold and Pamela Bright (South Bend, IN, University of Notre Dame Press, 1995), 123–41. This text contains essays by many leading Augustine scholars, including Van Fleteren, Bright, Markus, Teske, Babcock, Cavadini, Patout Burns, and others.

50. John Rist, *Augustine: Ancient Thought Baptized* (Cambridge: Cambridge University Press, 1995), 23–40.

51. Robert Markus, *Signs and Meanings: Word and Text in Ancient Christianity* (Liverpool: Liverpool University Press, 1996).

52. Brian Stock, *Augustine the Reader: Meditation, Self-Knowledge, and the Ethics of Interpretation* (Cambridge, MA: Belknap Press of Harvard University Press, 1996).

53. "But what am I loving when I love you? Not beauty of body nor transient grace, not this fair light which is now so friendly to my eyes, not melodious song in all its lovely harmonies, not the sweet fragrance of flowers or ointments or spices, not manna or honey, not limbs that draw me to carnal embrace: none of these do I love when I love my God. And yet I do love a kind of light, a kind of voice, a certain fragrance, a food and an embrace, when I love my God: a light, voice, fragrance, food and embrace for my inmost self, where something limited to no place shines into my mind, where something not snatched away by passing time sings for me, where something no breath blows away yields to me its scent, where there is savor undiminished by famished eating, and where I am clasped in a union from which no satiety can tear me away. This is what I love when I love my God" (*Confessions* X.6.8).

54. Tarcisius Van Bavel, "The Double Face of Love in Augustine," *Augustinian Studies* 17 (1986): 169–81. See also in the same volume W. Schoedel's critique of Van Bavel's article, "Augustine on Love: A Response," 183–85.

55. Raymond Canning, *The Unity of Love for God and Neighbour in St. Augustine* (Heverlee-Leuven: Augustinian Historical Institute, 1993).

56. Canning recalls that Matthew 25:40 reads: "And the King will answer them, 'Truly, I say to you, as you did it to one of the least of these my brethren, you did it to me.'" Verse 45 reads: "Then he will answer them, 'Truly, I say to you, as you did it not to one of the least of these, you did it not to me.'" Canning comments on Augustine's use of Matthew 25:40 and 45: "Of the more than ninety explicit and implicit references related to [Matt 25:] v. 40, 45, no fewer than 76 are met in homilies, and the majority of these in the *Ennarationes in psalmos*. Augustine's explicit use of v. 40, 45 is most concentrated in his preaching both at Hippo and at Carthage during the years 410–413 [as refugees from the fall of Rome are flooding into North Africa]. But v. 40, 45 and/or directly related verses…occur in his works at every stage." (Canning, *The Unity of Love*, 342).

57. *Teaching Christianity* I.3.3, 4.4, 22.20, 31.34, 32.35.

58. See O. O'Donovan, "*Usus* and *Fruitio* in Augustine, De Doctrina Christiana I,*" *Journal of Theological Studies*, new series, 33/2 (1982): 361–97; W. R. O'Connor, "The *uti/frui* Distinction in Augustine's Éthics," *Augustinian Studies* 14 (1983): 169–81.

59. Drobner, "Studying Augustine," 25. See also Rowan Williams, "Language, Reality and Desire in Augustine's *De doctrina*," *Literature and Theology* 3/2 (1989): 138–50; and, Luc Verheijen, "*Le premier livre du De Doctrina Christiana d'Augustin: Un traite de 'telicologie' biblique*," in *Augustiniana Traiectina*, ed. J. den Boeft and J. van Oort (Paris: Études Augustiniennes, 1987), 169–87.

60. See Tarcisius Van Bavel, "*Fruitio, delectatio*, and *voluptas* in Augustine," *Augustinus*, 38 (1993): 499–510. The *frui/uti* distinction draws from Stoic and Neo-Platonic thought.

61. Van Bavel's book *The Longing of the Heart: Augustine's Doctrine on Prayer* (Leuven: Peeters, 2009) is a posthumous publication that offers the reader delightful experience of Van Bavel's lifelong research and writing on Augustine.

62. J. Patout Burns, *The Development of Augustine's Doctrine of Operative Grace* (Paris: Études augustiniennes, 1980).

63. Agostino Trapé, OSA, *Agostino: Introduzione alla Dottrina della Grazia I: Natura e grazia* (Roma: Citta Nuova, 1987); *Vol. II: Grazia*

*e liberta* (Roma: Citta Nuova, 1990); and Rebecca Harden Weaver, *Divine Grace and Human Agency: A Study of the Semi-Pelagian Controversy* (Washington, DC: The Catholic University of America Press, 1996).

64. Basil Studer, OSB, "*Sacramentum et exemplum chez saint Augustin*," *Recherches augustiniennes* 10 (1975): 87–141; Joanne McWilliam, "The Christology of the Pelagian Controversy," *Studia Patristica*: Papers presented at the Tenth International Conference on Patristic Studies in Oxford 1979, vol. 17:3, ed. E. Livingstone (Leuven: Peeters, 1982), 1221–44; Robert Dodaro, OSA, "*Sacramentum Christi*: Augustine on the Christology of Pelagius," *Studia Patristica*: Papers presented at the Eleventh International Conference on Patristic Studies in Oxford 1991, vol. 27, ed. E. Livingston (Leuven: Peeters, 1993), 274–80.

65. Dodaro, "*Sacramentum Christi*," 488.

66. For recent work on these topics, see James Wetzel, *Augustine and the Limits of Virtue* (Cambridge: Cambridge University Press, 2008); and, "Predestination, Pelagianism, and Foreknowledge," in *The Cambridge Companion to Augustine*, ed. Eleonore Stump and Norman Kreutzmann (Cambridge: Cambridge University Press, 2001), 49–58.

67. Elaine Pagels, *Adam, Eve, and the Serpent* (New York: Random House, 1988); Rosemary Radford Reuther, *Sexism and God Talk: Toward a Feminist Theology* (Boston: Beacon Press, 1983).

68. Peter Brown, *The Body and Society: Men, Women, and Sexual Renunciation in Early Christianity: Twentieth Anniversary Edition with a New Introduction* (New York: Columbia University Press, 2008), xxiv.

69. For another historical study, see *Women in Late Antiquity— Pagan and Christian Lifestyles* by Gillian Clark (Oxford: Clarendon Press, 1993).

70. Judith Chelius Stark, ed. *Feminist Interpretations of Augustine*, Re-reading the Canon Series (University Park, PA: Penn State University Press, 2007). Contributors to this volume include Rosemary Radford Reuther, Anne-Marie Bowery, Felicia McDuffie, Virginia Burrus and Catherine Keller, Rebecca Moore, Margaret Miles, Joanne McWilliam, Ann E. Matter, Julius Chelius Stark, Julie B. Miller, Penelope Deutscher, and Ann Conrad Lammers.

71. Kari Elizabeth Borresen, ed., *The Image of God: Gender Models In Judaeo-Christian Tradition* (Minneapolis: Augsburg Fortress Publishers, 1995). Contributors include Borresen herself (the introduction and two essays), Phyllis A. Bird, Anders Hultgard, Lone Fatum, Giulia

Sfameni Gasparro, Kari Vogt, Jane Dempsey Douglass, and Rosemary Radford Reuther.

72. See *The Trinity* XII.7.10 for an example of Augustine's exegesis of Genesis 1:27. For an expansive study of sacred text, context, and hermeneutics, see Willemien Otten, "Views on Women in Early Christianity: Incarnational Hermeneutics on Tertullian and Augustine," in *Hermeneutics, Scriptural Politics, and Human Rights: Between Text and Context*, ed. Bas de Gaay Fortman, Kurt Martens, M. A. Mohammed Salih (New York: Palgrave Macmillan, 2009).

73. Kari Elizabeth Borresen, "God's Image: Is Woman Excluded. Medieval Interpretation of Gen 1,27 and I Cor 11,7", in Borresen, *The Image of God*, 210–35. See also Borresen, "In Defence of Augustine: How Feminine Is *Homo*?" in *Collecteana Augustiniana*, ed. B Bruning, M. Lamberigts, J. VanHoutem (Leuven: Augustinian Historical Institute, 1990), 411–28; Borresen, "Patristic Feminism: The Case of Augustine," *Augustinian Studies* 25 (1994): 139–52; and, Borresen, *Subordination and Equivalence: The Nature and Role of Woman in Augustine and Thomas Aquinas*, trans. Charles Talbot (Washington, DC: University Press of America, 1981).

74. On the social level, Augustine considered the subordination of women to men in society to be a result of original sin, and something that will not exist in heaven. See *The Literal Meaning of Genesis* IX.6.10; *City of God* XXII.17—18; *Expositions of the Psalms* 188.2. See also Larissa Carina Seelbach, "Augustine on Concubinage and Women's Dignity" *Studia Patristica* XLIII (2007), 245–49.

75. Rosemary Radford Reuther, "*Imago Dei*: Christian Tradition and Feminist Hermeneutics" in Borresen, *The Image of God*, 267–91. Margaret Miles provides a feminist critique of *Confessions* in her *Desire and Delight: a New Reading of Augustine's Confessions* (New York: CITY Crossroad, 1992; Eugene, OR: Wipf & Stock Publishers, 2006). See also her *Carnal Knowing: Female Nakedness and Religious Meaning in the Christian West* (Boston: Beacon Press, 1989). Another extensive and detailed study of Augustine's writings on women is Kim Power's *Veiled Desire: Augustine's Writings on Women* (London: Darton, Longman and Todd, 1995).

76. Augustine, *Marriage and Virginity*, *The Works of Saint Augustine, A Translations for the 21st Century*, I/9, trans. David Hunter, ed. John E. Rotelle, OSA (Hyde Park: New City Press, 2005). This volume

contains translations of Augustine's *The Excellence of Marriage, Holy Virginity, The Excellence of Widowhood, Adulterous Marriages,* and *Continence.* See also David Hunter, *Marriage in the Early Church* (Eugene, OR: Wipf and Stock, 2001).

77. David Hunter, "'Augustinian Pessimism': A New Look at Augustine's Teaching on Sex, Marriage, and Celibacy," *Augustinian Studies* 25 (1994): 153–77. See also his "Augustine on the Body," in *A Companion to Augustine,* ed. Mark Vessey, Blackwell Companions to the Ancient World (Oxford: Blackwell Publishing, 2012), 355–64.

78. Tarcisius Van Bavel, "Augustine's View on Women," *Augustiniana* 39 (1989): 5–53.

## 7. Meeting Augustine Anew: New Studies of His Life and Other Resources

1. Henry Chadwick, *Augustine of Hippo: A Life* (Oxford: Oxford University Press, 2009), 1.

2. See Frances Young, "The Confessions of St. Augustine: What Is the Genre of This Work?" *Augustinian Studies* 30:1 (1999): 1–16.

3. See, for example, Peter Brown and Geoffrey Barraclough, *The World of Late Antiquity AD 150–750* (New York: W. W. Norton, 1989).

4. Possidius, *The Life of Saint Augustine,* The Augustine Series, trans. Michele Cardinal Pellegrino, ed. John E. Rotelle, OSA (Villanova, PA: Augustinian Press: 1988). See esp. the Introduction, 22–27, for Pellegrino's analysis.

5. Erika Hermanowicz, *Possidius of Calama: A Study of the North African Episcopate in the Age of Augustine* (Oxford: Oxford University Press, 2008). See also Jane E. Merdinger, *Rome and the African Church in the Time of Augustine* (New Haven, CT: Yale University Press, 1997).

6. In his historical method, Tillemont is heir to the work of Cesare Cardinal Baronius (1538–1607), who wrote the first modern, extensive *Annals of Ecclesiastical History* based on a return to the sources.

7. Louis-Sebastien Le Nain de Tillemont, *The Life of Augustine, Part One: Childhood to Episcopal Consecration, a Translation of Memoirs pour servir a l'histoire ecclesiastique des six permeirs siecles,* vol. XIII, trans. Frederick Van Fleteren and George Berthold (New York: Peter

Lang, 2010); and *The Life of Augustine, Part Two: The Donatist Contro-versy, A Translation of Memoirs pour servir a l'histoire ecclesiastique des six permeirs siecles,* vol. XIII, trans. Frederick Van Fleteren (New York: Peter Lang, 2012). Van Fleteren provides a very helpful introduction and supplies extensive annotation.

8. John J. O'Meara, *The Young Augustine: The Growth of St. Augustine's Mind Up to His Conversion* (London: Longman, 1954; New York: Alba House, 1965/2001). The 1965 and 2001 editions have updated bibliographies.

9. Pierre Courcelle, *Recherches sur les Confessions de Saint Augustin* (Paris: E. De Boccard, 1950/1968). This work was the first extensive analysis of *Confessions* in many centuries.

10. Augustine takes Plotinus's *Enneads* to read in his sickbed shortly before his death. See Peter L. Brown, *Augustine of Hippo: A Biography* (Los Angeles: University of California Press, 1967/2000), 430.

11. "It cannot be without significance either that in his account in the *Confessions* of his comparison of the Scriptures with the Neo-Platonist books, the memory of the later seizing of St. Paul seems to have influenced him when he wrote: 'Therefore (*itaque*) most avidly did I seize (*arripui*) that venerable writing of Your Spirit; and chiefly the Apostle Paul'" (7:27, italics in original). O'Meara, *The Young Augustine*, 193. Augustine never reports "seizing" the Books of the Platonists.

12. See the memorial tribute to O'Meara by Frederick Van Fleteren, "In Memory of John J. O'Meara 1915–2003," *Augustinian Studies* 35:1 (2004): 2–42. This article contains a complete bibliography of O'Meara's writings. There is also the Festschrift in his honor *From Augustine to Eriugena: Essays on Neoplatonism and Christianity in Honor of John O'Meara,* ed. F. X. Martin, OSA, and J. A. Richmond (Washington, DC: Catholic University of America Press, 1991). Roland Teske, SJ, has also written extensively on the role of Neo-Platonism in Augustine's thought. He concentrates on the influence of Plotinus on Augustine. See two collections of his essays: *Augustine of Hippo: Philosopher, Exegete, and Theologian* (Milwaukee: Marquette University Press, 2009); and *To Know God and the Soul: Essays on the Thought of St. Augustine* (Washington, DC: The Catholic University of America Press, 2008). Robert J. O'Connell, SJ, favors Courcelle's approach. See his *The Origin of the Soul in St. Augustine's Later Works* (New York: Fordham University Press, 1987); and *St. Augustine's Confessions: The Odyssey of the Soul* (New

York: Fordham University Press, 1989). For another insight into this debate, see Philip Carey, "Saint Augustine and the Fall of the Soul: Beyond O'Connell and His Critics," *Augustinian Studies* 37/2 (2006): 292–95.

13. Frederic van der Meer's *Augustine the Bishop* (London: Sheed and Ward, 1961) appeared seven years after the first edition of O'Meara's biography. It takes up the story of Augustine's life at his ordination. Van der Meer's text focuses mostly on the worship, preaching, and piety of the church in Hippo with Augustine as its leader. It does not enjoy the benefit of later twentieth-century studies in the history of North Africa society and religion. Van der Meer also evaluates Augustine's teaching as foundational for the later scholastic theology of the Middle Ages, without parsing the uniqueness of his thought and ministry in his own time and culture. The book is intriguing but dated. A more recent insight into Augustine's monastic life and episcopal ministry is found in Luc Verheijen, OSA, *Saint Augustine: Monk, Priest, Bishop* (Villanova, PA: Augustinian Historical Institute, Villanova University Press, 1978).

14. Peter Brown, *Augustine of Hippo: A Biography* (Los Angeles, University of California Press, 1967/2000).

15. Henry Chadwick critiques Brown's work as a "biography without theology" in *Augustine of Hippo: A Life*, 120. Brown agrees: see Brown, *Augustine of Hippo*, 495.

16. See chapter 3.

17. Brown, *Augustine of Hippo*, 488.

18. Gerald Bonner, *St. Augustine of Hippo: Life and Controversies* (Norwich, England: The Canterbury Press, 1986; London: SMC Press, Ltd, 1963).

19. His 1970 Saint Augustine Lecture at Villanova University was entitled "Augustine and Pelagius in the Light of Modern Research" (Villanova, PA: Augustinian Institute, Villanova University Press, 1972); see also, "Rufinus of Syria and African Pelagianism," *Augustinian Studies* 1 (1970): 31–47; "Pelagianism and Augustine, Part I," *Augustinian Studies* 23 (1992): 33–51; "Pelagianism and Augustine, Part II," *Augustinian Studies* 24 (1993): 27–47.

20. The Catholic University of America also appreciated Bonner's approach to Augustine and named him distinguished professor from 1991 to 1994.

21. See also Gerald Bonner, *Freedom and Necessity: St. Augustine's Teaching on Divine Power and Human Freedom* (Washington, DC: The Catholic University of America Press, 2007); Gerald Bonner and Boniface Ramsey, eds., *Monastic Rules of St. Augustine* (New York: New City Press, 2004). There is a select biography of Bonner's works in the Festschrift in his honor by Robert Dodaro, OSA, and George Lawless, OSA, eds., *Augustine and His Critics* (London: Routledge, 2000).

22. Chapter 2, pages 25–26.

23. Henry Chadwick, *Augustine: A Very Short Introduction* (Oxford: Oxford University Press, 1986/2001).

24. Chadwick provides a synthesis of Courcelle's and O'Meara's opposing views regarding Augustine's conversion to Neo-Platonism or to Christianity: "It was momentous that he [Augustine] brought together Plotinus' negative, impersonal language about the One or Absolute and the biblical concept of God as love, power, justice and forgiveness" (Chadwick, *Augustine of Hippo*, 33).

25. Henry Chadwick, *Augustine of Hippo: A Life* (Oxford: Oxford University Press, 2009).

26. Ibid., ix.

27. Ibid., 65ff.

28. Ibid., 57.

29. The definition of *theology* as "faith seeking understanding" is usually attributed to St. Anselm of Canterbury. But the inspiration for Anselm's formulation is found in Augustine's *Sermon* 43.9: "Understand, in order to believe; believe, in order to understand." The importance Augustine put on thoughtful, informed faith is clear: "The very act of believing is nothing other than to think with assent. Not everyone, after all, who thinks believes, for many think in order not to believe. But everyone who believes thinks, and a believer thinks when believing and, in thinking, believes...for, without thinking, there is not faith at all" (*On The Predestination of the Saints* 2.5).

30. Miles Hollingworth, *St. Augustine of Hippo, An Intellectual Biography* (Oxford: Oxford University Press, 2013); *The Pilgrim City: St. Augustine of Hippo and his Innovation in Political Thought* (London: T&T Clark International, 2010).

31. Serge Lancel, *Saint Augustin* (Paris: Librairie Artheme Fayard, 1999).

32. Serge Lancel, *St. Augustine*, trans. Antonia Neville (London: SCM Press, 2002).

33. For a review of the French edition of Lancel's biography, see Eugene TeSelle, *Augustinian Studies* 31/2 (2000): 267–76.

34. Goulven Madec, *Portrait de saint Augustin* (Paris: Desclee de Brouwer, 2008).

35. Thomas F. Martin, OSA, *Augustine of Hippo: Faithful Servant, Spiritual Leader*, ed. Allan D. Fitzgerald, OSA (New York: Prentice Hall, 2011).

36. George Lawless, OSA, *Augustine of Hippo and his Monastic Rule* (Oxford: Clarendon Press, 1987); *The Monastic Rules of Augustine: A Commentary*, ed. Gerald Bonner, trans. Sr. Agatha Mary, SBP, and Gerald Bonner, The Augustine Series (Hyde Park, NY: New City Press, 2004); Adolar Zumkeller, OSA, *Augustine's Rule: A Commentary* (Villanova, PA: The Augustinian Historical Institute, Augustinian Press, 1987).

37. See Philip Cary, *Augustine's Invention of the Inner Self* (Oxford: Oxford University Press, 2003) for an exploration of this topic.

38. James O'Donnell, *Augustine: A New Biography* (New York: Harper, 2006).

39. Frederick Van Fleteren in *Augustinian Studies* 36:2 (2005): 447–52.

40. Garry Wills, *Saint Augustine: A Life* (New York: Penguin Books, 2005).

41. George Lawless, OSA, in *Augustinian Studies* 31:2 (2000): 243–53.

42. Formerly *Revue des études augustiniennes* (1955–2002). See www.patristique.org.

43. Formerly *The Second Century*.

44. Jonathan P. Yates assumed the editor's role in 2013. See Michael Cameron's tribute to Fitzgerald in *Augustinian Studies* 43 (2012): 3–4.

45. *Augustine Through the Ages: An Encyclopedia*, Allan Fitzgerald, OSA, ed. (Grand Rapids, MI: Wm. B. Eerdmans, 1999/2009).

46. Willemien Otten and Karla Pollmann, eds., *Oxford Guide to the Historical Reception of Augustine* (New York: Oxford University Press, USA, 2013). See Pollmann's general introduction, "The Proteanism of Authority: The reception of Augustine from his death to the present," in *OGHRA*, 1:3–14.

47. William Harmless, SJ, *Augustine in His Own Words* (Washington, DC: The Catholic University of America Press, 2010).

48. William Harmless, SJ, *Desert Christians: An Introduction to the Literature of Early Monasticism* (Oxford: Oxford University Press, 2004); *Augustine and the Catechumenate* (Collegeville, MN: Liturgical Press, 1995); see also his excellent study *Mystics* (Oxford: Oxford University Press, 2007).

49. Mary T. Clark, RCSJ, *Augustine of Hippo: Selected Writings, Classics of Western Spirituality* (Mahwah, NJ: Paulist Press, 1984).

50. Vernon J. Bourke, *The Essential Augustine* (Indianapolis: Hackett Publishing, 1964/1974).

51. Joseph T. Kelley, *Saint Augustine of Hippo: Selections from Confessions and Other Essential Writings* (Rutland, VT: SkyLight Publications, 2010).

52. Augustine, *Selected Writings on Grace and Pelagianism*, trans. Roland Teske, SJ, ed. John E. Rotelle, OSA (Hyde Park: New City Press, 2011), with introduction and notes by Roland Teske, SJ. This volume contains *Miscellany of Questions in Response to Simplician, The Punishment and Forgiveness of Sins and the Baptism of Little Ones, The Spirit and the Letter, Nature and Grace, The Predestination of the Saints, The Gift of Perseverance.*

53. Augustine, *Trilogy on Faith and Happiness*, trans. Roland Teske, SJ, ed. Boniface Ramsey (Hyde Park: New City Press, 2010), with notes and introduction by Roland Teske, SJ. This volume contains *The Happy Life, The Advantage of Believing*, and *Faith in the Unseen.*

54. *The Monastic Rules of Augustine: A Commentary*, ed. Gerald Bonner (Hyde Park: New City Press, 2004).

55. Augustine, *Essential Sermons*, trans. Edmund Hill, OP, ed. Daniel E. Doyle, OSA, and Boniface Ramsey (Hyde Park: New City Press, 2007), with an introduction by Daniel Doyle, OSA. This volume draws together in one place major sermons of Augustine from among the over 550 sermons published in eleven volumes in the New City Press series.

56. Augustine, *Prayers from the Confessions*, trans. Maria Boulding, OSB, ed. John E. Rotelle, OSA (Hyde Park: New City Press, 2003), with a forward by John E. Rotelle, OSA.

57. See, for example, E. M. Atkins and Robert Dodaro, OSA, eds., *Augustine: Political Writings* (Cambridge: Cambridge University Press,

2001); J. H. S. Burleigh, ed., *Augustine: Early Writings* (Philadelphia: Westminster Press, 1953); John Burnaby, ed., *Augustine: Later Writings* (Philadelphia: Westminster Press, 1955).

58. John Doody, Kevin L. Hughes, and Kim Paffenroth, eds., *Augustine and Politics* (Lanham, MD: Lexington Books, 2005); Robert P. Kennedy, Kim Paffenroth, and John Doody, eds., *Augustine and Literature* (Lanham, MD: Lexington Books, 2005); Christopher T. Daly, John Doody, and Kim Paffenroth, eds., *Augustine and History* (Lanham, MD: Lexington Books, 2007); Kim Paffenroth and Kevin L. Hughes, eds., *Augustine and Liberal Education* (Lanham, MD: Lexington Books, 2008); Brian Brown, John A. Doody, and Kim Paffenroth, eds., *Augustine and World Religions* (Lanham, MD: Lexington Books, 2008); Phillip Cary, John Doody, and Kim Paffenroth, *Augustine and Philosophy* (Lanham, MD: Lexington Books, 2010).

59. Eleonore Stump and Norman Kretzmann, eds., *The Cambridge Companion to Augustine* (Cambridge: Cambridge University Press, 2001).

60. Mark Vessey, ed., *A Companion to Augustine* (Oxford: Blackwell Publishing, 2012).

61. James Wetzel, *Augustine: A Guide for the Perplexed* (New York: Continuum, 2010).

62. James Wetzel, "Predestination, Pelagianism, and foreknowledge," *The Cambridge Companion to Augustine*, ed. Eleonore Stump and Norman Kretzmann (Cambridge: Cambridge University Press, 2001), 49–58; "The Force of Memory: Reflections on the Interrupted Self," *Augustinian Studies* 38/1 (2007): 147–59; "Will and Interiority in Augustine: Travels in an Unlikely Place," *Augustinian Studies* 33/2 (2002): 139–60.

63. Mary T. Clark, RCSJ, *Augustine* (New York: Continuum, 1994/ 2000/ 2005).

64. Thomas F. Martin, OSA, *Our Restless Heart: The Augustinian Tradition* (New York: Orbis, 2003.

65. Lancel, *St. Augustine*, 537.

66. Lancel, *Saint Augustin*, xviii.

# REFERENCES TO AUGUSTINE'S WORKS

## Letters

# BIBLIOGRAPHY

Arendt, Hannah. *Love and Saint Augustine*. Edited by Joanna Vec-
    chiarelli Scott and Judith Chelius Stark. Chicago: University of
    Chicago Press, 1929/1966.
Arnold, Duane W. H., and Pamela Bright, eds. *De Doctrina Christiana: A
    Classic of Western Culture*. Vol. 9, *Christianity and Judaism in
    Antiquity*. South Bend, IN: University of Notre Dame Press, 1995.
Atkins, E. M., and Robert Dodaro, OSA, eds. *Augustine: Political Writ-
    ings*. Cambridge: Cambridge University Press, 2001.
Augustine. *City of God*. Translated by Henry Bettensen. 3rd ed. New
    York: Penguin, 2003.
————. *City of God*. Translated by Markus Dods. New York: Hen-
    drickson, 2009.
————. *The City of God Against the Pagans*. Translated by R. W.
    Dyson. Cambridge: Cambridge University Press, 1998.
————. *Confessions*. Translated by R. S. Pine-Coffin. New York: Pen-
    guin, 1961.
————. *Confessions*. Translated by Frank J. Sheed. 2nd ed. New York:
    Sheed and Ward, 1970.
————. *Confessions*. Translated by Frank J. Sheed. 2nd ed. Hackett,
    2006.
————. *Confessions*. Translated by Gary Wills. New York: Penguin
    Classics, 2008.
————. *Confessions*. Translated by Henry Chadwick. 2nd ed. Oxford:
    Oxford University Press, 2009.

————. *Confessions (Study Edition)*. Translated by Maria Boulding, OSB. 2nd ed. Hyde Park, NY: New City Press, 2012.

————. *Confessions. The Works of Saint Augustine: A Translation for the 21st Century*. Translated by Maria Boulding, OSB. 1st ed. Hyde Park, NY: New City Press, 1997.

————. *Ennarationes in Psalmos/Les Commentaires Des Psaumes*. Vol. 1–111 *Oeuvres De Saint Augustin*. Edited by M. Dulaey. Paris: *Institut d'études augustiniennes*, 2009.

————. *Expositions of the Psalms. The Works of Saint Augustine: A Translation for the 21st Century*. Translated by Maria Boulding, OSB, edited by John E. Rotelle, OSA. Introduction by Michael Fiedrowicz. Vol. III/15. Hyde Park: New City Press, 2000.

————. *Love Song: A Fresh Translation of Augustine's Confessions*. Translated by Shirwood Hirt. New York: Harper and Row, 1971.

————. *The Monastic Rules of Augustine. The Augustine Series*. Edited by Boniface Ramsey. Translated by Sister Agatha Mary and Gerald Bonner, edited by Gerald Bonner. Hyde Park: New City Press, 2004.

————. *On Christian Teaching. Oxford World's Classic*. Translated by R. P. H. Green. 3rd ed. Oxford: Oxford University Press, 2008.

————. *Saint Augustine: Essential Sermons*. Translated by Edmund Hill, OP, edited by Daniel E. Doyle, Boniface Ramsey. Hyde Park: New City Press, 2007.

Ayres, Lewis O. *Augustine and the Trinity*. Cambridge: Cambridge University Press, 2010.

————. "'Where does the Trinity Appear?' Augustine's Apologetics and 'Philosophical' Readings of the *De Trinitate*." *Augustinian Studies* 43, no. 1/2 (2012): 109–26.

Baker-Brian, Nicholas. *Manicheism: An Ancient Faith Rediscovered*. London: T&T Clark, 2011.

Barnes, Michael. "Re-Reading Augustine's Theology of the Trinity." In *The Trinity: An Interdisciplinary Symposium on the Trinity*. Edited by Stephen T. Davies, Daniel Kendall, and Gerard O'Collins, 145–76. New York: Oxford University Press, 1999.

Bearsley, Patrick. "Augustine and Wittgenstein on Language." *Philosophy* 58 (1983): 229–36.

Beduhn, Jason. *Augustine's Manichean Dilemma, Vol. 2: Making a Catholic Self, 388–401 CE*. Vol. 2. Philadelphia: University of Pennsylvania Press, 2013.

———. *Augustine's Manichean Dilemma, Vol. 1: Conversion and Apostasy, 373–388 CE*. Vol. 1. Philadelphia: University of Pennsylvania Press, 2009.

———. "What Augustine (may have) Learned from the Manicheans." *Augustinian Studies* 43, no. 1/2 (2012): 35–48.

Bond, Lawrence H. "Mystical Theology." In *Introducing Nicholas of Cusa: A Guide to a Renaissance Man*, edited by Christopher Bellitto, Thomas M. Izbicki, and Gerald Christianson, 205–31. Mahwah, NJ: Paulist Press, 2004.

Bonner, Gerald. "Augustine and Pelagianism, Part II." *Augustinian Studies* 24 (1993): 27–47.

———. *Augustine and Pelagius in the Light of Modern Research*. Villanova, PA: Augustinian Institute: Villanova University Press, 1972.

———. *Freedom and Necessity: St. Augustine's Teaching on Divine Power and Human Freedom*. Washington, DC: The Catholic University of America Press, 2007.

———. "Pelagianism and Augustine, Part 1." *Augustinian Studies* 23 (1992): 33–51.

———. "Rufinus of Syria and African Pelagianism." *Augustinian Studies* 1 (1970): 31–47.

———. *St. Augustine of Hippo: Life and Controversies*. 2nd ed. Norwich, UK: The Canterbury Press, 1986.

Borresen, Kari Elizabeth. "God's Image: Is Woman Excluded? Medieval Interpretation of Gen 1,27 and I Cor 11,7." In *The Image of God: Gender Models in Judaeo-Christian Tradition*, edited by Kari Elizabeth Borresen, 210–35. Minneapolis: Augsburg Fortress Publishers, 1995.

———. *The Image of God: Gender Models in Judaeo-Christian Tradition*. Minneapolis: Augsburg Fortress Publishers, 1995.

———. "In Defence of Augustine: How Feminine is 'Homo?'" In *Collectanea Augustiniana*, edited by B. Bruning, M. Lamberigts, and J. van Houtem, 410–28. Leuven: Augustinian Historical Institute, 1990.

————. "Patristic Feminism: The Case of Augustine." *Augustinian Studies* 25 (1994): 139–52.

————. *Subordination and Equivalence: The Nature and Role of Women in Augustine and Thomas Aquinas.* Translated by Charles Talbot. Washington, DC: The Catholic University of America Press, 1981.

Bourke, Vernon J. *The Essential Augustine.* Indianapolis: Hackett Publishing, 1974.

Bright, Pamela. *The Book of Rules of Tyconius: Its Purpose and Inner Logic.* South Bend, IN: University of Notre Dame Press, 2009.

Brown, Brian, John Doody, and Kim Paffenroth, eds. *Augustine and World Religions.* Augustine in Conversation: Tradition and Innovation. Lanham, MD: Lexington Books, 2008.

Brown, Peter. *Augustine of Hippo.* Los Angeles: University of California Press, 1967/2000.

————. *The Body and Society: Men, Women, and Sexual Renunciation in Early Christianity: Twentieth Anniversary Edition with a New Introduction.* New York: Columbia University Press, 2008.

————. *Power and Persuasion in Late Antiquity: Towards a Christian Empire.* Madison, WI: University of Wisconsin Press, 1992.

————. *Religion and Society in the Age of Saint Augustine.* 2nd ed. Wipf & Stock Publishers, 2007.

Brown, Peter, and Geoffrey Barraclough. *The World of Late Antiquity AD 150–750.* New York: W. W. Norton, 1989.

Burke, Kenneth. *The Rhetoric of Religion: Studies in Logology.* Los Angeles: University of California Press, 1961/1970.

Burleigh, J. H. S., ed. *Augustine: Early Writings.* Philadelphia: Westminster Press, 1953.

Burnaby, John, ed. *Augustine: Later Writings.* Philadelphia: Westminster Press, 1955.

Burnell, Peter. "Is the Augustinian Heaven Inhuman? The Arguments of Martin Heidegger and Hannah Arendt." *Augustinian Studies* 30, no. 2 (1999): 283–92.

Burns, J. Patout. *The Development of Augustine Doctrine of Operative Grace.* Paris: Études Augustiniennes, 1980.

Burt, Donald X., OSA. *Augustine's World: An Introduction to His Speculative Philosophy.* Lanham, MD: University Press of America, 1996.

————. *Friendship and Society: An Introduction to Augustine's Practical Philosophy*. Grand Rapids, MI: Wm. B. Eerdmans Publishing, 1999.

Cameron, Michael. *Christ Meets Me Everywhere: Augustine's Early Figurative Exegesis*. Oxford Studies in Historical Theology. Oxford: Oxford University Press, 2012.

————. "An Encomium for Allan D. Fitzgerald, O.S.A., Editor of Augustinian Studies." *Augustinian Studies* 43 (2012): 3–4.

Canning, Raymond. *The Unity of Love for God and Neighbour in St. Augustine*. Heverlee-Leuven: Augustinian Historical Institute, 1993.

Caputo, John D., and Michael Scanlon, OSA, eds. *Augustine and Postmodernism: Confession and Circumcession*. Indiana Series in the Philosophy of Religion. Bloomington, IN: Indiana University Press, 2005.

Cary, Phillip. *Augustine's Invention of the Inner Self*. Oxford: Oxford University Press, 2003.

————. "Book Review: Augustine and the Jews." *Augustinian Studies* 40, no. 2 (2009).

————. "Saint Augustine and the Fall of the Soul: Beyond O'Connell and His Critics." *Augustinian Studies* 37, no. 2 (2006): 292–95.

Cary, Phillip, John Doody, and Kim Paffenroth, eds. *Augustine and Philosophy*. Augustine in Conversation: Tradition and Innovation. Lanham, MD: Lexington Books, 2010.

Casiday, A. M. C. *Tradition and Theology in St. John Cassian*. Oxford Early Christian Studies. Oxford: Oxford University Press, 2007.

Cavadini, John. "The Structure and Intention of Augustine's *De Trinitate*." *Augustinian Studies* 23 (1992): 103–23.

————. "Trinity and Apologetics in the Theology of St. Augustine." *Modern Theology* 29 (2013): 48–82.

Chadwick, Henry. *Augustine of Hippo: A Life*. Oxford: Oxford University Press, 2009.

————. *Augustine: A Very Short Introduction*. Oxford: Oxford University Press, 1986/2001.

Clark, Gillian. *Women in Late Antiquity: Pagan and Christian Lifestyles*. Oxford: Clarendon Press, 1993.

Clark, Mary T., RCSJ. *Augustine*. 3rd ed. New York: Continuum, 2005.

————. *Augustine of Hippo: Selected Writings*. Classics of Western Spirituality. Mahwah, NJ: Paulist Press, 1984.

————. "*De Trinitate.*" In *The Cambridge Companion to Augustine*, edited by Eleonore Stump and Norman Kretzmann, 91–102. Cambridge: Cambridge University Press, 2001.

Connolly, William. *The Augustinian Imperative: A Reflection on the Politics of Morality*. Newbury Park, CA: Sage Publications, 1993.

Conybeare, Catherine. *The Irrational Augustine*. Hyde Park: New City Press, 2006.

————. "Reading the *Confessions.*" In *A Companion to Augustine*, edited by Mark Vessey, 99–110. Oxford: Wiley-Blackwell, 2012.

————. "Spaces between Letters: Augustine's Correspondence with Women." In *Voices in Dialogue: Reading Women in the Middle Ages*, edited by Linda Olsen and Kathryn Kerby-Fulton, 57–72. South Bend, IN: University of Notre Dame Press 2005.

Courcelle, Pierre. *Recherches Sur Les Confessions De Saint Augustin*. Paris: E. DeBoccard, 1950/1968.

Coyle, Kevin J. "Saint Augustine's Manichean Legacy." *Augustinian Studies* 34 (2003): 1–22.

Daly, Christopher T., John Doody, and Kim Paffenroth, eds. *Augustine and History*. Augustine in Conversation: Tradition and Innovation. Lanham, MD: Lexington Books, 2007.

Dawson, David. "Sign Theory, Allegorical Readings, and the Motions of the Soul in *De Doctrina Christiana.*" In *De Doctrina Christiana: A Classic of Western Culture*, edited by Duane W. H. Arnold and Pamela Bright, 123–41. South Bend, IN: University of Notre Dame Press, 1995.

De Paulo, Craig, ed. *The Influence of Augustine on Heidegger*. Lewiston, ME: Edwin Mellen Press, 2006.

Derrida, Jacques. "Composing Circumfession." In *Augustine and Postmodernism: Confession and Circumfession*, edited by John D. Caputo and Michael Scanlon, OSA, 19–27. Bloomington, IN: Indiana University Press, 2005.

Derrida, Jacques, and Geoffrey Bennington. *Jacques Derrida. Religion and Postmodernism*, edited by Mark C. Taylor. Translated by Geoffrey Bennington. Chicago: University of Chicago Press, 1999.

Dimasio, Antonio. *Descartes' Error*. 2nd ed. New York: Putman, 2005.

Dodaro, Robert, OSA. "Augustine's Secular City." In *Augustine and His Critics*, edited by Robert Dodaro, OSA, and George Lawless, OSA. London: Routledge, 2000.

—. *Christ and the Just Society in the Thought of Augustine*. Cambridge: Cambridge University Press, 2008.

—. "Eloquent Lies, Just Wars and the Politics of Persuasion: Reading Augustine's City of God in a "Postmodern" World." *Augustinian Studies* 25 (1994): 77–137.

—. "*Sacramentum Christi*: Augustine on the Christology of Pelagius." In *Studia Patristica: Paper Presented at the Eleventh International Conference on Patristic Studies in Oxford 1991*, edited by E. Livingstone. Vol. 27, 274–80. Leuven: Peters, 1993.

Dodaro, Robert, OSA, and George Lawless, OSA. *Augustine and His Critics: Essays in Honour of Gerald Bonner*. London: Routledge, 2000.

Dolbeau, Francois. *Vingt-Six Sermons Au Peuple*. Paris: Études augustiniennes, 1996.

Donnelly, Dorothy F., ed. *The City of God: A Collection of Critical Essays*. New York: Peter Lang, 1995.

Donnelly, Dorothy F., and Mark A. Sherman, eds. *Augustine's De Civitate Dei: An Annotated Bibliography of Modern Criticism, 1960–1990*. New York: Peter Lang, 1991.

Doody, John, Kevin L. Hughes, and Kim Paffenroth, eds. *Augustine and Politics*. Augustine in Conversation: Tradition and Innovation. Lanham, MD: Lexington Books, 2005.

Dossey, Leslie. *Peasant and Empire in Christian North Africa*. Berkeley: University of California Press, 2010.

Drobner, Hubertus. "Psalm 21 in Augustine's *Semones ad Populem*: Catecheses on *Christus Totus* and Rules of Interpretation." *Augustinian Studies* 37, no. 2 (2006).

—. "Studying Augustine: An Overview of Recent Research." In *Augustine and His Critics: Essays in Honour of Gerald Bonner*, edited by Robert Dodaro, OSA, and George Lawless, OSA, 18–34. London: Routledge, 2000.

Ebbeler, Jennifer. *Disciplining Christians: Correction and Community in Augustine's Letters*. Oxford Studies in Late Antiquity. Oxford: Oxford University Press, 2012.

Enos, Richard Leo. *The Rhetoric of Saint Augustine of Hippo: De Doctrina Christiana and the Search for a Distinctly Christian Rhetoric.* Waco, TX: Baylor University Press, 2008.

Evers, Alexander. *Church, Cities, and People: A Study of the Plebs in the Church and Cities of Roman Africa in Late Antiquity.* Interdisciplinary Studies in Ancient Culture and Religion. Vol. 11. Leuven: Peeters, 2010.

Faggioli, Massimo. *Vatican II: The Battle for Meaning.* Mahwah, NJ: Paulist Press, 2012.

Fiedrowicz, Michael. *Psalmus Vox Totius Christi: Studien Zu Augustins "Ennarrationes in Psalmos."* Freiburg: Herder, 1997.

Fitzer, Joseph. "The Augustinian Roots of Calvin's Eucharistic Theology." *Augustinian Studies* 7 (1976): 69–98.

Fitzgerald, Allan, OSA, ed. *Augustine through the Ages: An Encyclopedia.* Wm. B. Eerdmans Publishing, 1999.

———. "Tracing the Passage from a Doctrinal to an Historical Approach to the Study of Augustine." *Revue des études augustiniennes et patristiques* 50 (2004): 295–310.

Forest, Aimé. "L'augustinisme de Maurice Blondell." *Sciences écclesiastiques* 14 (1962): 175–93.

Fredriksen, Paula. *Augustine and the Jews: A Christian Defense of Jews and Judaism.* 2nd ed. New Haven, CT: Yale University Press, 2010.

———. "The *Confessions* as Autobiography." In *A Companion to Augustine*, edited by Mark Vessey, 87–98. Oxford: Wiley-Blackwell, 2012.

Frend, W. H. C. *The Donatist Church: A Movement of Protest in Roman North Africa.* 2nd ed. Oxford: Oxford University Press, 2003.

Gadamer, Hans-Georg. *Wahrheit und Methode. Grundzuge einer Philosophischen Hermeneutick.* Gesammelte Werke. 2nd ed. Vol. 1. Tübigen: J. C. B. Mohr, 1986.

Gaume, Matthew Alan, Anthony Dupont, and Mathijs Lamberigts, eds. *The Uniquely African Controversy: Studies on Donatist Christianity.* Late Antique History and Religion. Vol. 7. Leuven: Peeters, forthcoming.

Gehl, P. F. "An Augustinian Catechism in Fourteenth Century Tuscany: Prosper's Epigrammatica." *Augustinian Studies* 19 (1985): 93–100.

Grondin, Jean. *Introduction to Philosophical Hermeneutics*. Yale Studies in Hermeneutics. Translated by Joel Weinsheimer. New Haven, CT: Yale University Press, 1996.

Grossi, Vittorino, OSA. "*L'Auctoritas di Agostino nella Dottrina del 'Peccatum Originis' da Cartagine (418) a Trento (1546)."* *Augustinianum* 31 (1991): 329–60.

———. "*La Giustificatione secondo Girolamo Serpando nel Contesto dei Dibattiti Tridentini."* *Analecta Augustiniana* 41 (1978): 5–24.

———. "Trent, Council of." In *Augustine through the Ages, an Encyclopedia*, edited by Allan Fitzgerald, OSA, 843–45. Grand Rapids, MI: Wm. B. Eerdmans Publishing, 1999.

Guitton, Jean. *The Modernity of St. Augustine*. Baltimore: Helicon Press, 1959.

Handley, Mark A. "Disputing the End of African Christianity." In *Vandals, Romans and Berbers: New Perspectives on Late Antique North Africa*, edited by A. H. Merrills. Aldershot, UK: Ashgate, 2004.

Harmless, William, SJ. *Augustine and the Catechumenate*. Collegeville, MN: Liturgical Press, 1995.

———. *Augustine in His Own Words*. Washington, DC: The Catholic University of America Press, 2010.

———. *Desert Christians: An Introduction to the Literature of Early Monasticism*. Oxford: Oxford University Press, 2004.

———. "A Love Supreme: Augustine's 'Jazz' of Theology." *Augustinian Studies* 43, no. 1/2 (2012): 149–77.

———. *Mystics*. Oxford: Oxford University Press, 2007.

Harrison, Carol. *Rethinking Augustine's Early Works: An Argument for Continuity*. Oxford: Oxford University Press, 2005.

Heidegger, Martin. *The Phenomenology of Religious Life*. Translated by Jennifer Anna Gosetti-Ferencei and Matthias Fritsch. 2nd ed. Bloomington, IN: Indiana University Press, 2004.

Hermanowicz, Erika. *Possidius of Calma: A Study of the North African Episcopate in the Age of Augustine*. Oxford: Oxford University Press, 2008.

Hollingworth, Miles. *The Pilgrim City: St. Augustine of Hippo and His Innovation in Political Thought*. London: T&T Clark International, 2010.

———. *St. Augustine of Hippo: An Intellectual Biography*. Oxford: Oxford University Press, 2013.

Holt, Laura. "Augustine in Review." *The Heythrop Journal* 46 (2005): 199–207.

———. "A Survey of Recent Works on Augustine." *The Heythrop Journal* 49 (2007): 292–308.

———. "What Are They For? Reading Recent Books on Augustine." *The Heythrop Journal* 54 (2013): 101–19.

Hombert, Pierre Marie. *Gloria Gratiae. Se Glorifier En Dieu, Principe Et Fin De La Theologie Augustinienne De La Grace.* Collection des études augustiniennes. Paris: Institut des études augustiniennes, 1996.

Hugo, John J. "St. Augustine at Vatican II." *The Homiletic and Pastoral Review* 67 (1966): 765–72.

Hunter, David. "Augustine on the Body." In *A Companion to Augustine*, edited by Mark Vessey, 353–64. Oxford: Blackwell Publishing, 2013.

———. "'Augustinian Pessimism:' A New Look at Augustine's Teaching on Sex, Marriage, and Celibacy." *Augustinian Studies* 25 (1994): 153–77.

Inowlocki, Sabrina. "Book Review: Augustine and the Jews." *Augustinian Studies* 40, no. 2 (2009).

Inowlocki, Sabrina, Phillip Cary, and Elena Procario-Foley. "Book Review: Augustine and the Jews." *Augustinian Studies* 40, no. 2 (2009): 279–94.

Kannengiesser, Charles. "Fifty Years of Patristics." *Theological Studies* 50, no. 4 (1989): 633–56.

Kelley, Joseph T. *Saint Augustine of Hippo: Selections from Confessions.* Rutland, VT: SkyLight Publications, 2010.

Kennedy, Robert, Kim Paffenroth, and John Doody, eds. *Augustine and Literature.* Augustine in Conversation: Tradition and Innovation. Lanham, MD: Lexington Books, 2005.

Kisiel, Theodore. *The Genesis of Heidegger's Being and Time.* Berkeley, CA: University of California Press, 1995.

Klingshirn, W. E. *Caesarius of Arles: Life, Testament, Letters.* Liverpool: Liverpool University Press, 1994.

———. *Caesarius of Arles: The Making of a Christian Community in Late Antique Gaul.* Cambridge: Cambridge University Press, 1994.

Kretzmann, Norman. "Faith Seeks, Understanding Finds: Augustine's Charter for Christian Philosophy." In *Christian Philosophy*, edited by T. P. Flint, 1–36. South Bend, IN: University of Notre Dame Press, 1990.

Kriseller, P. O. *Studies in Renaissance Thought and Letters.* Rome: Edizioni di Storia e Letteratura, 1956.

La Bonnardière, Anne-Marie. *Biblia Augustiniana.* Vol. 1–7. Paris: Institut des études augustiniennes, 1960–74.

———. *"Recherches de chronologie augustinienne."* Revue des études augustiniennes 10 (1965): 165–77.

———. *Saint Augustin et la Bible. Bible de Tous Les Temps.* Paris: Beauchense.

Lamberigts, Mathijs. "Jansenius." In *Augustine through the Ages, an Encyclopedia,* edited by Allan Fitzgerald, OSA, 459–60. Grand Rapids, MI: Wm. B. Eerdmans Publishing, 1999.

———. "Pelagius and Pelagians." In *Oxford Handbook of Early Christian Studies,* edited by Susan Ashbrook Harvey and David G. Hunter, 258–79. Oxford: Oxford University Press, 2008.

Lamberigts, M., and L. Kenis, eds. *L'augustinisme a l'ancienne faculte de theologie de Louvain.* Betl. Vol. 111. Louvain: University of Louvain, 1986.

Lancel, Serge. *St. Augustin.* Paris: Librairie Artheme Fayard, 1999.

———. *St. Augustine* [Saint Agustin]. Translated by Antonia Neville. London: SCM Press, 2002.

Lane, A. N. S. "Calvin's Use of the Fathers and the Medievals." *Calvin Theological Journal* 16 (1981): 149–205.

Lawless, George, OSA. *Augustine and His Monastic Rule.* New York: Oxford University Press, 1990.

———. "Augustine of Hippo: An Annotated Reading List." *Listening: Journal of Religion and Culture* 26 (Fall 1991): 173–88.

———. "Book Review of Gary Wills' *Confessions of Saint Augustine.*" *Augustinian Studies* 31, no. 2 (2000): 243–53.

Legaspi, Michael C. *The Death of Scripture and the Rise of Biblical Studies.* Oxford Studies in Historical Theology. Oxford: Oxford University Press, 2010.

Lepelley, Claude. *"Circumcelliones."* In *Augustinus-Lexikon,* edited by Cornelius Mayer, OSA. Vol. I, 246–52. 1986–94.

Liev, Samuel. *Manichaeism in the Later Roman Empire and Medieval China.* 2nd ed. Tübigen: Mohr, 1992.

Louis-Sebastien, Le Nain de Tillemont. *The Life of Augustine, Part One: Childhood to Episcopal Consecration* [*Memoirs pour servir a l'histoire ecclesiastique des six permeirs siecles*, Volume XIII]. Translated by Frederick Van Fleteren and George Berthold. Vol. 1. New York: Peter Lang, 2010.

————. *The Life of Augustine, Part Two: The Donatist Controversy* [*Memoirs pour servir a l'histoire ecclesiastique des six permeirs siecles*, Volume XIII]. Translated by Frederick Van Fleteren. Vol. 2. New York: Peter Lang, 2012.

Lyotard, Jean-Francois. *The Confession of St. Augustine*. Cultural Memory in the Present. Translated by Richard Beardsworth. Stanford, CA: Stanford University Press, 2000.

Madec, Goulven. "Analyse du 'De Magistro.'" *Revue des études augustiniennes* 21 (1975): 63–71.

————. "Christus." In *Augustinus-Lexikon*, edited by Mayer Cornelius, OSA, and Erich Feldmann. Vol. 1, 845–908. Basel: Schwabe, 1987.

————. "*Christus Scientia et Sapientia Nostra: le principe de coherence de la doctrine augustinienne.*" *Recherches augustiniennes* 10 (1975): 77–85.

————. *Portrait de Saint Augustine*. Paris: Desclee de Brouwer, 2008.

Mallard, William. *Language and Love: Introducing Augustine's Religious Thought through the* Confessions. Translated by William Mallard. University Park, PA: Pennsylvania State University Press, 1994.

Marin de San Martin, Luis, OSA. *The Augustinians: Origin and Spirituality*. Translated by Brian Lowery, OSA. Roma: Curia Generale Agostiniana, 2013.

Markus, Robert A. *The End of Ancient Christianity*. Cambridge: Cambridge University Press, 1991.

————. "Evolving Disciplinary Contexts for the Study of Augustine, 1950–2000: Some Personal Reflections." *Augustinian Studies* 32, no. 2 (2001): 189–00.

————. "The Legacy of Pelagius: Orthodoxy, Heresy, and Conciliation." In *The Making of Orthodoxy: Essays in Honour of Henry Chadwick*, edited by Rowan Williams, 214–34. Cambridge: Cambridge University Press, 1989.

————. *Sacred and Secular: Studies on Augustine and Latin Christianity*. Aldershot: Variorum, 1994.

——. *Saeculum: History and Society in the Theology of St. Augustine.* Cambridge: Cambridge University Press, 1970/1988.

——. *Signs and Meanings: Word and Text in Ancient Christianity.* Liverpool: Liverpool University Press, 1996.

Marrou, Henri. *The Resurrection and Saint Augustine's Theology of Human Value.* Villanova, PA: The Augustinian Institute-Villanova University Press, 1965.

Martin, F. X., OSA, and J. A. Richmond, eds. *From Augustine to Eriugena: Essays on Neoplatonism and Christianity in Honor of John O'Meara.* Washington, DC: The Catholic University of America Press, 1991.

Martin, Thomas, OSA. *Augustine of Hippo: Faithful Servant, Spiritual Leader.* Library of World Biography Series., edited by Allan Fitzgerald, OSA. New York: Prentice Hall, 2011.

——. *Our Restless Hearts: The Augustinian Tradition.* New York: Orbis, 2003.

Mathison, R. W. "For Specialists Only: The Reception of Augustine and His Theology in Fifth Century Gaul." In *Collecteana Augustiniana: Augustine, Presbyter Factus Sum*, edited by J. T. Lienhard, E. C. Muller, and Roland Teske, SJ. Vol. 2, 29–41. New York: Peter Lang, 1993.

Matter, E. Ann. "*De Cura Feminarum*: Augustine the Bishop, North African Women, and the Development of a Theology of Female Nature." In *Feminist Interpretations of Augustine*, edited by Judith Chelius Stark, 203–14. University Park, PA: Penn State University Press, 2007.

Matthews, Gareth B. "Post-Medieval Agustinianism." In *The Cambridge Companion to Augustine*, edited by Eleonore Stump and Norman Kretzmann, 267–79. Cambridge: Cambridge University Press, 2001.

McGrath, Sean J. "Alternative Confessions, Conflicting Faiths: A Review of the Influence of Augustine on Heidegger." *American Catholic Philosophical Quarterly* 82, no. 2 (2008): 317–35.

McWilliam, Joanne. "Augustine's Letters to Women." In *Feminist Interpretations of Augustine*, edited by Judith Chelius Stark, 289–02. University Park, PA: Penn State University Press, 2007.

——. "The Christology of the Pelagian Controversy." Chap. 3, In *Studia Patristica: Papers Presented at the Tenth International Con-*

*ference on Patristic Studies in Oxford 1979*, edited by E. Livingstone. Vol. 17, 1221–44. Leuven: Peeters, 1982.

Meconi, David Vincent, and Eleonore Stump, eds. *The Cambridge Companion to Augustine*. 2nd ed. Cambridge: Cambridge University Press, 2014.

Menn, Stephen. *Descartes and Augustine*. Cambridge: Cambridge University Press, 1998.

Merdinger, Jane. *Rome and the African Church in the Time of Augustine*. New Haven: Yale University Press, 1997.

Milbank, Arabella. "Review." *Journal of the Medieval Reading Group at the University of Cambridge* 16: 7/20/2013.

Miles, Margaret. *Carnal Knowing: Female Nakedness and Religious Meaning in the Christian West*. Boston: Beacon Press, 1989.

———. *Desire and Delight: A New Reading of Augustine's Confessions*. 2nd ed. New York: Wipf & Stock Publishers, 2006.

Milweski, D. J. "Augustine's 124 Tractates on the Gospel of John: The *Status Quaestionis* and the State of Neglect." *Augustinian Studies* 33, no. 1 (2002): 61–77.

Monfasani, John. "Humanism." In *Augustine through the Ages: An Encyclopedia*, edited by Allan Fitzgerald, OSA, 714–15. Grand Rapids, MI: Wm. B. Eerdmans Publishing, 1999.

Morreto, Giovanni. "*Schleiermacher und Augustinus*." In *Internationaler Schleiermacher Kongress*, 365–80. Berlin: W. de Gruyter, 1984.

Muller, Richard A. "Reformation, Augustinianism in the." In *Augustine through the Ages, an Encyclopedia*, edited by Allan Fitzgerald, OSA, 705–7. Grand Rapids, MI: Wm. B. Eerdmans Publishing, 1999.

Murray, Michael V., ed. *Theorems on Existence and Essence*. Medieval Philosophical Texts in Translation. Translated by Michael V. Murray. Vol. 7, 1973.

O'Connell, Robert J., SJ. *The Origin of the Soul in St. Augustine's Later Works*. New York: Fordham University Press, 1987.

O'Connor, W. R. "The *uti/frui* Distinction in Augustine's Ethics." *Augustinian Studies* 14 (1984): 169–81.

O'Daly, Gerard. *Augustine's City of God: A Reader's Guide*. 2nd ed. Oxford: Oxford University Press, 2004.

O'Donnell, James J. *Augustine: Confessions (3 Vols.)*. Oxford: Oxford University Press, 1992.

———. *Augustine: A New Biography*. New York: Harper, 2006.

O'Donovan, O. "*Usus* and *Fruitio* in Augustine, *De Doctrina Christiana I.*" *Theological Studies* 33, no. 2 (1982): 361–97.

O'Meara, John. *The Young Augustine: The Growth of St. Augustine's Mind Up to His Conversion*. 3rd ed. New York: Alba House, 2001.

Ortega, Mariano Martin. "The Augustinian Charism and Vatican II." In *Augustinian Spirituality and the Charism of the Augustinians*, edited by John E. Rotelle, OSA, 140–53. Villanova, PA: Augustinian Press, 1995.

Otten, Willemien. "Between Praise and Appraisal: Medieval Guidelines for the Assessment of Augustine's Intellectual Legacy." *Augustinian Studies* 43, no. 1/2 (2012): 201–18.

————. "Views on Women in Early Christianity: Incarnational Hermeneutics on Tertullian and Augustine." In *Hermeneutics, Scriptural Politics, and Human Rights: Between Text and Context*, edited by Bas de Gaay Fortman, Kurt Martens, and M. A. Mohammed Salih. New York: Palgrave Macmillan, 2009.

Otten, Willemien, and Karla Pollmann, eds. *Oxford Guide to the Historical Reception of Augustine*. New York: Oxford University Press, 2013.

Paffenroth, Kim, and Kevin L. Hughes, eds. *Augustine and Liberal Education*. Augustine in Conversation: Tradition and Innovation. Lanham, MD: Lexington Books, 2008.

Paffenroth, Kim, and Robert Kennedy, eds. *A Reader's Companion to Augustine's* Confessions. Louisville, KY: Westminster John Knox Press, 2003.

Pagels, Elaine. *Adam, Eve, and the Serpent*. New York: Random House, 1988.

Peckhold, C. C. "Theo-Semiotics and Augustine's Hermeneutical Jew: Or, What's a Little Supersessionism among Friends?" *Augustinian Studies* 37, no. 1 (2006): 27–42.

Pelagius. *Pelagius's Commentary on St. Paul's Epistle to the Romans*. Oxford Early Christian Studies. Translated by Theodore de Bruyn. 2nd ed. Oxford: Clarendon Press, 2002.

Pelikan, Jaroslav. "*Canonica Regula*: The Trinitarian Hermeneutics of Augustine." In *Collectanea Augustiniana: Augustine, "Second Founder of the Faith*," edited by Joseph Schnaubelt, OSA, and Frederick Van Fleteren, 329–43. New York: Peter Lang, 1990.

————. *The Mystery of Continuity: Time and History, Memory and Eternity, in the Thought of St. Augustine.* Charlottesville, VA: University of Virginia Press, 1986.

Possidius. *The Life of Saint Augustine.* The Augustine Series. Translated by Michele Cardinal Pellegrino, edited by John E. Rotelle, OSA. Villanova, PA: Augustinian Press, 1988.

Power, Kim. *Augustine Writings on Women.* London: Darton, Longman and Todd, 1995.

Quillen, Carol Everhart. "Plundering the Egyptians: Petrarch and Augustine's *De Doctrina Christiana.*" In *Reading and Wisdom: The 'De Doctrina Christiana' of Augustine in the Middle Ages,* edited by Edward D. English, 153–71. South Bend, IN: University of Notre Dame Press, 1995.

————. "Renaissance to the Enlightenment." In *Augustine through the Ages: An Encyclopedia,* edited by Allan Fitzgerald, OSA. Grand Rapids, MI: Wm. B. Eerdmans Publishing, 1999.

————. *Rereading the Renaissance: Petrarch, Augustine, and the Language of Humanism.* Recentiores: Later Latin Texts and Context. Ann Arbor, MI: University of Michigan Press, 1998.

Quinn, John, OSA. *A Companion to the Confessions of St. Augustine.* New York: Peter Lang, 2002.

Quy, Joseph, OSA, and Joseph Lam C. *Theologishe Verwandtschaft: Augustinus Von Hippo Und Joseph Ratzinger/Papst Benedikt XVI.* Wuerzburg: Echter, 2009.

Rahner, Karl. *Foundations of Christian Faith.* New York: Seabury Press, 1978.

Ramsey, Boniface, ed. *The City of God. The Works of Saint Augustine: A Translation for the 21st Century.* Translated by William Babcock. Vol. II/6. Hyde Park: New City Press, 2013.

Ratzinger, Joseph. *The Fathers.* Huntington, IN: Our Sunday Visitor, 2008.

————. *Popolo e Casa Di Dio in Sant'Agonstino.* Milano: Jaca Book SpA, 1978/2005.

————. *Volk und Haus Gottes in Augustins Lehre Von Der Kirche.* Munchen: Karl Zink Verlag, 1954.

Rees, Brinley Roderick. *Pelagius: Life and Letters.* Rochester, NY: Boydell, 2004.

Reuther, Rosemary Radford. "*Imago Dei*: Christian Tradition and Feminist Hermeneutics." In *The Image of God: Gender Models in Judaeo-Christian Tradition*, edited by Kari Elizabeth Borresen, 267–91. Minneapolis: Augsburg Fortress Publishers, 1995.

———. *Sexism and God Talk: Toward a Feminist Theology*. Boston: Beacon Press, 1983.

Ricoeur, Paul. *Time and Narrative*. Translated by Kathleen Blamey, Kathleen McLaughlin, and David Pelauer. Vol. 1–3. Chicago: University of Chicago Press, 1984/1988/1990.

Rist, John. *Augustine: Ancient Thought Baptized*. Cambridge: Cambridge University Press, 1996.

Rubenstein, Richard. *Aristotle's Children: How Christians, Muslims, and Jews Rediscovered Ancient Wisdom and Illuminated the Middle Ages*. New York: Houghton-Mifflin-Harcourt, 2003.

Ruegg, Walter, and Hilde De Ridder-Symoens, eds. *A History of the University in Europe: Universities in the Middle Ages*. 2nd ed. Vol. 1. Cambridge: Cambridge University Press, 2003.

Rush, Ormond. *Still Interpreting Vatican II: Some Hermeneutical Principles*. Mahwah, NJ: Paulist Press, 2004.

Ruy Chais, Jules. "Maurice Blondell et saint Augustin." *Revue des études augustiniennes* 11 (1966): 55–84.

Saak, E. L. "Scholasticism, Late." In *Augustine through the Ages: An Encyclopedia*, edited by Allan Fitzgerald, OSA, 754–59. Grand Rapids, MI: Wm. B. Eerdmans Publishing, 1999.

Scanlon, Michael, OSA. "The Augustinian Tradition: A Retrieval." *Augustinian Studies* 20 (1989): 61–92.

———. "Karl Rahner: A Neo-Augustinian Thomist." *The Thomist* 43 (1979): 178–85.

———. "Theology, Modern." In *Augustine through the Ages, an Encyclopedia*, edited by Allan Fitzgerald, OSA, 825–26. Grand Rapids, MI: Wm. B. Eerdmans Publishing, 1999.

Schiller, Isabella, Dorothea Weber, and Clemens Weidmann. *Zeitshcrift Fur Klassische Philologie, Patristick und lateinische Tradition: Sermones Erfurt 1, 5, 6*. Wiener Studien. Vol. 121. Wien: Verlag der Oesterreicheschen Akademie Wissenschaften, 2008.

———. *Zeitshcrift Fur Klassische Philologie, Patristick und lateinische Tradition: Sermones Erfurt 2, 3, 4*. Wiener Studien. Vol. 122. Wien: Verlag der Oesterreichischen Akademie der Wissenschaften, 2009.

Schnaubelt, Joseph, OSA, and Frederick Van Fleteren, eds. *Collectanea Augustiniana: Augustine, "Second Founder of the Faith."* New York: Peter Lang, 1990.

Schoedel, W. "Augustine on Love: A Response (to the *Double Face of Love in Augustine* by Van Bavel)." *Augustinian Studies* 17 (1986): 183–85.

Secretariat for Justice and Peace. *Augustine, 'Father of Christian Political Activism.'* Edited by Curia Generalizia Agostiniana. Roma: Pubblicazioni Agostiniane, 2007.

Seelbach, Larissa Carina. "Augustine on Concubinage and Women's Dignity." *Studia Patristica* XLIII (2007): 245–49.

Selman, Francis. *Aquinas 101: A Basic Introduction to the Thought of Saint Thomas Aquinas.* South Bend, IN: Ave Maria Press, 2007.

Shaw, Brent. *Sacred Violence: African Christians and Sectarian Hatred in the Age of Augustine.* Cambridge: Cambridge University Press, 2011.

Stark, Judith Chelius, ed. *Feminist Interpretations of Augustine.* Re-Reading the Canon Series. University Park, PA: Penn State University Press, 2007.

Steinhauser, Kenneth B. *The Apocalypse Commentary of Tyconius: A History of its Reception and Influence.* European University Studies, xxiii. Vol. 310. Frankfurt: Peter Lang, 1987.

————. "Manuscripts." In *Augustine through the Ages, an Encyclopedia,* edited by Allan Fitzgerald, OSA, 525–33. Grand Rapids, MI: Wm. B. Eerdmans Publishing, 1999.

Steinmetz, D. C. *Misericordia Dei: The Theology of Johannes Von Staupitz in its Late Medieval Setting.* Leiden: Brill, 1968.

Stock, Brian. *Augustine the Reader: Meditation, Self-Knowledge, and the Ethics of Interpretation.* Cambridge, MA: Harvard University Press, 1996.

Stone, Harold, S. "Cult of Augustine's Body." In *Augustine through the Ages: An Encyclopedia,* edited by Allan Fitzgerald, OSA, 256–59. Grand Rapids, MI: Wm. B. Eerdmans, 1999.

Stone, M. F. W. "Augustine and Medieval Philosophy." In *The Cambridge Companion to Augustine,* edited by Eleonore Stump and Norman Kretzmann, 253–66. Cambridge: Cambridge University Press, 2001.

Studer, Basil, OSB. "*Sacramentum et Exemplum chez Saint Augustin.*" *Recherches augustiniennes* 10 (1975): 87–141.

Stump, Eleonore. "Augustine on Free Will." In *The Cambridge Companion to Augustine*, edited by Eleonore Stump and Norman Kretzmann, 124–27. Cambridge: Cambridge University Press, 2001.

Tack, Theodore, OSA. *As One Struggling Christian to Another: Augustine's Christian Ideal for Today*. Collegeville, MN: The Liturgical Press, 2001.

Tanner, Norman P., SJ, ed. *Decrees of the Ecumenical Councils*. Vol. I, II. Georgetown: Georgetown University Press, 1990.

Tertullian. *De Praescriptione*. Tertulliani Opera. Edited by Corpus Christianorum. Series Latina I. Turnhout, Belgium: Brepols, 1954.

TeSelle, Eugene. "Book Review: *Saint Augustin* by Serge Lancel." *Augustinian Studies* 31, no. 2 (2000).

Teske, Roland, SJ. *Augustine of Hippo: Philosopher, Exegete, and Theologian*. Milwaukee, WI: Marquette University Press, 2009.

————. *Paradoxes of Time in Saint Augustine*. Milwaukee: Marquette University Press, 1996.

————. *To Know God and the Soul: Essays on the Thought of St. Augustine*. Washington, DC: The Catholic University of America Press, 2008.

Thonnard, F. J. "*Saint Augustine et les grand courants de la philosophie contemporaine.*" *Revue des études augustiniennes* 1 (1955): 68–80.

Tilley, Maureen A., ed. *Donatist Martyr Stories: The Church in Conflict in Roman North Africa*. Translated Texts for Historians. Translated by Maureen A. Tilley. Vol. 24. Liverpool: Liverpool University Press, 1997.

————. "Family and Financial Conflict in the Donatist Controversy: Augustine's Pastoral Problem." *Augustinian Studies* 43, no. 1/2 (2012): 49–64.

Trape, Agostino, OSA. *Agostino: Introduzione alla Dottina della Grazia I: Natura e Grazia*. Roma: Citta Nuova, 1987.

————. *Agostino: Introduzione alla Dottina della Grazia II: Grazia e Liberta*. Roma: Citta Nuova, 1990.

Trapp, Damasus. "*Adnotationes.*" *Augustinianum* 5 (1965): 150.

Van Bavel, Tarcisius, OSA. "Augustine's Views on Women." *Augustiniana* 39 (1989): 5–53.

————. *Christians in the World.* New York: Catholic Book Publishing Company, 1980.

————. "The Double Face of Love in Augustine." *Augustinian Studies* 17 (1986): 169–81.

————. "*Fruitio, Delectatio,* and *Voluptas* in Augustine." *Augustinus* 38 (1993): 499–510.

————. *The Longing of the Heart: Augustine's Doctrine on Prayer.* Leuven: Peters, 2009.

Van der Meer, Frederic. *Augustine the Bishop.* London: Sheed and Ward, 1961.

Van Fleteren, Frederick. "Book Review: *Augustine: A New Biography* by James J. O'Donnell." *Augustinian Studies* 36, no. 2 (2005): 447–52.

————. "In Memory of John J. O'Meara, 1915–2003." *Augustinian Studies* 35, no. 1 (2004): 2–42.

————. *Martin Heidegger's Interpretations of* Augustine: Sein und Zeit und Ewigkeit. Lewiston, ME: The Edwin Mellen Press, 2005.

Van Oort, J., Otto Wermelinger, and Gregor Wurst, eds. *Augustine and Manichaeism in the Latin West: Proceedings of the Fribourg-Utrecht International Symposium of the International Association for Mission Studies, Nag Hammadi, and Manichaean Studies.* Leiden: Brill, 2001.

Verheijen, Luc. "*Le premier livre du* De Doctrina Christiana *d'Augustin: un traite de Telicologie Biblique.*" In *Augustiniana Traiectina,* edited by J. den Boeft and J. van Oort, 169–87. Paris: Études augustiniennes, 1987.

————. *Saint Augustine: Monk, Priest, Bishop.* Villanova, PA: Augustinian Historical Institute: Villanova University Press, 1978.

Vessey, Mark, ed. *A Companion to Augustine.* Blackwell Companions to the Ancient World. Oxford: Blackwell Publishing, 2012.

————. "Response to Catherine Conybeare: Women of Letters." In *Voices in Dialogue: Reading Women in the Middle Ages,* edited by Linda Olsen and Kathryn Kerby-Fulton, 73–96. South Bend, IN: University of Notre Dame Press, 2005.

Vessey, Mark, Karla Pollmann, and Allan Fitzgerald, OSA, eds. *History, Apocalypse, and the Secular Imagination: New Essays on Augustine's City of God.* Bowling Green, OH: Bowling Green State University, Philosophy Documentation Center, 1999.

Weaver, Rebecca Harden. *Divine Grace and Human Agency: A Study of the Semi-Pelagian Controversy*. Washington, DC: The Catholic University of America Press, 1996.

Wetzel, James. *Augustine and the Limits of Virtue*. Cambridge: Cambridge University Press, 1992.

——. *Augustine's City of God: A Critical Guide*. Cambridge Critical Guides. Cambridge: Cambridge University Press, 2012.

——. "The Force of Memory: Reflections on the Interrupted Self." *Augustinian Studies* 38, no. 1 (2007): 147–59.

——. "Predestination, Pelagianism and Foreknowledge." In *The Cambridge Companion to Augustine*, edited by Eleonore Stump and Norman Kretzmann. Cambridge: Cambridge University Press, 2001.

——. "Snares of Truth: Augustine on Free Will and Predestination." In *Essays in Honour of Gerald Bonner*, edited by Robert Dodaro, OSA, and George Lawless, OSA, 124–41. London: Routledge, 2000.

——. "Will and Interiority: Reflections on the Interrupted Self." *Augustinian Studies* 33, no. 2 (2002): 139–60.

Wiles, James W. *A Scripture Index to the Works of St. Augustine in English Translation*. Lanham, MD: University Press of America, 1995.

Wilks, Michael. *The Problem of Sovereignty in the Later Middle Ages*. Cambridge Studies in Medieval Life and Thought. Vol. 9. Cambridge: Cambridge University Press, 1964.

Williams, Rowan. *Arius*. 3rd ed. Grand Rapids, MI/Cambridge: Wm. B. Eerdmans Publishing, 2002.

——. "Good for Nothing?" *Augustinian Studies* 25 (1994): 9–24.

——. "Insubstantial Evil." In *Augustine and His Critics*, edited by Robert Dodaro, OSA, and George Lawless, OSA, 105–23, 2000.

——. "Language, Reality and Desire in Augustine's *De Doctrina*." *Literature and Theology* 3, no. 2 (1989): 138–50.

Wills, Gary. *Saint Augustine: A Life*. New York: Penguin Books, 2005.

Wittgenstein, Ludwig. *Philosophical Investigations*. Translated by G. E. M. Anscombe, P. M. S. Hacker, and Joachim Schulte, edited by P. M. S. Hacker, Joachim Schulte. 4th ed. Oxford: Wiley-Blackwell, 2009.

Young, Frances. "The *Confessions* of St. Augustine: What is the Genre of this Work?" *Augustinian Studies* 30, no. 1 (1999): 1–16.

Zumkeller, Adolar, OSA. *"Die Augustinerschule des Mittelalters: Vertreter und Philosophisch-Theologische Lehre."* Analecta Augustiniana 27 (1964): 167–262.

————. *Augustine's Rule: A Commentary.* Villanova, PA: Augustinian Press 1987.

————. *Theology and History of the Augustinian Order in the Middle Ages.* The Augustine Series, edited by John E. Rotelle, OSA. Villanova, PA: Augustinian Press, 1996.

# INDEX

# WHAT ARE THEY SAYING ABOUT Series

# WHAT ARE THEY SAYING ABOUT Series

What Are They Saying About Paul and the Law?
*by Veronica Koperski*

What Are They Saying About the Pastoral Epistles?
*by Mark Harding*

What Are They Saying About Catholic Ethical Method?
*by Todd A. Salzman*

What Are They Saying About New Testament Apocalyptic?
*by Scott M. Lewis, SJ*

What Are They Saying About Environmental Theology?
*by John Hart*

What Are They Saying About the Catholic Epistles?
*by Philip B. Harner*

What Are They Saying About Theological Method?
*by J. J. Mueller, SJ*

What Are They Saying About Mark?
*by Daniel J. Harrington, SJ*

What Are They Saying About the Letter to the Hebrews?
*by Daniel J. Harrington, SJ*

What Are They Saying About John? (Revised Edition)
*by Gerard S. Sloyan*

What Are They Saying About the Historical Jesus?
*by David B. Gowler*

What Are They Saying About Fundamentalisms?
*by Peter A. Huff*